How to be good at English Language Arts

How to be good at English Language Arts

Senior editors Laura Sandford, Rona Skene, Monica Woods
Project art editor Anna Scully
Editors Jolyon Goddard, Caryn Jenner, Sarah MacLeod, Mani Ramaswamy, James Smart
Designers Kelly Adams, Lauren Arthur, Gilda Pacitti
Illustrators Adam Brackenbury, Edwood Burn
Senior US editor Kayla Dugger
US executive editor Lori Hand

Authors Geoff Barker, Catherine Casey, Helen Dineen, Tom Hanlon, Cath Senker
Consultants Jane Burstein, Janet Gough

Managing editors Christine Stroyan, Carine Tracanelli
Managing art editor Anna Hall
Production editor Gillian Reid
Senior production controller Jude Crozier

Jacket designer Vidushi Chaudhry
Jacket design development manager Sophia MTT
Publisher Andrew Macintyre
Art director Karen Self
Design director Phil Ormerod
Publishing director Jonathan Metcalf

First American Edition, 2022
Published in the United States by DK Publishing
1450 Broadway, Suite 801, New York, NY 10018

Copyright © 2022 Dorling Kindersley Limited
DK, a Division of Penguin Random House LLC
22 23 24 25 26 10 9 8 7 6 5 4 3 2 1
001–327410–Aug/2022

All rights reserved.
Without limiting the rights under the copyright reserved above, no part of this publication may be reproduced, stored in or introduced into a retrieval system, or transmitted, in any form, or by any means (electronic, mechanical, photocopying, recording, or otherwise), without the prior written permission of the copyright owner.

A catalog record for this book
is available from the Library of Congress.
ISBN: 978-0-7440-4847-6

DK books are available at special discounts when purchased in bulk for sales promotions, premiums, fund-raising, or educational use. For details, contact: DK Publishing Special Markets, 1450 Broadway, Suite 801, New York, NY 10018
SpecialSales@dk.com

Printed and bound in China

For the curious
www.dk.com

This book was made with Forest Stewardship Council™ certified paper—one small step in DK's commitment to a sustainable future. For more information go to www.dk.com/our-green-pledge

Contents

1 Grammar

Grammar rules!	10
Nouns	12
Pronouns	14
Using pronouns	16
Determiners	18
Adjectives	20
Using more than one adjective	22
Noun phrases	24
Verbs	26
Adverbs	28
Adverb phrases and clauses	30
Using adverb phrases	32
Prepositions	34
What is a sentence?	36
Types of sentences	38
Clauses	40
Relative clauses	42
Multiclause sentences	44
Conjunctions	46
Tenses	50
Talking about the past	52
Talking about possibility	56
Conditional and subjunctive	58

Facts, questions, and instructions **60**

Verbals **62**

Active and passive sentences **64**

2 Punctuation

Why those dots and marks matter **68**

Starting and ending sentences **70**

Punctuating direct speech **72**

Apostrophes to show possession **74**

Apostrophes to show contractions **76**

Commas **78**

Semicolons **82**

Colons **84**

Parentheses, dashes, and ellipses **86**

Hyphens and dashes **88**

3 How words work

Studying words **92**

Roots and root words **94**

Breaking words into parts **96**

Prefixes **98**

What is a suffix? **102**

Vowel suffixes **104**

Doubling letters for suffixes **106**

Consonant suffixes **108**

The power of suffixes **110**

Plurals **112**

Homophones **114**

Silent and unstressed letters **116**

Synonyms **118**

4 Reading stories, plays, and poems

Why read? **122**

Features of stories, plays, and poems **124**

Genres **126**

What is the setting? **130**

Why the setting matters **132**

Characters **134**

Understanding characters **136**

Who's telling the story? **138**

Introducing plot **140**

The three-act structure **142**

Reading plays **144**

Performance **146**

What is a poem? **148**

Making sense of poetry **150**

Asking about a story **152**

How to work out meaning	**154**
The effects of language	**156**
Figurative language	**158**
What are inferences?	**160**
How to make inferences	**162**
Understanding the tone	**164**
Exploring dialogue	**166**
Analyzing poetry	**168**
Finding the main idea	**170**
Identifying themes	**172**
Comparing and contrasting fiction	**174**
Summarizing	**178**
Proving your point	**180**
Using evidence from the text	**182**

5 Reading nonfiction

Types of nonfiction	**186**
Reading informative texts	**188**
Magazines and newspapers	**190**
Reading online media	**192**
Narrative nonfiction	**194**
Letters	**196**
Reading speeches	**198**

Sales materials	**200**
What's the writer's purpose?	**202**
Audience	**204**
Levels of formality	**206**
Language for different purposes	**208**
Different viewpoints	**212**
Layout and structure	**214**
New words and terms	**216**
Finding information	**218**
Inferring meaning	**220**
Facts and opinions	**222**
Comparing and contrasting nonfiction	**224**
Summarizing multiple paragraphs	**228**

6 Writing

How to write well	**232**
The stages of writing	**234**
Coming up with ideas	**236**
Research	**238**
Learning from other writers	**240**
Collaboration and synthesis	**242**
Organizing ideas	**244**
Identifying your audience and purpose	**246**

Choosing the form	248
Writing in the right style	250
Writing sentences	252
Using sentences effectively	254
Writing paragraphs	256
Transition words	258
Using language techniques	260
Descriptive writing	262
Planning a story	264
Plot and structure	266
Starting and ending a story	268
Creating a setting	270
Creating characters	272
Choosing a narrator	274
Narrative techniques	276
Planning a poem	278
Writing a poem	280
Writing about poetry	282
Writing to inform and explain	284
How to present information clearly	286
How to write a formal letter	288
How to write an informal email and letter	290
Writing persuasively	292
Writing to argue	294
Writing a speech	296
Answering an essay prompt	298
Introduce, cite, explain	300
Revision, editing, and proofreading	304
Glossary	306
Further reading	310
Index	314

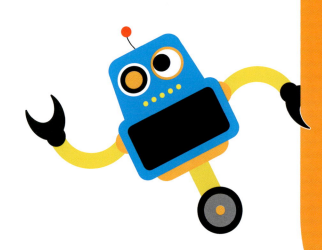

Grammar is the scaffolding that holds language up. Without grammar, it would be difficult to understand what you read and the sentences you write wouldn't make sense— in fact, they wouldn't be sentences at all! Grammar covers everything from nouns and verbs to prepositions and relative clauses. These all play a part in helping you think, speak, and write more clearly.

GRAMMAR

Grammar rules!

The rules of grammar tell us how to use words and build sentences. We learn grammar naturally as we grow up, from talking, listening, and reading. Grammar helps us communicate clearly, and it's not scary—it's something that we use every single day.

Grammar is about how words are used to make sentences.

What is grammar?

Grammar is the way in which language is organized and structured. Grammar helps us use different types of words, along with the right punctuation, to build sentences. By correctly using parts of speech such as nouns, verbs, adverbs, and adjectives, we can communicate more clearly.

TRY IT OUT

Don't be afraid of making mistakes in your writing. You can always ask an adult and find out how to fix things. Your teacher can also help point you to good reference books and reliable websites.

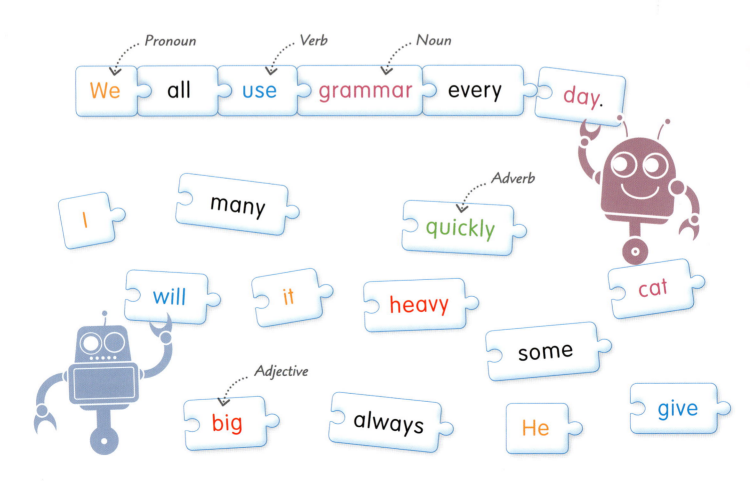

Why is grammar important?

Having a good grasp of grammar helps us understand what we hear and read. When we're speaking and writing, grammar allows us to express our thoughts clearly so that others can understand our meaning.

When grammar isn't used correctly, confusion can result. These were all genuine mistakes made on signs!

The word "eating" is confusing and should be removed: no one wants to eat a customer!

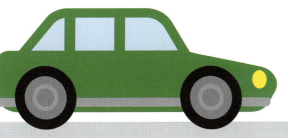

Here, "fine" should read "fined," the past tense of the verb "to fine." Right now, it appears to be an adjective meaning "satisfactory."

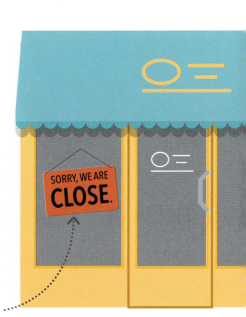

This appears to be an adjective meaning "near." It should read "closed," the past tense of the verb "to close," to mean that the store is shut.

Practice makes perfect

We can all continue to improve our grammar skills as we get older. With writing, the more grammar you know, the more you can say and understand. Keep listening, reading, and learning—and your efforts will be rewarded!

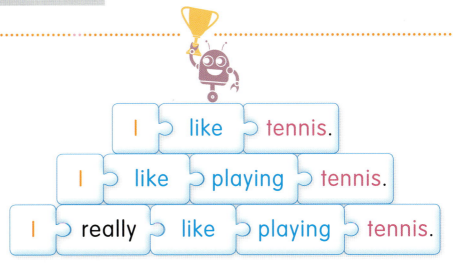

Nouns

A noun identifies a person, place, or thing, including objects, feelings, and groups of things. Nouns play an important part in almost every sentence.

Nouns are called **singular** when they refer to one thing and **plural** when they refer to a group of things.

What is a noun?

A noun is the name of somewhere, someone, or something. Nouns are often the name of things we can see, taste, smell, hear, or touch, but feelings and thoughts can also be nouns. Nouns can be divided into five categories.

SEE ALSO
Adjectives 20
Noun phrases 24
What is a sentence? 36

People
These nouns identify people: doctor, farmer, Alice, children.

Places
These nouns identify places: England, Tokyo, city, beach.

Things
These nouns identify things: swing, sandpit, cheese, car.

Feelings or qualities
Also called abstract nouns: friendship, joy, truth.

Groups of things
Also called collective nouns: a flock of birds, a bunch of grapes.

Types of nouns

Nouns may be common nouns or proper nouns, depending on what they are describing.

Common nouns
Common nouns identify people, things, or places in general.

> **TRY IT OUT**
> Count the nouns you can see around you. Which are common nouns and which are proper nouns?

teacher   teddy bear   city

Mr. Smith   Ted   New York

Proper nouns
Proper nouns name a particular person, thing, or place. They begin with a capital letter.

Nouns in sentences

Most sentences contain at least one noun. Nouns may be the subject or object of the sentence.

Jack is the subject of this sentence.

Jack — shouted in — anger.

This collective noun is the subject of the sentence.

The grass is the object of this sentence.

A — herd — of — cows — chewed the — grass.

These proper nouns begin with a capital letter.

Next — month, — Carlos — is flying to — France.

Pronouns

A pronoun is a short word that can stand in for a noun, usually after the first time the noun is mentioned. Pronouns remind us who or what is being described.

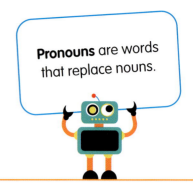

Pronouns are words that replace nouns.

What is a pronoun?

A pronoun replaces a noun or group of nouns. It helps us avoid repeating the same word. We also use pronouns when we don't know which noun to use.

SEE ALSO	
Nouns	12
What is a sentence?	36
Relative clauses	42

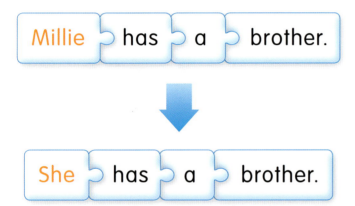

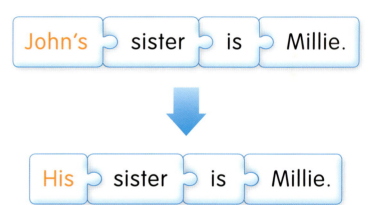

People pronouns

"He" and "she" are traditionally used for male and female people. But people can choose their own pronouns. It's important to respect someone's chosen pronouns. Ask if you are unsure.

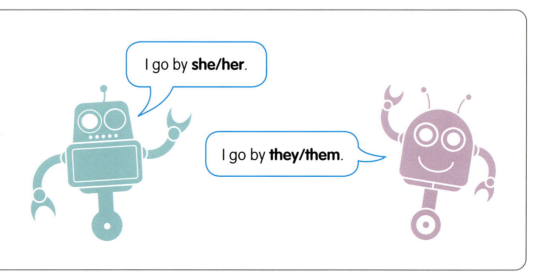

GRAMMAR • PRONOUNS

What can pronouns do?

Pronouns always stand in for nouns, but they can perform several different jobs. This means we need different groups of pronouns to show their specific role in the sentence.

> **SPEAK UP**
> Try talking with a friend without using any pronouns. See how awkward it sounds—and how difficult it is!

1 **Replace the subject of a sentence** (I, you, he, she, it, we, they, and so on).

2 **Replace the object of a sentence** (me, you, him, her, it, us, them, and so on).

3 **Show who owns or has something** (my, mine, your, his, her, our, their, and so on).

4 **Ask questions** to find out information (who, whom, whose, which, what, and so on).

5 **Point things out** to indicate what is being described (this, that, these, those, and so on).

6 **Give more information** using a relative clause (who, that, which, and so on).

Using pronouns

There are many different pronouns in English. Choosing the right pronouns and thinking about when and where to use them will help you write more clearly.

Which pronoun to use?

It's important to use the correct pronoun. Match it to the person or object it replaces and to the role it plays in the sentence.

SEE ALSO	
Nouns	12
Pronouns	14
Relative clauses	42

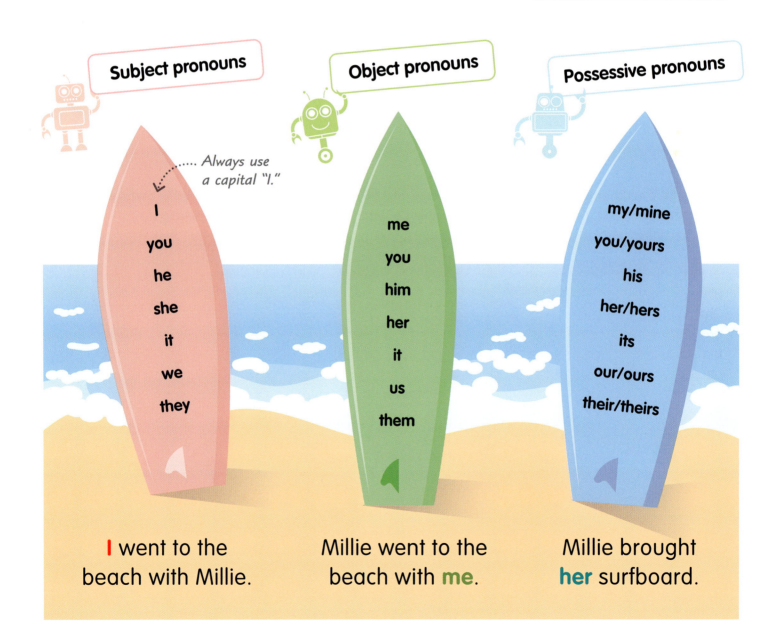

Subject pronouns
Always use a capital "I."
I, you, he, she, it, we, they

Object pronouns
me, you, him, her, it, us, them

Possessive pronouns
my/mine, you/yours, his, her/hers, its, our/ours, their/theirs

I went to the beach with Millie.

Millie went to the beach with **me**.

Millie brought **her** surfboard.

GRAMMAR • USING PRONOUNS

"Self" pronouns

"Self" pronouns always refer back to the subject. Intensive pronouns are used for emphasis. Reflexive pronouns show the subject did something to or for themselves.

INTENSIVE EXAMPLE

The children built the sandcastle themselves.

..... Emphasizes that the children did it themselves without help

REFLEXIVE EXAMPLE

Millie dug herself a hole in the sand.

..... Clarifies that Millie dug the hole for herself

Common mistakes

1 When you include yourself and another person in a sentence, always put the other person first. Check that you're using the correct pronoun to describe yourself by temporarily leaving out the other person. Would you say, "Me went to the beach" or "I went to the beach"?

✗ Me and Millie went to the beach.
✗ Millie and me went to the beach.
✔ Millie and I went to the beach.

We don't find out who loves what until the second sentence. Confusing!

✗ She loves it. Millie goes surfing every day.
✔ Millie loves surfing. She does it every day.

..... Here, we already know that "she" is Millie and "it" is surfing.

2 When you use a pronoun to avoid repeating a noun, it's important to make it clear who or what the pronoun refers to. Use the noun first, then replace it with a pronoun.

Determiners

Determiners are words like "the," "some," "a," and "this." They tell the reader which object or person is being talked about—and they always go in front of the noun.

> **Determiners** make it clear what or who you're referring to.

What is a determiner?

A determiner is a word that introduces a noun, giving readers more information about it. There are many different types of determiners, including articles, possessives, quantifiers, and demonstratives.

SEE ALSO
Nouns — 12
Pronouns — 14

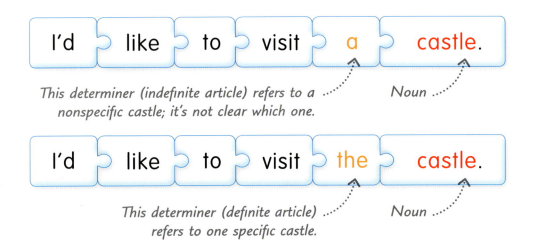

I'd like to visit **a** castle.

This determiner (indefinite article) refers to a nonspecific castle; it's not clear which one. — Noun

I'd like to visit **the** castle.

This determiner (definite article) refers to one specific castle. — Noun

Articles
are divided into "indefinite" (a/an) and "definite" (the).

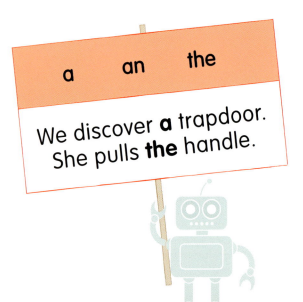

a   an   the

We discover **a** trapdoor.
She pulls **the** handle.

Possessives
show who owns or "possesses" something.

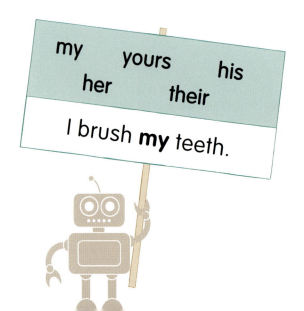

my   yours   his
her   their

I brush **my** teeth.

GRAMMAR • DETERMINERS

Pronoun or determiner?

Possessive pronouns can also be called possessive determiners when they sit before a noun.

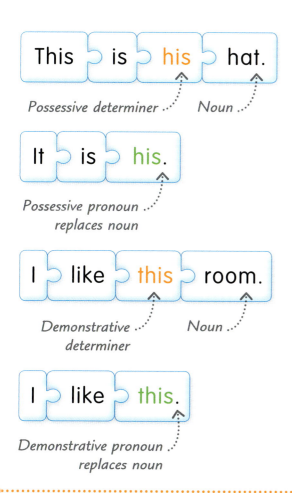

Using "a" or "an"

If a noun starts with a consonant sound, we use the article "a." If it starts with a vowel sound, we use the article "an."

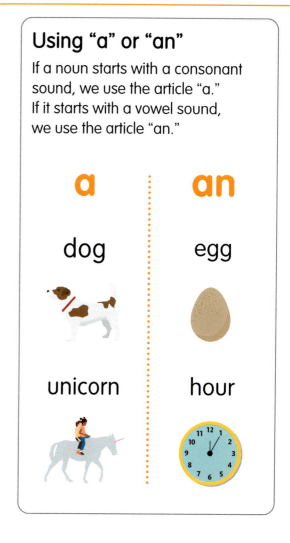

Quantifiers
show the amount of something.

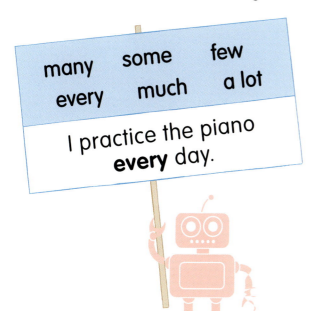

Demonstratives
point to something that is close or distant in space or time.

GRAMMAR • ADJECTIVES

Adjectives

Adjectives are words that describe nouns. They tell us more about people, places, and things. We can use adjectives to describe, identify, and compare.

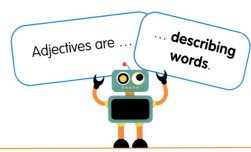

Adjectives are... ...describing words.

What is an adjective?

Adjectives give us more information and detail about a noun. They tell us what a noun is like, and we can use them to be more specific about a person, place, or thing.

SEE ALSO
Using more than one adjective — 22
Using language techniques — 260
Creating a setting — 270

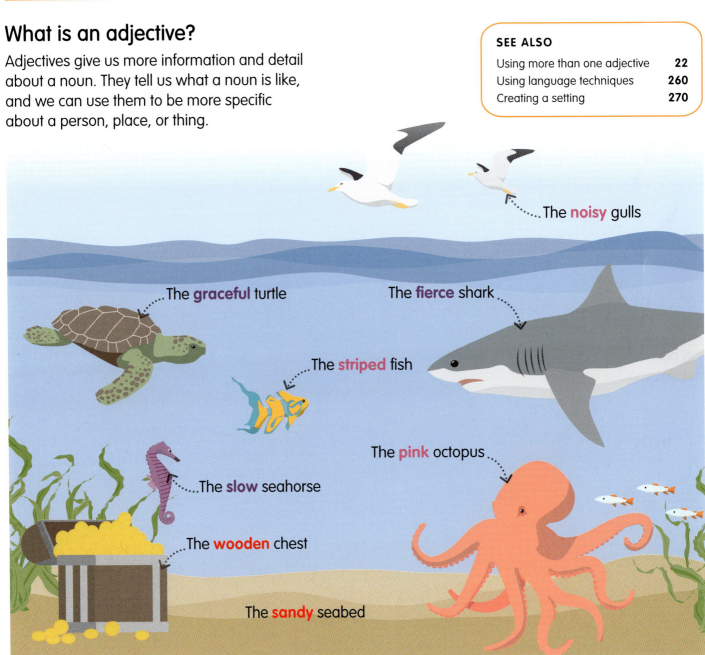

The noisy gulls
The graceful turtle
The fierce shark
The striped fish
The pink octopus
The slow seahorse
The wooden chest
The sandy seabed

1 Adjectives can describe what a noun looks like, smells like, feels like, tastes like, or sounds like.

2 They might describe the characteristics of a person, place, or thing.

3 Adjectives can also be used to describe what a noun is made out of.

GRAMMAR • ADJECTIVES

Where do adjectives go?

Adjectives can go before or after a noun. Putting the adjective after the noun gives it extra emphasis. When adjectives are used like this, they are called predicate adjectives.

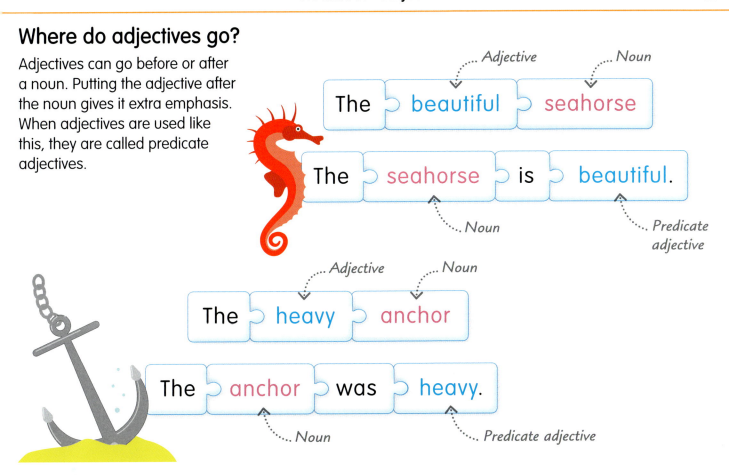

Why use adjectives?

Adjectives help the reader or listener understand more about the person, place, or thing being described. Adjectives also help us compare or tell the difference between nouns.

Adjectives create an image of the noun in our minds.

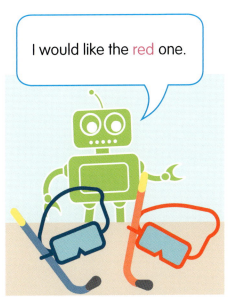

We can use adjectives to tell things apart.

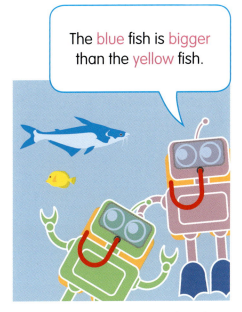

Add "-er" or "-est" to adjectives when comparing nouns.

Using more than one adjective

Multiple means more than one. Sometimes we might use multiple adjectives to help us describe or identify a person, place, or thing more effectively.

Remember, an **adjective** describes a noun.

Why use more than one adjective?
Using more than one adjective gives a reader or listener more information about the noun. This can be useful when describing or identifying a noun.

SEE ALSO
Adjectives	20
Commas	78
The effects of language	156

1 Using multiple adjectives to describe things
Using more than one adjective can create a stronger, more powerful image of the thing you are describing. This is great for stories and poems.

A shark   A striped shark   A long, striped shark   A long, hungry, striped shark

2 Using multiple adjectives to identify things
Using more than one adjective makes it clearer which item, person, or place you are describing. This is especially useful if there are several similar things.

The big, brown seal took my flipper!

GRAMMAR • USING MORE THAN ONE ADJECTIVE

Which adjective comes first?

Saying the phrase aloud can help you find the best order. You can also consider if the adjective is subjective or objective.

Subjective adjectives, like beautiful, soft, or lonely, are based on feelings or opinions. Objective adjectives, like wooden, spotted, or blue, are based on facts. When adjectives go before a noun, objective adjectives go closer to the noun than subjective adjectives.

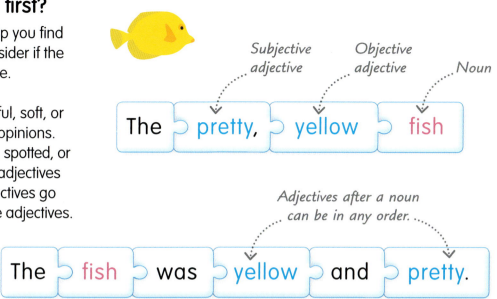

The **pretty,** *yellow* fish
— Subjective adjective / Objective adjective / Noun

The fish was *yellow* and **pretty**.
Adjectives after a noun can be in any order.

Punctuation with multiple adjectives

Sometimes we use commas to separate adjectives. This depends on the adjectives used. We might use a comma to separate adjectives when:

1 The adjectives could be used in any order and make sense.

The beautiful, delicate shell

The delicate, beautiful shell

..... *A comma can be placed between the adjectives.*

2 The word "and" could be used between the adjectives.

The slimy and slippery seaweed

The slimy, slippery seaweed

..... *The word "and" can be replaced with a comma.*

3 The adjectives both describe the noun separately and equally.

The green and spotty seahorse

The green, spotty seahorse

These adjectives are equally important for describing the noun.

SPEAK UP

Say these phrases out loud.
Which sounds correct?

The huge, golden fish
The golden, huge fish

Noun phrases

A phrase is a small group of words that forms part of a sentence. A noun phrase contains a noun, plus other words that provide extra information about the noun.

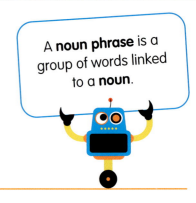

A **noun phrase** is a group of words linked to a **noun**.

How to build a noun phrase

Noun phrases always contain a noun. They can also include a determiner, which comes before the noun. Expanded noun phrases give extra detail and might include an adjective before the noun and additional information after it.

SEE ALSO	
Nouns	12
Determiners	18
Adjectives	20

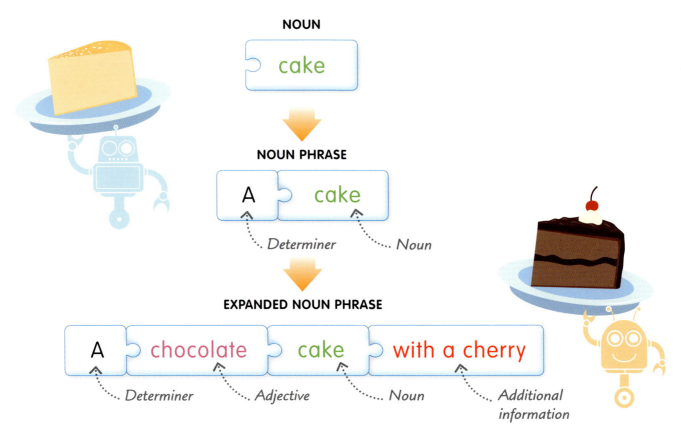

TRY IT OUT

Write an expanded noun phrase about each of these robots. How might you describe them?

Using noun phrases

You use noun phrases in a sentence just as you would use a noun. Sentences can contain more than one noun phrase.

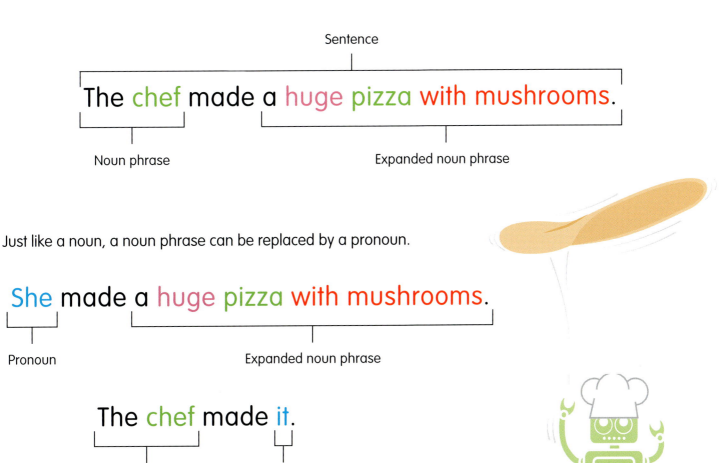

Just like a noun, a noun phrase can be replaced by a pronoun.

How to identify a noun phrase

A noun phrase is built up from words linked to the noun that form a unit of meaning. Use this checklist to identify noun phrases.

✔ A noun phrase contains a noun, plus other words.

✔ These other words tell you more about the noun.

✔ They may be determiners or adjectives (which come before the noun) …

✔ … or additional information (which comes after the noun).

✔ A noun phrase can be replaced by a pronoun.

Verbs

A verb is a word used to describe an action, state, or event. Without verbs, we wouldn't be able to express complete thoughts and ideas.

Verbs are **doing**, **being**, and **happening** words.

What is a verb?

Every sentence contains at least one verb. A verb tells you about doing (an action), being or having (a state), and happening (an event).

SEE ALSO
Pronouns	14
Clauses	40
Tenses	50
Verbals	62

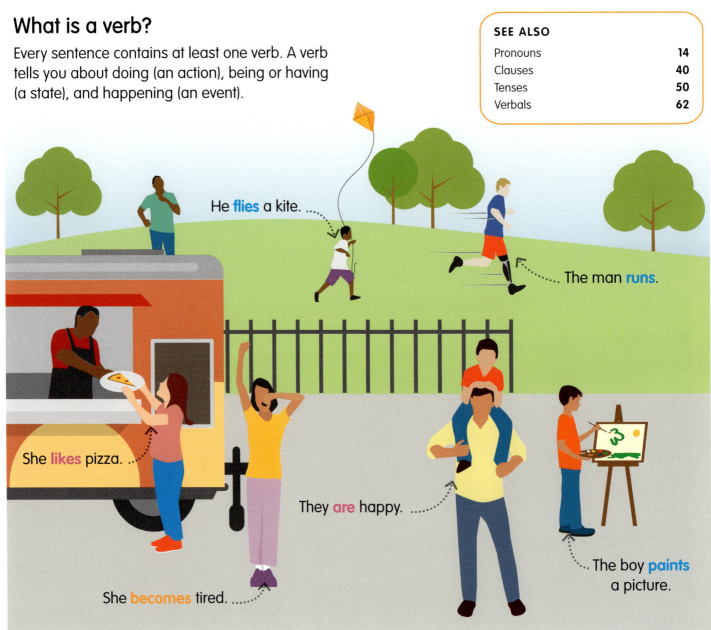

He **flies** a kite.
The man **runs**.
She **likes** pizza.
They **are** happy.
She **becomes** tired.
The boy **paints** a picture.

Action
Something that you do by yourself or to something or someone else.

State
Something that you are, you have, you think, or you feel.

Event
Something that is happening to you that is transforming you in some way.

How to use a verb

A verb connects with a subject (which usually comes before the verb) to make a sentence. Sentences can't do without verbs! Most verbs have one form if you're talking about "I," "we," "you," or "they" and a different form for "he," "she," or "it".

> **SPEAK UP**
>
> Read the examples below aloud to hear the difference the "s" makes.

Use the verb without an "s" in a sentence where the subject is "I," "we," "you," or "they":

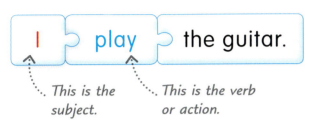

This is the subject. · This is the verb or action.

Add an "s" to the verb in a sentence where the subject is "he," "she," or "it":

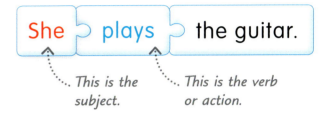

This is the subject. · This is the verb or action.

"To be" and "to have"

"To be" and "to have" are both irregular verbs, which means they don't follow the regular pattern. Many verbs are irregular and have different forms that we have to learn. The examples given here are in the present tense, but these verbs can also be used with different tenses (see pages 50–55).

TO BE

- ✔ I am thirsty.
- ✘ I is thirsty.
- ✔ You/we/they are tired.
- ✘ You/we/they is tired.
- ✔ He/she/it is late.
- ✘ He/she/it are late.

TO HAVE

- ✔ I have a cold.
- ✘ I has a cold.
- ✔ You/we/they have the tickets.
- ✘ You/we/they has the tickets.
- ✔ He/she/it has a class.
- ✘ He/she/it have a class.

Linking verbs

"To be" is also a linking verb. Linking verbs act as an equals sign—they provide information about the subject by connecting them to an adjective or to another noun.

Subject · Linking verb · Adjective

Adverbs

Adverbs tell us more about a verb, an adjective, or another adverb. There are many different types of adverbs and different ways to use them in a sentence.

Adverbs are used to describe verbs, adjectives, or other adverbs.

What are adverbs?

Adverbs describe verbs, adjectives, and other adverbs. They often tell us how, when, where, or why something is happening. Adverbs can also show how often, how much, to what extent, or the possibility of something.

SEE ALSO	
Verbs	26
Adverb phrases and clauses	30
Prepositions	34

How

The tennis player *accidentally* broke his racket.
(Adverb) (Verb)

When

The children *played* basketball *earlier today*.
(Verb) (Adverb) (Adverb)

Where

The gymnast was *outside* working on his routine.
(Adverb) (Verb)

Why

She ran the fastest and *therefore* won the race.
(Adverb) (Verb)

Types of adverbs

Adverbs work in lots of different ways—some important types are shown below. Some words can be adverbs, adjectives, or nouns depending on how they are used. Here are some of the most common types of adverbs.

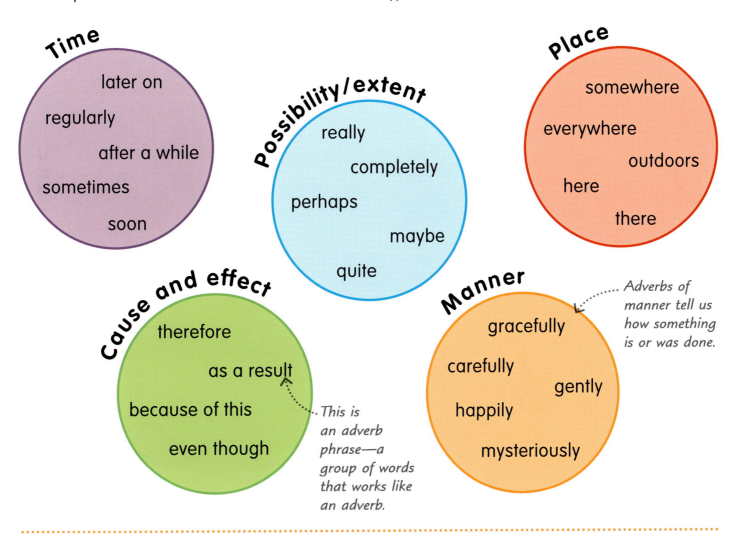

Time: later on, regularly, after a while, sometimes, soon

Possibility/extent: really, completely, perhaps, maybe, quite

Place: somewhere, everywhere, outdoors, here, there

Cause and effect: therefore, as a result, because of this, even though

This is an adverb phrase—a group of words that works like an adverb.

Manner: gracefully, carefully, gently, happily, mysteriously

Adverbs of manner tell us how something is or was done.

Where to put adverbs

Adverbs can be used in different positions within a sentence. They can be at the front, middle, or end of clauses. (A clause is a group of words with a subject and a verb.) Varying the position of adverbs in your sentences can make your writing or speech more interesting.

Front position: **Perhaps** I will go for a swim.

Middle position: The dancer was **really** nervous.

End position: The hockey game will be starting **soon**.

Adverb phrases and clauses

Adverbs, adverb phrases, and adverb clauses are sometimes grouped together as adverbials. They tell us more about a verb, adjective, or adverb. Adverbials have several useful functions.

What are adverbials?

Adverbials are used to describe verbs, adjectives, or adverbs. They are used in the same way whether they're a single word, a phrase, or a clause.

> **SEE ALSO**
> Adverbs 28
> Using adverb phrases 32

An adverbial can be one word—an **adverb**.

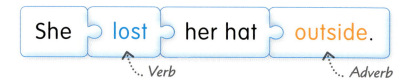
She lost her hat outside.
…Verb …Adverb

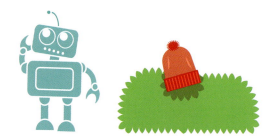

An adverbial can be a **phrase**.

She lost her hat in the classroom.
…Verb …Adverb phrase

An adverbial can be a **clause**.

She lost her hat after she had lunch.
…Verb …Adverb clause

TRY IT OUT

Identify the adverbials in these examples …

She ate her snack as soon as the class finished.

He sat in silence, then let out a chuckle.

GRAMMAR • **ADVERB PHRASES AND CLAUSES**　　31

What do adverbials tell us?

Adverbials tell us different things about a verb, adjective, or adverb, such as when, where, why, how, how much, or how often.

1 Adverbials can tell us **when** an action happens, is happening, or has happened.

We **have** sports *on Wednesday afternoons*.
　Verb　　　　　　Adverbial

2 Adverbials can tell us **where** an action happens, is happening, or has happened.

I **play** the drums *in the music room at school*.
　Verb　　　　　　　Adverbial

3 Adverbials can tell us **why** an action happens, is happening, or has happened.

I **forgot** my homework *because I was in a rush*.
　Verb　　　　　　　　Adverbial

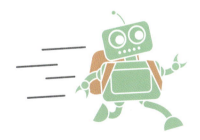

4 Adverbials can tell us **how** (or how much or how often) an action happens, is happening, or has happened.

I **ate** my lunch *as quickly as I could*.
　Verb　　　　　Adverbial

Using adverb phrases

An adverb phrase is a group of words that describes a verb or clause. Adverb phrases can add extra information and color. They're also useful for linking and comparing.

Adverb phrases can help us emphasize when, where, or how something is done.

Where to put adverb phrases

Adverb phrases can be used at the beginning, middle, or end of a sentence. They can help you emphasize when, where, or how something is done.

SEE ALSO	
Adverbs	28
Adverb phrases and clauses	30
Transition words	258

End position

Tom dreams of lions every night.

Every night, Tom dreams of lions.

Front position

A hawk perches on a tree.

On a tree, a hawk perches.

The ranger approached the snake cautiously.

Cautiously, the ranger approached the snake.

GRAMMAR • USING ADVERB PHRASES

Punctuating adverb phrases

A comma is used after a adverb phrase when it is used at the start of a sentence.

After school, we feed the ducks.

Adverb phrase

TRY IT OUT

Rewrite these sentences, putting the adverb phrase at the beginning of the sentence. Remember to put a comma after the adverb phrase.

We went to the park with Maria yesterday morning.

I can see a shimmering rainbow in the sky.

Linking and comparing

Sometimes adverb phrases are used to order text or compare and contrast ideas. Adverb phrases can link to previous sentences or paragraphs to develop cohesion within a text.

1 Adverb phrases can be used to **order text**:

As soon as we arrived, I decided to explore the forest.

After a while, I saw a brightly coloured parrot.

2 Adverb phrases can be used to **compare and contrast**:

Like the rhino, the antelope doesn't eat meat.

In contrast, the cheetah is a carnivore.

Prepositions

A preposition describes how different nouns in a sentence are connected in terms of place, time, or movement.

Prepositions describe where or when something is in relation to something else.

Prepositions of place, time, and movement

Using prepositions, we can describe precisely where or when certain people, places, or things (nouns) are in relation to others.

SEE ALSO	
Nouns	12
Pronouns	14
Adverbs	28
Conjunctions	46

◻ **Prepositions of place** tell us where things are.

◻ **Prepositions of time** tell us when things happen.

◻ **Prepositions of movement** are used to show movement from one place to another.

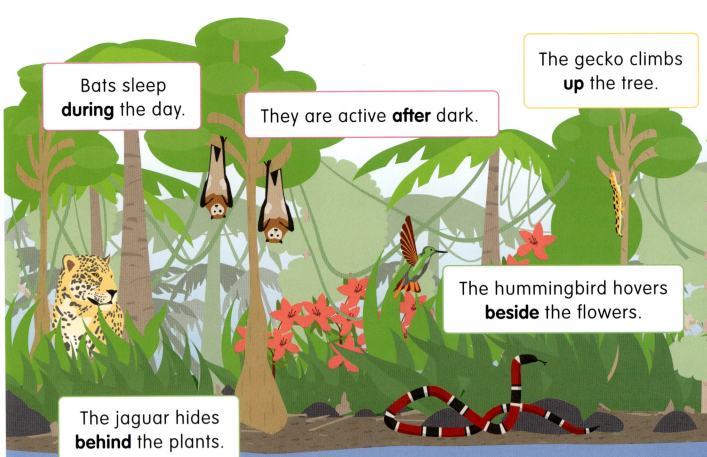

Bats sleep **during** the day.

They are active **after** dark.

The gecko climbs **up** the tree.

The hummingbird hovers **beside** the flowers.

The jaguar hides **behind** the plants.

The snake sits **in front of** the rocks.

GRAMMAR • PREPOSITIONS 35

Where do prepositions go?

A preposition is usually placed between two related nouns, pronouns, or noun phrases. It comes before the word or phrase it describes.

The gecko climbs **up** the tree.

- Noun: gecko
- Noun: tree
- The preposition shows where the nouns are in relation to each other.

A snake waits **below** it.

- Noun: snake
- Pronoun: it
- This preposition shows where the noun is in relation to the pronoun.

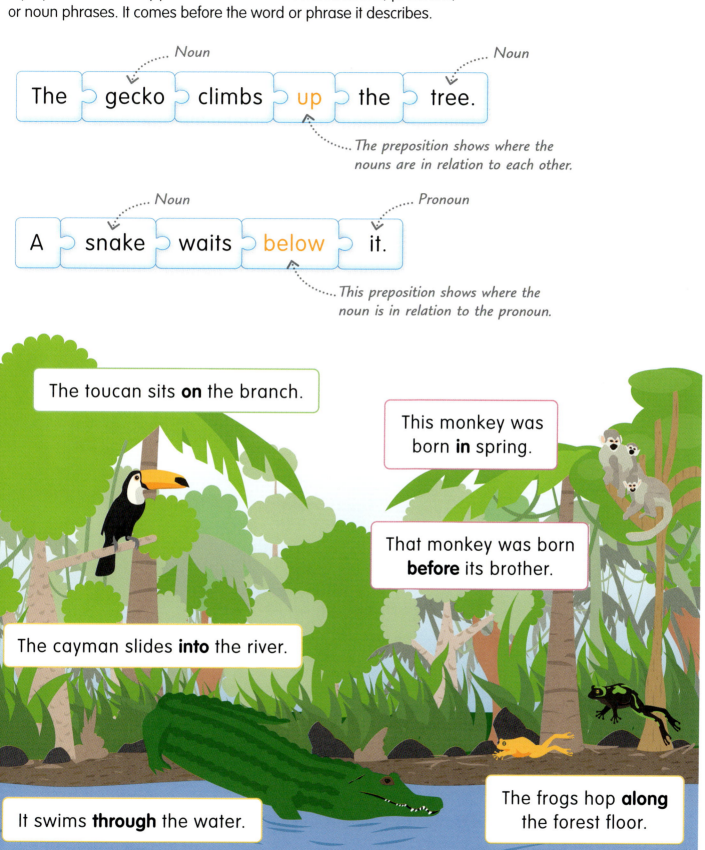

The toucan sits **on** the branch.

This monkey was born **in** spring.

That monkey was born **before** its brother.

The cayman slides **into** the river.

It swims **through** the water.

The frogs hop **along** the forest floor.

What is a sentence?

A sentence is a group of words that convey a complete thought. A sentence always contains a verb, usually has a subject, and sometimes includes an object.

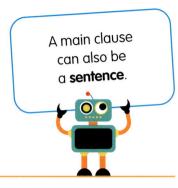

A main clause can also be a **sentence**.

Building blocks

We can use words a bit like building blocks to construct sentences and other, shorter groups of words, like phrases and clauses.

SEE ALSO
Noun phrases 24
Verbs 26
Clauses 40

1 Words
Every word has some meaning on its own. Words can be combined to build up meaning bit by bit.

2 Phrases
Groups of words that don't contain a subject and a verb are called phrases. They are not sentences.

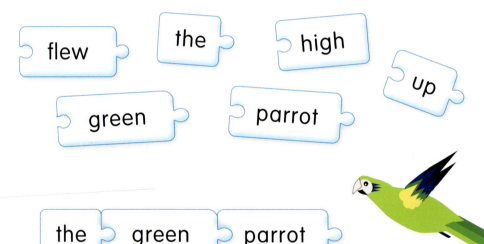

3 Clauses
A clause is a group of words containing a subject and a verb. A main clause can also be a sentence.

This clause contains a verb and makes sense on its own, so it is also a sentence.

Always use a capital letter at the start of a sentence.

4 Sentences
A complete thought that makes sense on its own is a sentence. It must always contain a verb.

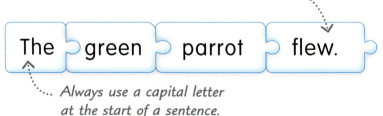

A sentence must end with a period, exclamation mark, or question mark.

GRAMMAR • WHAT IS A SENTENCE?

Parts of a sentence

All sentences include a verb. Most sentences also have a subject (or an implied subject) and they sometimes contain an object.

> **TRY IT OUT**
> Write five sentences about five things you can see.

The basketball player scored a point.

Verb — The verb describes the action.

Object — The object is the receiver of the action.

Subject — The subject is the person or thing doing the action.

Predicate — The predicate contains a verb and something about the object.

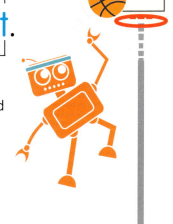

Is it a sentence?

It's important to be able to write accurate sentences. Remember: a sentence must contain a verb, be a complete thought, and make sense on its own.

The subject ("you") is not mentioned in the sentence. We call this an implied subject.

✘ **Jumping.**

"Jumping" is a verb, but it doesn't make sense on its own. This is not a sentence.

✘ **Where are?**

This contains a verb, but it's not a complete thought, so it's not a sentence. It needs a subject.

✔ **Run!**

This command (see page 39) has an implied subject: "you." It makes sense on its own.

✘ **The sun is.**

This is not a sentence. It has a subject and a verb but does not form a complete thought.

✘ **The ginger cat.**

This phrase does not contain a verb and it is not a complete thought, so it's not a sentence.

✔ **I am.**

This sentence contains a subject and a verb. It is most likely an answer to a question.

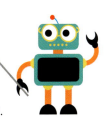

Types of sentences

There are four main types of sentences: statements, exclamations, commands, and questions. Each type of sentence does a different job.

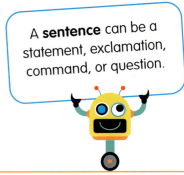

A **sentence** can be a statement, exclamation, command, or question.

Statements

Statements tell us something or give us information. Most sentences, like this one, are statements. Depending on how they are being used, statements can end with a period or an exclamation mark. They might also include other punctuation, such as commas in a list.

SEE ALSO
What is a sentence?   **36**
Starting and ending sentences   **70**

I think that's a clownfish.

I'm going to swim toward it.

What a huge shark that is!

How amazing!

Exclamations

Exclamations express strong emotions. They start with "what" or "how" and usually end with an exclamation mark. An exclamation is a complete sentence. An incomplete sentence that starts with "what" or "how" and ends with an exclamation mark is called an exclamatory fragment.

GRAMMAR • **TYPES OF SENTENCES** 39

Commands

Commands tell us to do something. They are punctuated with a period or exclamation mark and include an imperative verb (see page 61). The subject is often understood to be "you," like in the sentence "Stop!" Sometimes commands include a noun of address, for example, "Dad" in "Dad, open the window!"

> **TRY IT OUT**
>
> Can you think of any more statements, exclamations, commands, and questions to describe the picture below?

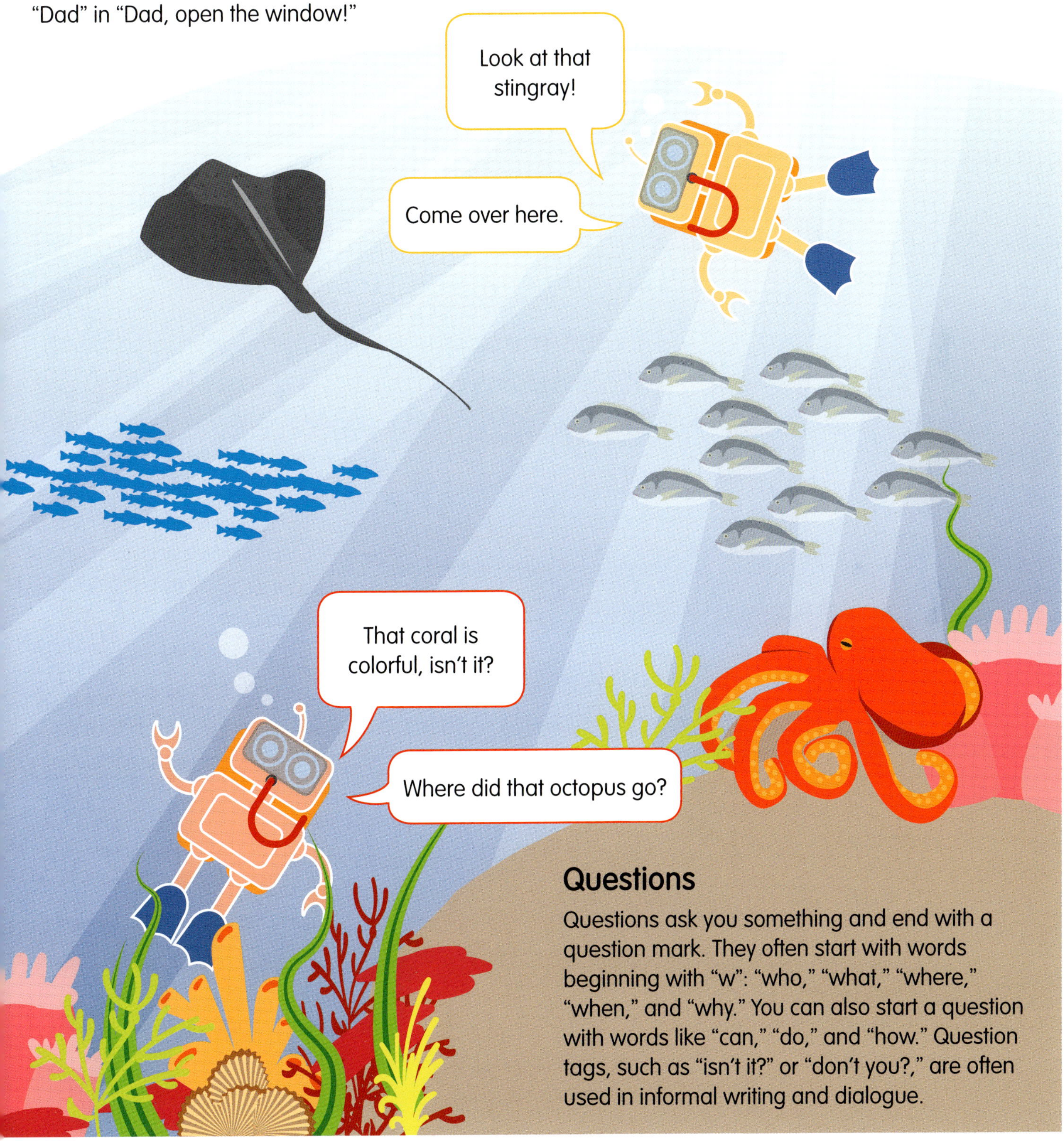

Look at that stingray!

Come over here.

That coral is colorful, isn't it?

Where did that octopus go?

Questions

Questions ask you something and end with a question mark. They often start with words beginning with "w": "who," "what," "where," "when," and "why." You can also start a question with words like "can," "do," and "how." Question tags, such as "isn't it?" or "don't you?," are often used in informal writing and dialogue.

Clauses

Sentences are made up of clauses that tell us what is happening. A clause can be a whole sentence on its own or it can form part of a sentence to add extra information.

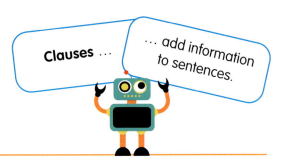

What is a clause?

A clause is a group of words that contains a subject (noun) and a verb to tell us who is doing what. Some clauses, like the examples below, can stand alone as sentences and some cannot.

SEE ALSO	
Noun phrases	24
Adverb phrases and clauses	30
Relative clauses	42
Multiclause sentences	44

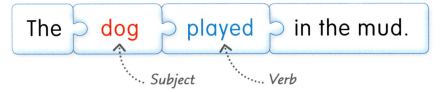

Is it a phrase or a clause?

A phrase does not include a subject or verb, so it cannot tell us what is happening. A phrase gives limited information. A clause has both a subject and a verb, giving us more information.

GRAMMAR • CLAUSES   41

Main clause

A **main clause** is also called an "independent clause" because it is a complete thought and can form a complete sentence.

This **main clause** stands alone as a sentence.

Ben bakes a cake.

....The subject of the clause

....The action (verb)

Subordinate clause

A **subordinate clause** is also called a "dependent clause" because it is not a complete thought and depends on the main clause in order to make sense. It can include a subordinating conjunction to join it to the main clause.

See page 48 for a list of **subordinating conjunctions**.

This **subordinate clause** cannot stand alone as a sentence.

When it's his sister's birthday

A subordinate clause often starts with a conjunction.

Ben bakes a cake when it's his sister's birthday.

When it's his sister's birthday, Ben bakes a cake.

....*Use a comma if the subordinate clause is before the main clause.*

Relative clauses

A relative clause tells us something about a noun. It is a type of subordinate clause that usually begins with a relative pronoun or a relative adverb.

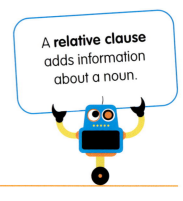

A **relative clause** adds information about a noun.

What is a relative clause?

A relative clause gives information about a noun. It is a type of subordinate clause, so it needs to be connected to a main clause, usually using a relative pronoun or a relative adverb. A relative clause can be embedded in the middle of a sentence, where it is separated by commas.

SEE ALSO	
Pronouns	14
Adverbs	28
Clauses	40
Multiclause sentences	44

This relative clause is embedded in the middle of the sentence and separated by commas.

My sister**, who is nine,** loves to ride her scooter.

Relative pronoun

I know the reason **why** the wheel came off the scooter.

Relative adverb

My sister rode her scooter over a rock **that** was on the path.

Relative pronoun

GRAMMAR • **RELATIVE CLAUSES**   43

Relative pronouns

The relative pronoun that you use in a relative clause depends on what you are writing about. Here are some common relative pronouns.

> **WORLD OF WORDS**
>
> Sometimes you don't need to use a relative pronoun. For example, you could leave out "that" and say, "The book I read yesterday was really exciting." Similarly, there's no need to add a comma if the relative clause helps you identify the subject of the sentence.

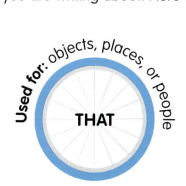

The book **that I read yesterday** was really exciting.

I'm going to my cousin's house, **which is near the ocean**.

He is the teacher **who runs the student council**.

He is the teacher **to whom the student council reports**.

Avi, **whose mother is a marathon runner**, won the race.

Relative adverbs

Relative adverbs can also be used to introduce a relative clause. Here are three common examples of relative adverbs.

The beach **where I went on holiday** was beautiful.

I remember the summer **when I learned how to ride a bike**.

I don't know **why I'm so hungry**.

Multiclause sentences

A clause is a group of words that contains a subject and a verb. A single-clause sentence is made up of just one main clause. A multiclause sentence has more than one clause—and at least one of these clauses must be a main clause.

A **single-clause** sentence has only one main clause.

A **multiclause** sentence has more than one clause.

Joining main clauses

A main clause can form a complete sentence and make sense on its own. Some sentences have two or more main clauses joined together, often by a coordinating conjunction, such as "or," "and," or "but."

SEE ALSO
Clauses 40
Relative clauses 42
Conjunctions 46

These sentences are **single-clause** sentences. They are each made up of **one main clause**.

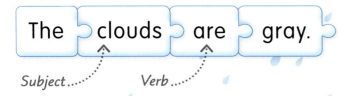

Subject ... *Verb*

A coordinating conjunction can join the two single-clause sentences to form a **multiclause sentence**.

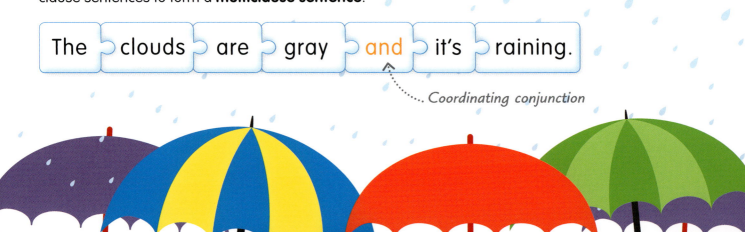

Coordinating conjunction

GRAMMAR • **MULTICLAUSE SENTENCES**　　45

Making a multiclause sentence

Multiclause sentences can have a mixture of main clauses (which are complete thoughts) and subordinate clauses (which don't make sense on their own).

Main clause with a subject and verb

He can't play outside.

Subordinate clause | Main clause

When it rains, he can't play outside.

Subordinate clause | Main clause | Subordinate clause

When it rains, he can't play outside because he'll get rusty.

Common mistakes

Here are some common mistakes with clauses. Being aware of these will help you get clauses right.

1 Sentence fragment
An incomplete sentence that is usually missing a subject or verb.

✗ Because of the rain

This is a phrase, not a sentence. It needs a subject and verb to be a sentence.

2 Comma splice
Joining main clauses with a comma instead of a coordinating conjunction.

✗ The clouds are gray, it's raining.

Instead of a comma, these sentences should be joined with a conjunction such as "and."

3 Too many clauses
Joining too many clauses together makes a sentence difficult to read.

✗ When it rains, he can't play outside because he'll get rusty, but this makes him very sad because he loves playing outside, even in the rain.

Conjunctions

Conjunctions, or joining words, connect words and ideas together. They can be useful little words when you're extending a sentence or adding information.

Words like "and," "but," and "so" **join ideas** together.

SEE ALSO
Clauses	40
Multiclause sentences	44
Transition words	258

Joining different parts of a sentence

Simple words like "and" or "but" help join different parts (clauses) of a sentence together and improve the flow. Both clauses also need to make sense on their own.

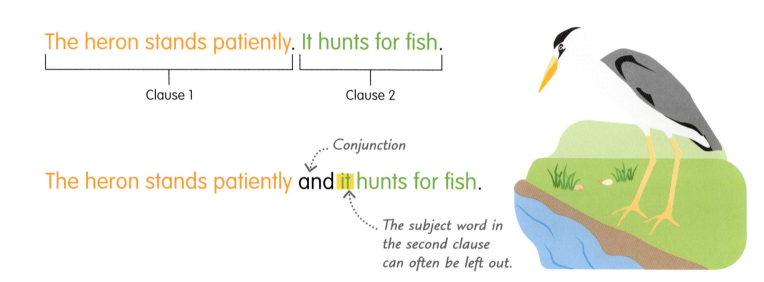

The heron stands patiently. It hunts for fish.

Clause 1 — Clause 2

Conjunction

The heron stands patiently and it hunts for fish.

The subject word in the second clause can often be left out.

Joining equally important ideas

Joining words, known as "coordinating conjunctions," link words or ideas that are just as important as the first idea. The most common coordinating conjunctions are "for," "and," "nor," "but," "or," "yet," wand "so"; you can remember them more easily by using FANBOYS.

Do you want to go for a walk or play tennis?

Coordinating conjunction

She hates to be late, so she always leaves early.

Linking to a less important idea

Sometimes a first idea, or main clause, is linked to a second, less important idea. This "subordinate clause" tells us more about the main clause, but it doesn't make sense on its own. You can use linking words, called "subordinating conjunctions," like "when," "because," "if," and "although."

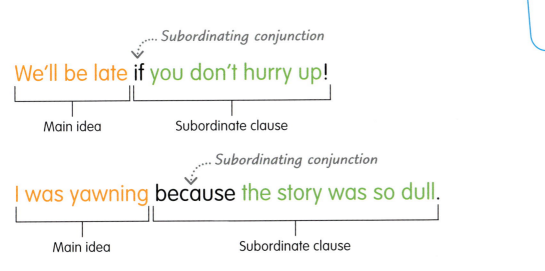

The **subordinate clause** can also go at the start of a sentence.

If the subordinate clause comes first, a **comma** separates the two clauses.

> **TRY IT OUT**
>
> Use a coordinating conjunction to extend each of these sentences, then substitute with a subordinating conjunction.
>
> I wanted to see the movie ...
>
> Vampire bats sleep during the day ...
>
> Your braces look great ...

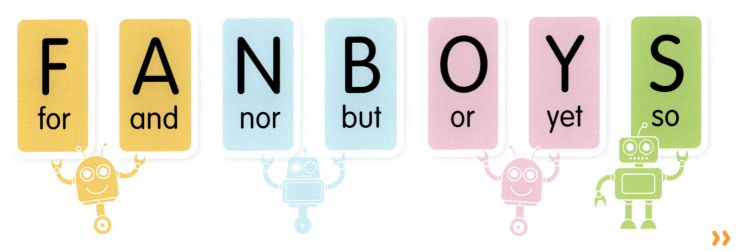

❯❯ Linking to a time or place

Subordinating conjunctions can also be used to connect an action or event to a time or place. Examples of these linking words of time and place are "once," "while," "when," "whenever," "where," "wherever," "before," and "after."

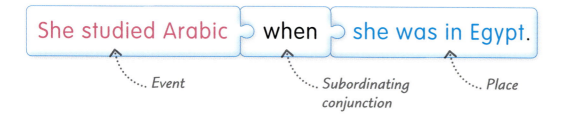

She studied Arabic ... Event | when ... Subordinating conjunction | she was in Egypt. ... Place

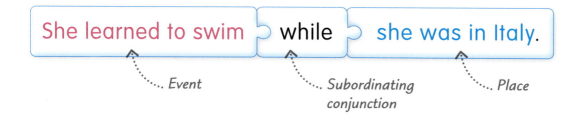

She learned to swim ... Event | while ... Subordinating conjunction | she was in Italy. ... Place

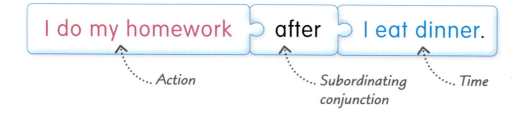

I do my homework ... Action | after ... Subordinating conjunction | I eat dinner. ... Time

Moving on …

In writing, there are linking words and phrases you can use to show that you are moving on—these are called transition words. For example, you can mark shifts in time using "first," "then," "next," "later," and "finally."

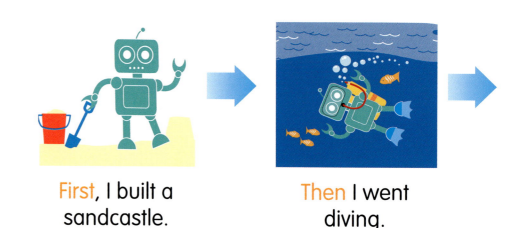

First, I built a sandcastle.

Then I went diving.

GRAMMAR • CONJUNCTIONS 49

Working in pairs

Sometimes conjunctions work in pairs, known as "correlative conjunctions." Common examples are "both" followed by "and," or "not only" followed by "but also." You might also use "either/or" or "neither/nor."

We'd like to visit both the zoo and the aquarium.

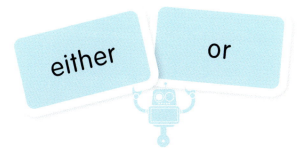

I will study either French or Spanish.

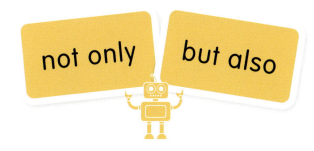

We'd like to visit not only the zoo but also the aquarium.

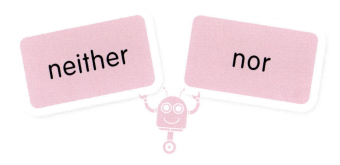

I will study neither French nor Spanish.

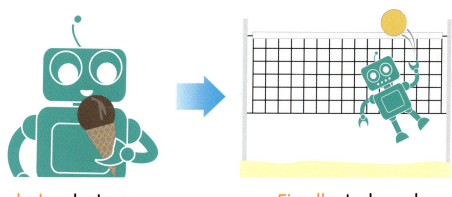

Later, I ate an ice cream.

Finally, I played volleyball.

TRY IT OUT

Build your own short sequence of events using "moving on" linking words. Start with "first." Continue with "then," followed by "next" or "later." You can end the sequence with "finally."

Tenses

When you're writing or speaking, you can use different words to show if something has already happened, is happening now, or will happen in the future.

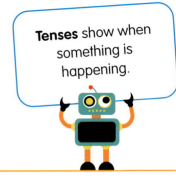

Tenses show when something is happening.

The past, present, and future

The tense of a verb tells us when it happens. This timeline shows how to use the past, present, and future tenses. Keep using the same tense to describe the same event: don't chop and change.

SEE ALSO

Verbs	26
What is a sentence?	36
Talking about the past	52
Talking about possibility	56

Past tense
The event has already happened.

I decided to paint a picture.

Present tense
The event is happening now.

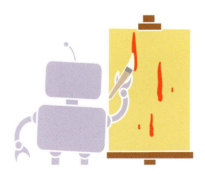

I paint a picture.
I am painting a picture.

Future tense
The event is going to happen.

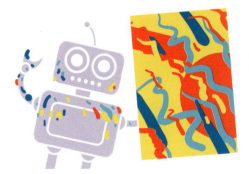

I will hang it on the wall.

SPEAK UP

Use tenses to talk about an action you **did** yesterday, an action you **are doing** today, and an action you **will do** tomorrow.

TRY IT OUT

Try writing a story in the past tense. Check that you have used the past tense all the way through.

Getting your verbs right

In a sentence, subjects and their verbs always have to agree. This means the verb needs the right ending.

Singular
When the subject of a sentence is singular, only one person or thing is doing the action or being something. Choose a singular form of the verb.

Plural
When the subject is plural, more than one person or thing is doing the action or being something. Choose a plural form of the verb.

Past tense, first-person singular

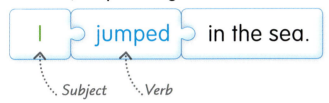
I jumped in the sea.
··· Subject ···Verb

Past tense, first-person plural

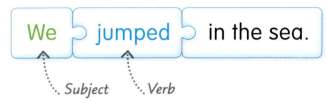
We jumped in the sea.
··· Subject ···Verb

Present tense, third-person singular

He/she/it jumps in the sea.

··· Usually, the third-person singular in the present tense ends with an "s" or "es."

Present tense, third-person plural

They jump in the sea.

Future tense, second-person singular

You will jump in the sea.

Future tense, second-person plural

You will jump in the sea.

Using the verb "to be"

Sometimes we use the verb "to be" with another word that ends in "-ing." This is the progressive or continuous tense—past, present, and future—and describes an ongoing action.

Past tense, first-person singular
I was jumping.

Present tense, second-person singular
You are jumping.

Future tense, third-person singular
Anna will be jumping.

Past tense, first-person plural
We were jumping.

Present tense, second-person plural
You are jumping.

Future tense, third-person plural
They will be jumping.

Talking about the past

Past tenses help us describe exactly when an action happened and whether it has finished or not. We can use the simple past, the present perfect, the past perfect, and the past progressive tenses.

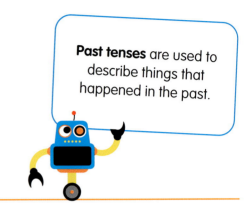

Past tenses are used to describe things that happened in the past.

Regular verbs in the simple past

The simple past is the most common past tense. It is used to talk about single actions that have already finished. Regular verbs take the ending "-ed," which sounds like "d," "t," or "ed."

SEE ALSO	
Verbs	26
Tenses	50
Vowel suffixes	104

For most regular verbs:

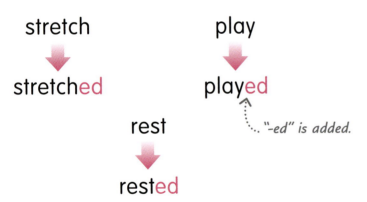

"-ed" is added.

If the verb ends with an "e":

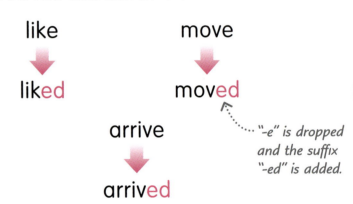

"-e" is dropped and the suffix "-ed" is added.

If the verbs ends with a consonant + "y":

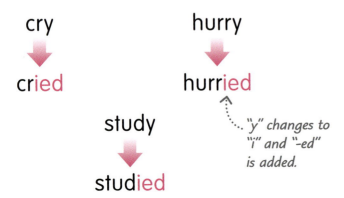

"y" changes to "i" and "-ed" is added.

When the verb ends with a short vowel sound + consonant:

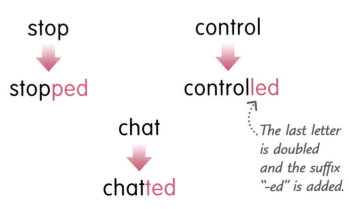

The last letter is doubled and the suffix "-ed" is added.

GRAMMAR • **TALKING ABOUT THE PAST**   53

Irregular verbs in the simple past

Some of the most common verbs in English are irregular. This means that they have their own verb form for the simple past, rather than using "-ed." We need to learn words like these individually.

be	go	say	know	eat	drink
↓	↓	↓	↓	↓	↓
was	went	said	knew	ate	drank

come	become	make	do	see
↓	↓	↓	↓	↓
came	became	made	did	saw

The present perfect

The present perfect tense is used to talk about past actions that are connected to the present somehow. They might have an impact on current actions or be statements that are still true today.

Adverbs like "just," "already," "ever," "never," and "yet" are often used with this tense.

The **present perfect** is formed from the present tense of "to have" and a past participle.

I have never eaten a cupcake.

·· The present tense of "to have."
·· Past participle

The **present perfect** can also describe actions or events that have finished very recently.

He has just finished his homework.

·· Adverbs slot in between the two parts of the verb phrase.

»

❯❯ The past perfect

The past perfect is used to talk about an event that happened before another event in the past. It is formed from the past tense of "to have" and a past participle (the form of the verb that usually ends in "-ed").

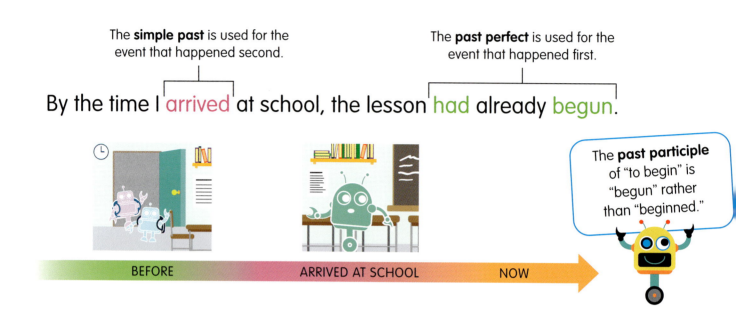

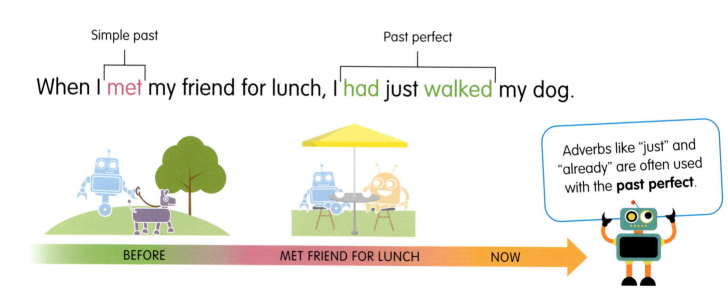

TRY IT OUT

The past perfect is useful when you're telling a story. Try talking about two things that happened last week and describe which one happened first using the past perfect.

The past progressive

The past progressive—also known as the past continuous—is used to talk about an event in the past that was still happening when another event took place. It is formed from the past tense of "to be" and another verb that ends in "-ing" (see "-ing endings" below).

They were sunbathing when it started to rain.

The past progressive is also used to talk about an action that went on for some time in the past but is now finished. In this example, she was working for a period of time in the past, but she is not working now.

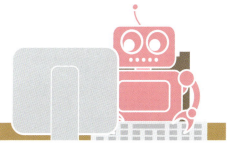

She was writing her essay all day yesterday.

"-ing" endings

To form "-ing" endings in the past progressive, add "-ing" to the base form of the verb. Remove the final "e" or change "ie" to "y" first if necessary.

wear → wearing

write → writing

tie → tying

✗ I was rode my bike.
✗ I was rideing my bike.
✓ I was riding my bike.

✗ I was ate breakfast.
✗ I was ating breakfast.
✓ I was eating breakfast.

Talking about possibility

We use modal auxiliary verbs to talk about how likely something is to take place in the future, from completely certain at one end of the scale to impossible at the other.

> We use **modal auxiliary verbs** to talk about possibility and the future.

What is a modal auxiliary verb?

A modal auxiliary verb is written before another verb or verb phrase to describe the possibility of it happening. There are nine main modal auxiliary verbs that express possibility from possible to certain. Adding "not" to these verbs expresses negative possibility, ranging from unlikely to impossible.

SEE ALSO	
Verbs	26
Tenses	50
Facts, questions, and instructions	60

can   may   shall   will   must
could   might   should   would

Add the word "not" after the modal auxiliary verb to express negative possibility.

I should get in.   I might get in.   I will not get in.

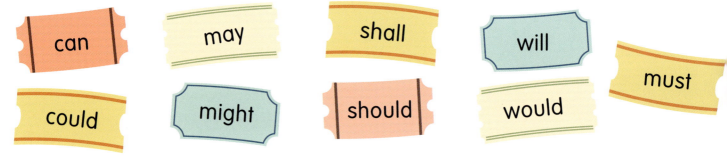

GRAMMAR • TALKING ABOUT POSSIBILITY   57

Other types of possibility

Modal auxiliary verbs can also show whether someone is doing an action because they plan to (intention), are able to (ability), have to (obligation), or are allowed to (permission).

I **will** go swimming tomorrow.
Expressing intention

I **can** go swimming tomorrow.
Expressing ability

I **must** go swimming tomorrow.
Expressing obligation

You **may** go swimming tomorrow.
Expressing permission

Word order

Modal auxiliary verbs are always written before the main verb or verb phrase in a sentence. In a statement, the modal auxiliary verb is written after the subject. In a question, the modal auxiliary verb is written before the subject.

In a statement, the subject comes first.

The main verb comes after the subject and modal auxiliary verb.

We **should** go for a walk.

Can we go for a walk?

In a question, the modal auxiliary verb comes first.

Conditional and subjunctive

We use the conditional and the subjunctive to imagine possible events and actions that don't exist now but could or would if the circumstances were right.

Use the **conditional** and **subjunctive** to describe imagined events and actions.

Using the conditional

We use the conditional to express when something could happen if something else happens first to cause it or allow it. So the main verb in a sentence in the conditional can only occur if certain circumstances are right.

SEE ALSO	
Verbs	26
Tenses	50
Talking about possibility	56

1 Conditional sentences usually start with "If …," with the conditional phrase written before the main verb. But they can also be written the other way around.

If it rains, you will get wet.

You will get wet if it rains.

2 When we want to express how likely the main verb is to happen, we can use a modal verb (see page 56), such as "might."

If you get wet, you might catch a cold.

3 When we want to express something that might have happened if the conditions had been right, we use the past tense.

If you had taken an umbrella, you would have stayed dry.

Using the subjunctive

The subjunctive is not very common in English. It is used to talk about imaginary things that are very unlikely to happen. It is also used to express wants and needs in formal or old-fashioned writing.

1 **The past subjunctive** is used to talk about imaginary events and wishes that are very unlikely to happen. A sentence in the past subjunctive usually begins with "If I …" or "I wish I …," followed by the word "were."

In informal English, people often use "was" instead of "were" here.

I wish I were a wizard, so I could use magic.

2 **The present subjunctive** is very formal and usually follows a verb that expresses a desire, a demand, or a recommendation for action. The clause containing the subjunctive verb is usually linked to the main clause with the word "that."

The subjunctive verb is written in the present tense with no "-s."

I insist that he leave at once.

What's the difference?

The conditional and subjunctive both express something that hasn't happened yet because the conditions haven't been met.

The **conditional** is used for things that could happen if the circumstances were right.

If I bounce on the trampoline, I can reach the tree.

The **subjunctive** is used to express things that probably couldn't or wouldn't ever happen.

If I were a bird, I could fly to the top of the tree.

Sometimes the form of a verb being used, such as the subjunctive or imperative (see page 61), is referred to as the verb's **"mood."**

Facts, questions, and instructions

We can use verbs for different purposes—called "moods"—to show whether we are stating facts, asking people questions, or telling them what to do.

Use the **indicative** mood to make statements, the **interrogative** mood to ask questions, and the **imperative** mood to give instructions.

Stating facts

The indicative mood
This mood is used to talk about facts or ideas we already know are true. We say that the verb is in the indicative mood because "to indicate" means to show or tell. A sentence with a verb in the indicative mood is called a statement.

Where to look for it
Factual books, reports, newspapers, stories, and information posters.

What it looks like
A statement always has a subject and a verb. It ends with a period.

> **SEE ALSO**
> Verbs — 26
> Types of sentences — 38
> Conditional and subjunctive — 58

This hill is very steep.
— Subject: hill
— Verb: is
— Period: .

Verb moods

The term "mood" doesn't mean your verb is happy or sad! It's about using the right form of a verb to show what its purpose is. The indicative mood states a fact, the interrogative mood asks a question, and the imperative mood expresses an order or an instruction.

GRAMMAR • FACTS, QUESTIONS, AND INSTRUCTIONS

Asking questions

The interrogative mood
To "interrogate" means to ask questions. We use the interrogative mood to get a "yes" or "no" answer or to find out more information.

Where to look for it
In conversation, quizzes, surveys, and interviews.

What it looks like
An auxiliary verb, or "helping verb" (like "do," "can," "is/are," or "has/have"), comes before the subject and main verb. A question word like "who," "why," "when," or "how" is added to find out more information. The sentence always ends with a question mark.

Giving instructions

The imperative mood
We use the imperative mood to ask or tell someone to do something. This includes giving other people advice, requests, instructions, or orders. You might also hear these verbs called commands or "bossy verbs."

Where to look for it
In rules, instructions, recipes, signs, and directions.

What it looks like
It's usually short, with no subject. The verb comes early in the sentence. The imperative mood uses a period or an exclamation mark.

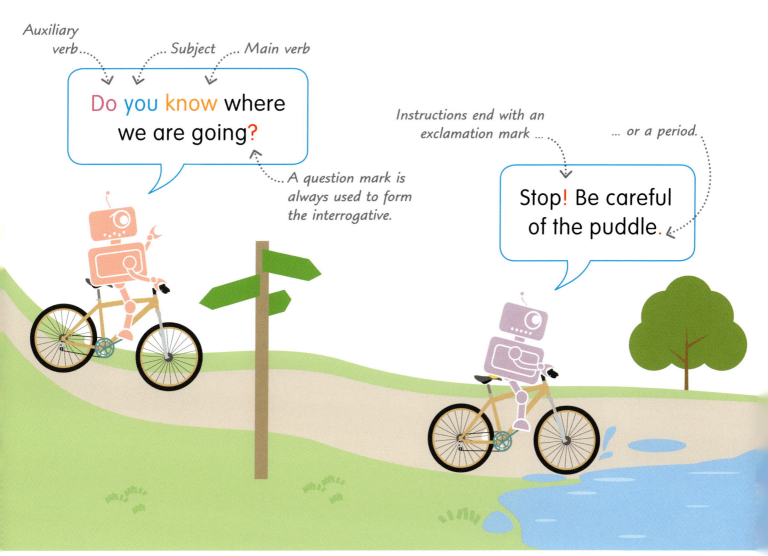

Auxiliary verb … Subject … Main verb

Do you know where we are going?

…A question mark is always used to form the interrogative.

Instructions end with an exclamation mark … … or a period.

Stop! Be careful of the puddle.

GRAMMAR • VERBALS

Verbals

Verbals are verbs that have changed their role to take on the job of nouns, adjectives, or adverbs. There are three basic types: gerunds, participles, and infinitives.

Verbals act like nouns, adjectives, or adverbs.

Gerunds

A gerund is a verb or a verb phrase which is used as a noun. It always ends in "-ing." You can check that it's being used as a noun by replacing it with the word "it."

SEE ALSO
Nouns — 12
Adjectives — 20
Verbs — 26

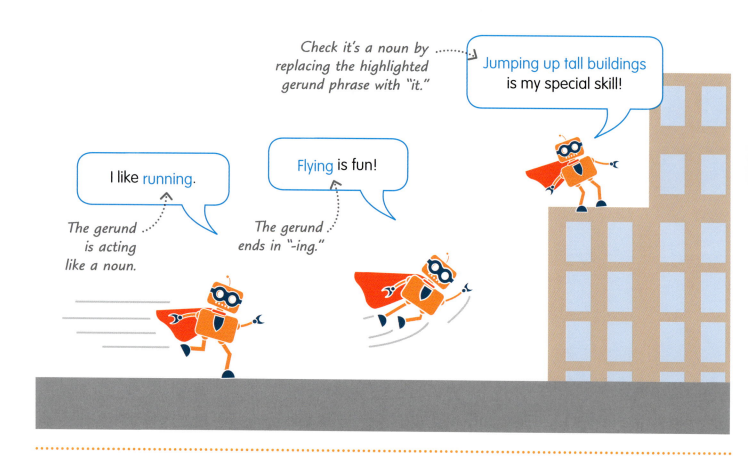

Check it's a noun by replacing the highlighted gerund phrase with "it."

Jumping up tall buildings is my special skill!

I like running.

The gerund is acting like a noun.

Flying is fun!

The gerund ends in "-ing."

How a gerund is formed

To form the gerund, add "-ing" to the base form of the verb. Remove the final "e" or change "ie" to "y" first.

walk walking

make making

lie lying

Participles

A participle is a verb that acts like an adjective, describing the state of a noun. There are both past and present participles.

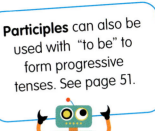

Participles can also be used with "to be" to form progressive tenses. See page 51.

Past participle

1 Usually ends with "-ed," "-t," "-en," or "-n"

2 Explains how the noun has been changed by a past action

Broken glass

... The participle describes the noun "glass."

Burnt toast

... The action describing the noun happened in the past.

Present participle

1 Ends with "-ing"

2 Describes the noun's current action

The shivering children

... The participle describes the noun "children."

The burning logs

... The action describing the noun is happening now.

Infinitives

The infinitive is the basic form of the verb. It usually comes after the word "to." Infinitives can act as nouns, adjectives, or adverbs.

To fly was her biggest dream.

... This infinitive is the subject of the sentence, so it acts like a noun.

This is the best time **to eat**.

... This infinitive tells us about the noun "time," so it acts like an adjective.

She fought **to win**.

... This infinitive describes why she fought, so it acts like an adverb.

Active and passive sentences

You can write sentences in two different ways: active and passive. Active sentences are direct and clear. Passive sentences may be used when we want to emphasize the action, which is shown by the verb, or when we don't know who's doing the action.

What are active and passive sentences?

In active sentences, the subject of the sentence performs an action (shown by the verb). In passive sentences, an action happens to the subject, and we may add the word "by" after the verb to show who or what is doing the action.

SEE ALSO	
Verbs	26
Verbals	62
Using sentences effectively	254

Using the **active voice**

Alex strokes the goat.

"**strokes**" is the active form

Using the **passive voice**

The goat is stroked by Alex.

"**is stroked**" is the passive form

GRAMMAR • ACTIVE AND PASSIVE SENTENCES 65

Forming the active and passive

Active sentences have a simple construction. Passive sentences, however, have a more complicated construction and include a form of the verb **to be**.

1 Active Active sentences follow a simple word order: subject + verb + object.

Rosa fed the chickens.

2 Passive We use a form of **to be** coupled with the past participle of the main verb to show what happens to the subject.

The chickens were fed by Rosa.

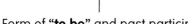

Form of **"to be"** and past participle

When to use each form

Usually, it's best to use the active voice if possible because it's livelier. The passive voice is often quite wordy, but you might use it to stress the action rather than who's doing it.

1 Active We use the active voice when we need to be clear about who does what.

Joe and Tia will collect the eggs.

2 Passive We use the passive voice when the action is important or it's not clear who's doing it.

The eggs will be collected later.

The stress is on the action.

Common mistakes

Don't mix up the active and passive in the same sentence. Be consistent in your use of one form or the other.

✔ The farmer ploughs the fields, and he sows the crops.

...... It sounds better when both verbs are active.

✘ The farmer ploughs the fields, and the crops are sown by him.

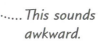

......This sounds awkward.

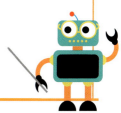

Punctuation marks may be small, but they are powerful. A period or comma, for example, can entirely change the meaning of a sentence. What would we do without question marks, exclamation marks, colons, and all the other dots and marks in the punctuation family? We rely on them to clarify meaning and make our writing easier to read.

PUNCTUATION

Why those dots and marks matter

Punctuation is an essential tool in writing. It can be surprising how much these little dots and marks affect the meaning of the words you write.

Punctuation is the use of spacing, marks, and signs in writing.

Making meaning clear

It's important to use punctuation correctly because getting it wrong can cause a lot of confusion and change the whole meaning of a sentence. Be particularly careful when you're using commas.

1 Add a comma to the first sentence, and you can save the cat's life! Commas can be very important in making the meaning of a sentence as clear as possible.

While Tom was eating the cat, the dog, and the rabbit tried to steal his meal.

While Tom was eating**,** the cat, the dog, and the rabbit tried to steal his meal.

2 Commas also give these two sentences different meanings. The first sentence says all toys are dangerous and should be banned. The second makes more sense: just dangerous toys should be banned.

Toys**,** known to be dangerous to children**,** should be banned.

Toys known to be dangerous to children should be banned.

Making tone clear

Punctuation helps convey the tone of writing. An exclamation mark (!) might point out when something exciting is happening, and a question mark (?) tells you when something is being asked. An ellipsis (…) can also show where there's a pause or a break in the writing.

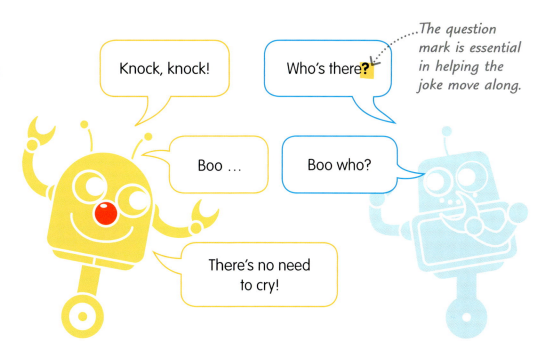

The question mark is essential in helping the joke move along.

Making things easier to read

To make writing easier to read, different words are separated from each other with a single space. Without spaces and punctuation, it's nearly impossible to read a piece of writing.

insectsaccountforatleastthreequartersofallknownanimalspeciesonearththeyhavecolonizedvirtuallyeverylandhabitatfromtheicyarctictosunscorcheddesertsonereasonfortheirsuccessistheirbodystructurewhichincludesastrongexternalexoskeletonthatprotectstheirdelicateinternalorgansandawiderangeofmouthpartstosuitdifferentdiets

Watch your handwriting

Punctuation marks are often small, so it's vital to be precise and accurate with your handwriting when making these marks. It's easy for a period to look like a comma.

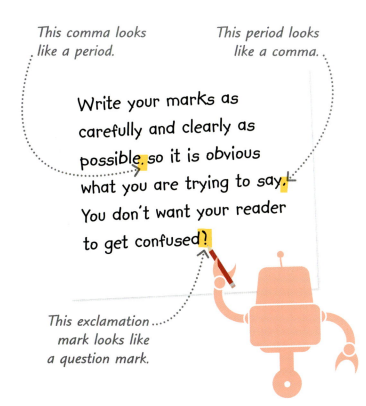

This comma looks like a period.

This period looks like a comma.

Write your marks as carefully and clearly as possible, so it is obvious what you are trying to say. You don't want your reader to get confused!

This exclamation mark looks like a question mark.

Starting and ending sentences

Using the correct punctuation and capital letters in sentences is important because it lets your reader know when one sentence ends and a new one begins.

Sentence punctuation

All sentences must start with a capital letter and end with a period, exclamation mark, or question mark. The punctuation depends on the type of sentence you are writing and how forceful the sentence is.

> **SEE ALSO**
> What is a sentence?   **36**
> Writing sentences   **252**

We always use a capital letter for the personal pronoun "I."

I think I will like this one.

The ride is starting.

I have a funny feeling about this**.**

Stop worrying**.**

1 Capital letters
No matter what type of sentence you are writing, the first word of the sentence must always have a capital letter. This tells the reader a new sentence is beginning.

2 Periods
Statements are sentences that tell you something and commands tell you to do something. We usually mark the end of these sentences with a period.

PUNCTUATION • **STARTING AND ENDING SENTENCES** 71

TRY IT OUT

Try writing some statements, exclamations, and questions about roller-coasters using the punctuation you have learned.

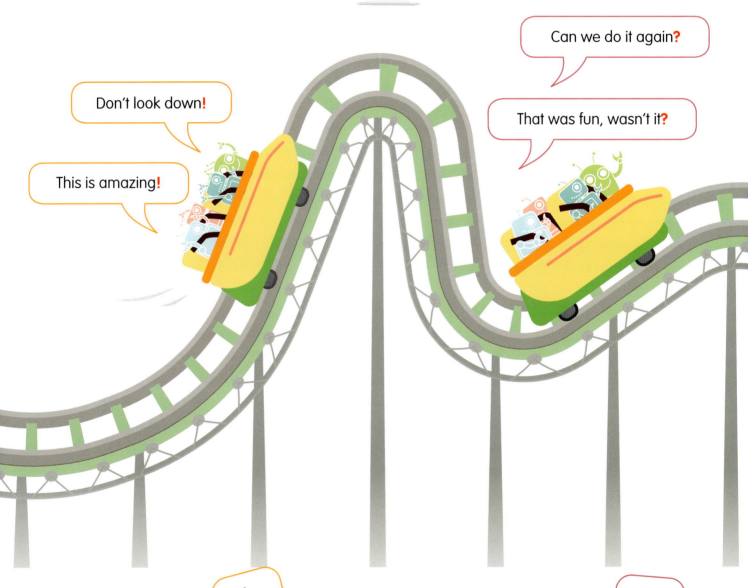

3 Exclamation marks
You use an exclamation mark at the end of a sentence to show strong feelings—such as anger, surprise, or excitement—or to show that a sentence is loud or forceful.

4 Question marks
A question is a sentence that asks something. You always use a question mark to end a question. This tells the reader that the sentence is asking something.

Punctuating direct speech

When you write down the exact words that someone has said, you are using direct speech. We place quotation marks at the start and end of any direct speech.

Quotation marks are also called **speech marks** or **inverted commas**.

What is direct speech?
Stories and reports may include speech. Direct speech is the exact words spoken. Reported speech is a summary of something that has been said.

> **SEE ALSO**
> Commas — 78
> Exploring dialogue — 166
> Narrative techniques — 276

Showing direct speech
In direct speech, we use quotation marks to show the precise words spoken by a person or character.

Opening quotation marks · · · · ·   Closing quotation marks · · · · ·

"Who left the door open?" asked Ali.

Who left the door open?

Showing reported speech
Reported speech is sometimes called indirect speech. No quotation marks are used.

Ali asked who had left the door open.

WORLD OF WORDS

Look at a website or a book. Can you find any examples of direct speech? How is it punctuated? You might see different ways of showing speech. For example, some texts use single instead of double quotation marks.

TRY IT OUT

Can you add quotation marks in the correct places in these sentences?

What are you doing? asked the man.

Sam said, We are growing sunflowers.

PUNCTUATION • PUNCTUATING DIRECT SPEECH

How to use quotation marks
Quotation marks go at the beginning and the end of the exact words that were spoken by the person or character.

WRITTEN SPEECH

"My sunflower is nearly as tall as me!" exclaimed Tom.

Ava asked, "Can we measure our sunflowers?"

"The sunflowers are growing really well," said the teacher.

Other punctuation used with direct speech
Here are some tips on how punctuation and capital letters are usually used with direct speech.

1 We use a capital letter after the quotation marks to start direct speech.

The teacher said, "**N**ext, you need to water the seeds."

2 Exclamation marks and question marks go inside the quotation marks.

"The sunflowers are so tall**!**" exclaimed the children.

3 We use a comma after the speech and inside the quotation marks.

"The sunflowers are looking wonderful**,**" the teacher commented.

4 If a speaker is identified before the speech, we use a comma before the quotation marks.

Sam asked**,** "What do plants need to grow?"

Apostrophes to show possession

An apostrophe (') is a punctuation mark that usually sits between two letters. It looks like a small straight or curly line. One of its uses is to show who owns what.

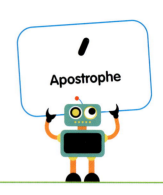

How to use apostrophes

We use an apostrophe to show who or what a thing belongs to. We usually do this by writing an apostrophe followed by the letter "s" at the end of the word for the owner.

SEE ALSO
Apostrophes to show contractions 76
Plurals 112

1 To write this phrase using an apostrophe, first identify the owner. Here, the owner is the spider.

The web of the spider

2 Next, we add an apostrophe and the letter "s" to "spider."

The spider's web

The apostrophe and "s" go after the word "spider."

WORLD OF WORDS

Bananas or banana's?

Look out for mistakes in signs using apostrophes. It's quite common for them to be wrong. Can you spot the mistakes in these labels?

To show who owns what

When there is a single owner, the way you use an apostrophe depends on whether the word for the owner ends in "s" or another letter. When there is more than one owner, the rules are a little more straightforward.

For singular words not ending in "s," write an apostrophe and the letter "s" after the owner.

This is Monica's dog.

The dog's fur is spotty.

For singular words ending in "s," either add an apostrophe and an "s" or just an apostrophe.

This is James's ball.

James' ball is yellow.

For plural words ending in the letter "s," just add an apostrophe after the letter "s."

The girls' rackets are red and blue.

The rackets' grips are brown.

For plural words not ending in the letter "s," write an apostrophe and the letter "s."

The mice's tails are long.

These are the children's pets.

Common mistakes

Apostrophes can be tricky to get right at first. Here are some tips to help you decide when and when not to use an apostrophe to show possession.

1 There is one exception to the rules on this page. When "it" is the owner, you never use an apostrophe.

✗ The dog chased it's tail.

✓ The dog chased its tail.

2 You use an apostrophe when there is an owner—not just because there is a letter "s."

✗ I love fish and chip's.

✓ I love fish and chips.

3 Look out for possessive pronouns like "theirs" and "ours." These words should not have apostrophes.

✗ The shoes were their's.

✓ The shoes were theirs.

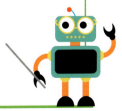

Apostrophes to show contractions

Apostrophes are a type of punctuation that we use to show that letters have been left out of a word. We call these words contractions.

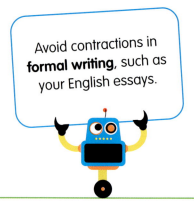

Avoid contractions in **formal writing**, such as your English essays.

Missing letters

Sometimes we leave out letters to combine or shorten words, creating contractions. We write an apostrophe where the letters have been left out of the original words.

SEE ALSO
Why those dots and marks matter 68
Apostrophes to show possession 74

you will
⬇
you'll

These letters are replaced with an apostrophe.

we are
⬇
we're

do not
⬇
don't

I am
⬇
I'm

cannot
⬇
can't

I have
⬇
I've

I would
⬇
I'd

she would
⬇
she'd

they are
⬇
they're

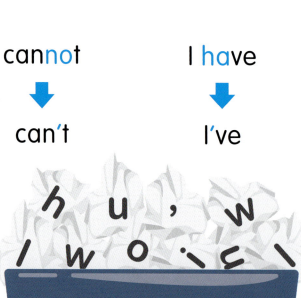

PUNCTUATION • APOSTROPHES TO SHOW CONTRACTIONS   77

It's or its?

Remember, we never use an apostrophe with "it" to show possession. To work out if you need to use an apostrophe, replace "it's" with "it is" or "it has" and see if the sentence still makes sense.

It is cold outside.

↓

It's cold outside.

It has been raining.

↓

It's been raining.

WORLD OF WORDS

What's in a name?

Sometimes you'll see apostrophes to show contractions in names. For example, "O" is short for "of" in names like O'Connor. The family name that follows keeps a capital letter.

O'Connor   L'Heureux
        d'Artagnan

TRY IT OUT

Write down the correct contractions for the following words:

he had	let us	you will
would not		we will
did not	has not	we have

Common mistakes

The apostrophe is a tiny punctuation mark, so it can be easy to make mistakes. Watch out for these common slips:

1 Sometimes we reduce phrases like "would have" and "could have" to "would've" and "could've." Although these contractions sound a bit like "would of" and "could of," this is incorrect.

✗ I would of liked some chocolate.

✓ I would've liked some chocolate.

✓ I would have liked some chocolate.

2 Make sure you check you've written an apostrophe in the correct place, which is exactly where you've left out letters. It's easy to put an apostrophe in the wrong spot!

✗ The cyclist did'nt see the puddle.

✓ The cyclist didn't see the puddle.

Commas

A comma is a punctuation mark that is used to organize our writing by separating words and clauses and to clarify meaning.

We pause briefly at a **comma** when we are reading.

Commas in lists

Commas are used to separate items in a list. This helps us avoid repeating the word "and" throughout. We use an "and" after the final comma.

SEE ALSO
Clauses   40
Conjunctions   46

The comma separates items in the list.

At the playground are swings, a slide, **and** a jungle gym.

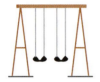  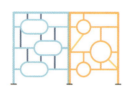

I'm growing carrots, potatoes, onions, **and** broccoli in the garden.

You need to bring a hat, sunscreen, **and** a bucket **and** spade.

We don't add a comma before "and" if it already joins the last two items in a list.

A comma before the **last item** in a list is sometimes called a **serial comma**.

PUNCTUATION • COMMAS

Commas in letters

Commas are used in dates and after greetings and closings when we write letters.

1 Use a comma after the day of the month, and after the day of the week if the date includes it.

September 3, 2021

Use a comma after the day of the month.

Friday, September 3, 2021

Use a comma after the day of the week.

Tuesday, October 12, 2021

Hello, Auntie Martina,

Thank you for the beautiful colored pencils and paper you sent me. I'm looking forward to using them to draw you a picture.

Lots of love,
Lucy

2 Use a comma after the greeting to the reader of your letter.

Hello, Grandma,

Dear Alice,

To my friend Max,

Good morning,

3 Use a comma after the closing phrase before you sign your name.

Yours sincerely,

Love,

Best wishes,

Many thanks,

SPEAK UP

Play a group game: "In the fruit bowl is …"

Each person adds another fruit to the list. Think about where you pause (add a comma) and where you say "and."

In the fruit bowl is an apple.

In the fruit bowl is an apple **and** a banana.

In the fruit bowl is an apple, a banana, **and** a clementine.

In the fruit bowl is an apple, a banana, a clementine, **and** a dragon fruit.

›› Commas and clauses

Commas are often used to separate clauses within a sentence, which makes sentences easier to read. When you're reading, a comma indicates a pause.

1 You can use a comma before a conjunction when the conjunction joins two main clauses.

It was raining, so I took the bus home.
........Conjunction

2 An adverb or adverb phrase at the start of a sentence is always separated from the main clause by a comma.

Excitedly, the children helped blow up the balloons.
....Adverb

3 Question tags turn statements into questions. Always use a comma before a question tag.

The balloons are all red, aren't they?
........Question tag

4 Use a comma before direct speech if the speaker is identified before the speech.

The teacher shouted, "Don't run!"
........Direct speech

Common mistakes

Commas should not be used on their own to join sentences. If the clauses both make sense on their own, a period or a conjunction should be used.

✗ I went to the beach, I bought a beach ball.

✓ I went to the beach. I bought a beach ball.

✓ I went to the beach and I bought a beach ball.

PUNCTUATION • COMMAS

Commas and meaning

Commas are often used to avoid confusion and make the meaning clear. A comma can sometimes completely change the meaning of the sentence.

> A **comma** can change the meaning of a sentence.

Let's eat Dad.   Let's eat, Dad.

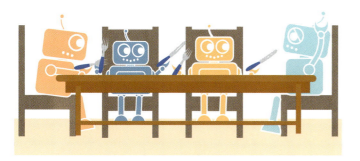

Adding extra information

We can use commas to mark extra information within sentences—this nonessential information is called a parenthetical. If we remove the information between the commas, the sentence will still make sense.

> **Parentheses** and **dashes** can also be used to add extra information. Parentheses add emphasis and dashes are used for an informal, chatty style.

The watering can, which had a hole, was useless.

The children, who had been waiting ages, were hungry.

The flowers, which were in full bloom, looked beautiful.

TRY IT OUT

Try finishing these sentences, using commas to add extra information.

Lara, who..

Inside the house, which............................

The goat, which....................................

Semicolons

A semicolon (;) is a punctuation mark that we use to join sentences and separate items in a list.

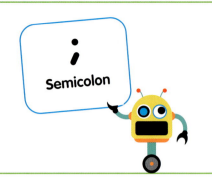

Joining two ideas

When two independent sentences are closely related, we can (but don't have to) use a semicolon to join them to make one, longer sentence. A semicolon is often used instead of a conjunction like "so" or "but."

SEE ALSO
Multiclause sentences	44
Conjunctions	46
Commas	78

Both parts of this sentence could stand alone, but because they are so closely related, we can join them using a semicolon.

It was a warm spring; the tulips were flowering early.

You can use either a period or semicolon here. Sometimes you might find a period is more effective.

The flowers were in bloom. The bees could drink the nectar.

Semicolons in lists

When we have a list that contains long phrases or groups of items, we use a semicolon to separate each of the items in the list. This makes the list much easier to read.

The semicolons separate each group.

He pruned the roses, peonies, and lilacs; weeded the flower bed, vegetable patch, and path; mowed the lawn; and watered the plants.

Put a semicolon before the last item in the list.

Common mistakes

People often use a comma when they should use a semicolon.

1 Never use a comma to join two sentences or main clauses—use a semicolon here instead.

✗ The flowers started to wilt, they didn't have enough water.

✓ The flowers started to wilt; they didn't have enough water.

2 Use semicolons, not commas, to break up long sentences that contain lists.

✗ The garden center is busy. Kids are picking flowers, adults are pushing carts, and workers are sorting seeds.

✓ The garden center is busy. Kids are picking flowers; adults are pushing carts; and workers are sorting seeds.

3 Use a comma (not a semicolon) to join a subordinate and main clause.

✗ After it rained; the flowers looked better.

✓ After it rained, the flowers looked better.

Colons

A colon (:) is a punctuation mark that we use to introduce an explanation, quotation, or list. Colons are very different from semicolons, which we use to join closely linked sentences.

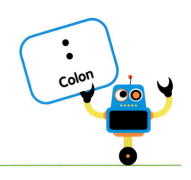

Introducing an explanation

A colon is handy when you want to add an explanation or extra information to a sentence. You write a colon after the first part of the sentence but before the explanation.

SEE ALSO	
Punctuating direct speech	72
Semicolons	82

The first part of the sentence introduces an idea.

The colon shows an explanation is coming.

The ice cream shop was popular: it had the biggest selection of flavors in the city.

The children couldn't believe what they saw: ice cream in every flavor imaginable.

The second part of the sentence gives the explanation.

The part after the colon explains what the children saw.

PUNCTUATION • COLONS 85

Introducing quotations

Colons can also be used to introduce a quotation. The statement that comes before the colon must be a complete sentence. The quotation written after the colon then explains that statement.

The girl asked the owner politely: "Please could I buy a strawberry ice cream?"

The quotation reveals what the girl said.

The owner warned the children: "Don't eat them too quickly!"

The colon introduces the quotation.

Introducing lists

Another use for a colon is to introduce a list. The first part of the sentence explains what the list will be about, then a colon is written followed by the list.

The shop owner was known for two things: his love of ice cream and his silly hat.

The colon is written before the list.

The child chose three flavors that he had never tried before: banana, coconut, and bubblegum.

TRY IT OUT

Pick up any book and see if you can spot any colons. Can you find one that introduces a list or quotation? What about a colon that has been used to add information or shed light on the clause before it?

Parentheses, dashes, and ellipses

Parentheses and dashes can be used in a similar way to commas to add nonessential information to a sentence. An added word or phrase is called a parenthetical. Ellipses (three dots in a row) are used to create a pause or suspense in a sentence.

A nonessential word or phrase added to a sentence is called a **parenthetical**.

Parentheses

When you want to add information that is useful (but not essential) to a sentence, you can use a pair of parentheses. They are put on either side of the added information. If you remove the parentheses and their contents, the remaining sentence must still make sense.

SEE ALSO
Commas	78
Hyphens and dashes	88
Using sentences effectively	254

The astronauts were heading to Mars **(**known as the red planet**)** for their mission.

Parentheses put more emphasis on their contents than commas.

( ) Parentheses

Dashes

Dashes create a stronger interruption than commas. They are also used to add drama or show a span of time or a range of numbers. If you remove a pair of em dashes and the text between them, the sentence must still make sense.

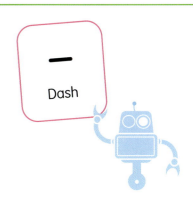
Dash

1 Use an em dash or a pair of em dashes with no space on either side to separate the interruption from the main sentence.

The journey—at over seven months—had been a long one.

The journey had been a long one—over seven months.

A dash joins the information to the sentence.

2 Use an en dash without a space on either side for ranges of numbers or spans of time.

They were almost there but only had 10–12 hours of oxygen left on board!

No space on either side

3 Use an em dash with no space on either side in the middle of a sentence to create a dramatic pause.

Mars was near—but perhaps not near enough.

Ellipses

An ellipsis (three dots in a row) can create a dramatic pause or suspense in a sentence. It can also show that words are missing, especially in dialogue.

Mars grew nearer...

This ellipsis creates a dramatic pause.

The astronauts were going to make it... just.

The captain exclaimed, "It's... it's beautiful!"

This ellipsis tells us the sentence is unfinished.

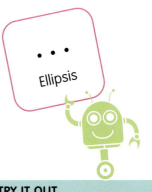
Ellipsis

TRY IT OUT

Try to find examples of parentheses, dashes, and ellipses in your own books. How have they been used?

Hyphens and dashes

Hyphens and dashes are used to join words together to form a single idea. They are very versatile: they can join adjectives, nouns, verbs, and even parts of words together.

Hyphens to join describing words

A hyphen is often used to join together two or more adjectives when those adjectives work together to form a single idea. Using a hyphen in this way helps avoid confusion and make the meaning clear.

> SEE ALSO
> Using more than one adjective   22
> Parentheses, dashes, and ellipses   86
> Prefixes   98

The hyphen joins the words that describe the noun.

A 16-year-old cat

Without a hyphen, this could suggest a bird is eating a spider.

A bird-eating spider

The runner isn't made of lightning. She is fast like lightning.

A lightning-fast runner

A smooth-skinned frog

Hyphens in numbers

We use hyphens to write numbers from twenty-one (21) to ninety-nine (99) and for fractions like two-thirds.

My grandfather is seventy-five today.

Hyphens in verbs

Sometimes hyphens appear in verbs after a prefix (such as "re" or "co") to make the meaning clear. This helps avoid confusion with verbs that would otherwise look the same but have a different meaning.

To "resent" is to feel angry about something you think is unfair.

I resent being told to eat my vegetables.

"Re-sent" has a totally different meaning. It means to send again.

I re-sent the email to my friend.

Dash or hyphen?

A dash (a longer line) and a hyphen (a shorter line) look similar but do different jobs: a dash joins phrases and a hyphen joins words.

1 Dashes
When you add information to a sentence, you can use a dash to join the extra information to the main sentence.

2 Hyphens
When you want to link words (or parts of words) together into a single unit or idea, you use a hyphen.

He was doomed—the monster had him cornered.

He was attacked by a man-eating shark.

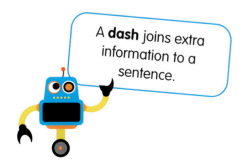

*A **dash** joins extra information to a sentence.*

*A **hyphen** joins two or more words.*

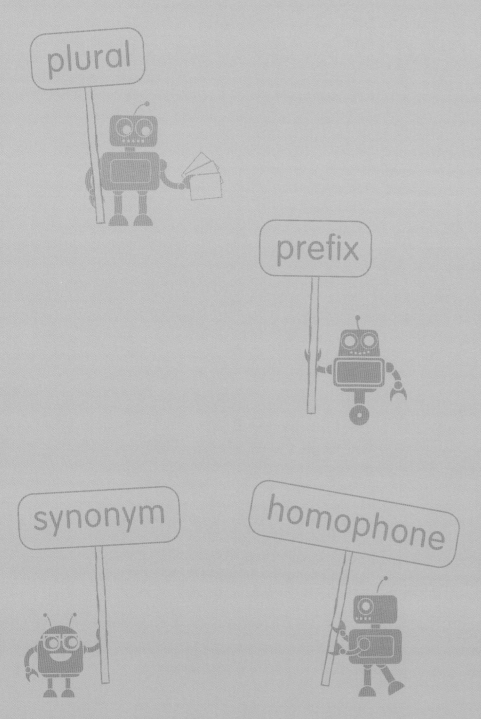

Understanding how words are put together helps you work out their meaning, spelling, and pronunciation. When you can identify a word's root, it can lead you to a whole tree's worth of words! The English language certainly includes a lot of words. It draws on Latin, Greek, and French, making it one of the richest European languages.

HOW WORDS WORK

Studying words

The study of words helps improve your understanding, spelling, and pronunciation of them. It can also increase your knowledge of other languages.

People who study words and language are called **linguists**.

Ways to study words

You can study words in different ways. For example, you may want to see if a word can be broken up into smaller, meaningful units. Or you might explore its history to find out how and when it entered the English language.

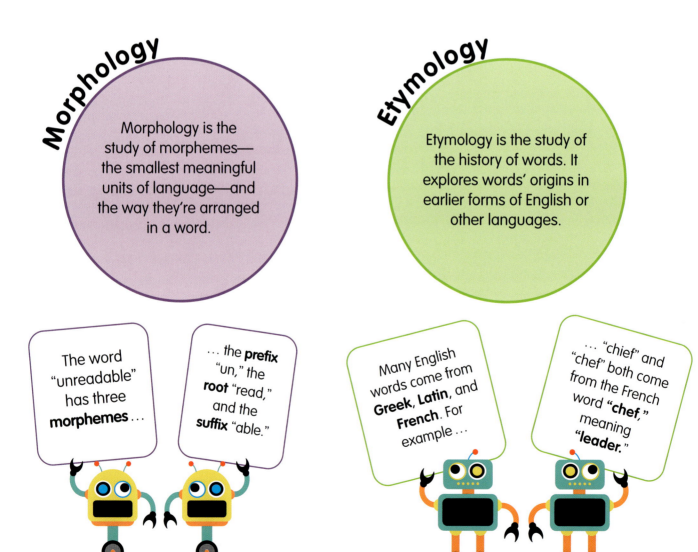

Morphology

Morphology is the study of morphemes—the smallest meaningful units of language—and the way they're arranged in a word.

The word "unreadable" has three **morphemes**…

… the **prefix** "un," the **root** "read," and the **suffix** "able."

Etymology

Etymology is the study of the history of words. It explores words' origins in earlier forms of English or other languages.

Many English words come from **Greek**, **Latin**, and **French**. For example…

… "chief" and "chef" both come from the French word **"chef,"** meaning **"leader."**

Dictionaries

A dictionary entry will tell you a word's spelling and meaning. It may also tell you the word's part of speech, how many syllables it has, and how to pronounce it.

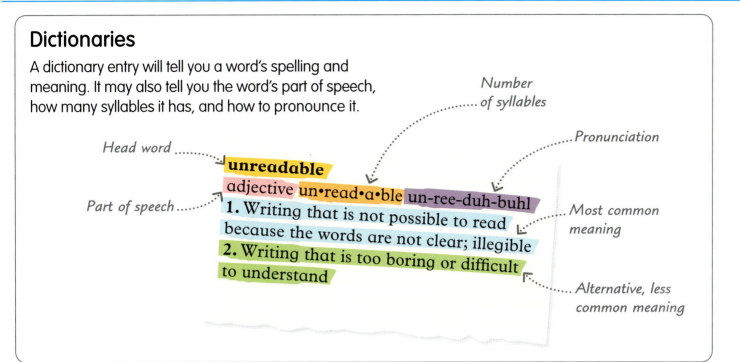

Orthography

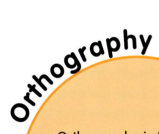

Orthography is the study of the rules of spelling. It also includes the rules on using capital letters and hyphens.

Phonology

Phonology is the study of the sounds that make up words. If you're not sure how a word is pronounced or sounds, you can check in a dictionary (see above).

Pronounced: FUH-nol-uh-jee

So many rules to learn!

WORLD OF WORDS

Lexicographers are people who compile and write dictionaries. They continuously scan all forms of writing for new words and also monitor which words are falling out of use.

Roots and root words

Roots and root words are the base parts of a word. It is from the roots that words grow and become other words, often by adding prefixes or suffixes.

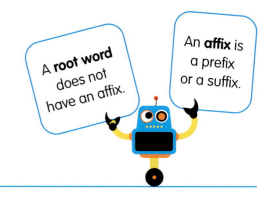

A **root word** does not have an affix.

An **affix** is a prefix or a suffix.

What are root words?

Root words are complete words that can **stand on their own** without a prefix or a suffix.

A **prefix** is a group of letters that goes at the **start** of a root word, changing its meaning.

A **suffix** is a group of letters that goes at the **end** of a root word, changing its meaning.

> **SEE ALSO**
> Breaking words into parts   96
> Prefixes   98
> What is a suffix?   102

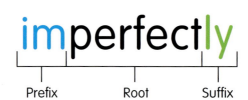

Roots and where they come from

Most English words originally came from other languages, often Latin or Greek. Knowing the definition of the root, or base part of the word, can help with spelling and with understanding the meaning of words.

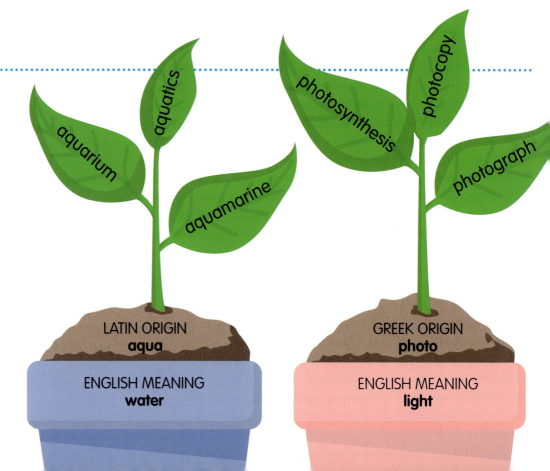

HOW WORDS WORK • **ROOTS AND ROOT WORDS** 95

Word families

Word families are groups of words that all have the root word in common, but often with different **affixes** (prefixes or suffixes). They share parts of the same spelling and are linked in meaning.

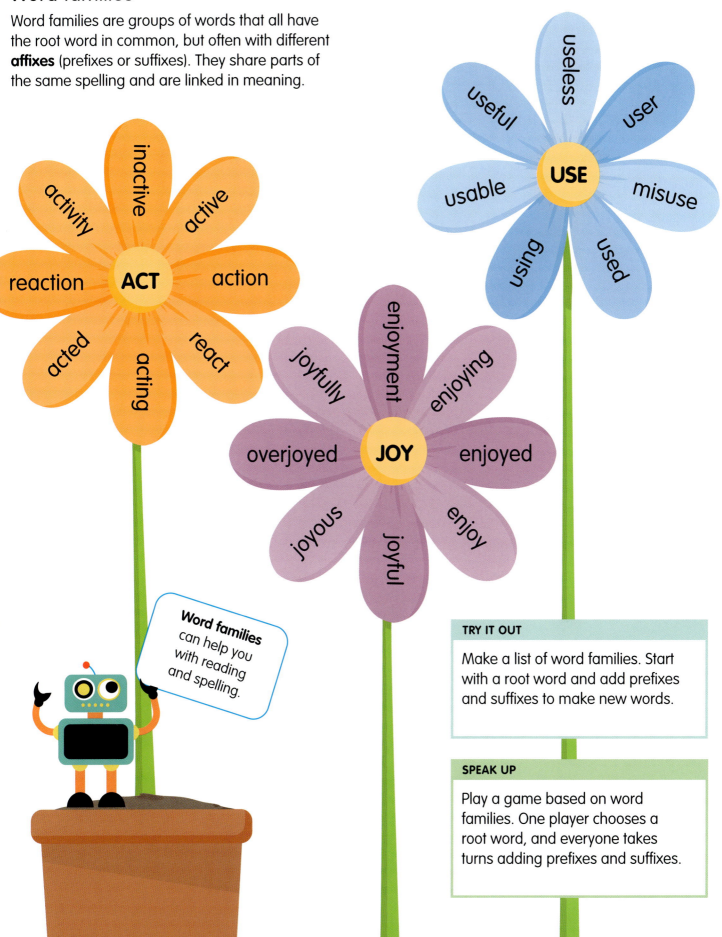

Word families can help you with reading and spelling.

TRY IT OUT

Make a list of word families. Start with a root word and add prefixes and suffixes to make new words.

SPEAK UP

Play a game based on word families. One player chooses a root word, and everyone takes turns adding prefixes and suffixes.

Breaking words into parts

Knowing how to break words into parts can help with your reading and spelling skills, as well as your understanding of the meanings of words.

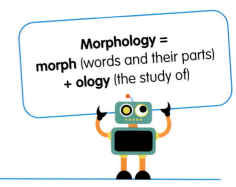

Morphology = **morph** (words and their parts) + **ology** (the study of)

How to break words into parts

If we break a word into parts and look at the meanings of each separate part, it can help us understand the word better. To do this, first find the root word, then look for any prefixes and suffixes that you recognize.

SEE ALSO
Studying words — 92
Roots and root words — 94
Prefixes — 98
What is a suffix? — 102

1 Root words

Root words are complete words that can stand alone without a prefix or suffix. For example, the word "cycle" can stand alone, but the affixes give the root word new meanings and spellings.

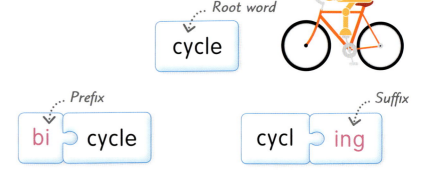

2 Roots and origins

A root is part of the word that forms the basic meaning. The origin of the root is often another language, such as Latin or Greek. For example, "ology" means "the study of." Knowing this helps us work out the meaning of words such as "technology" and "biology."

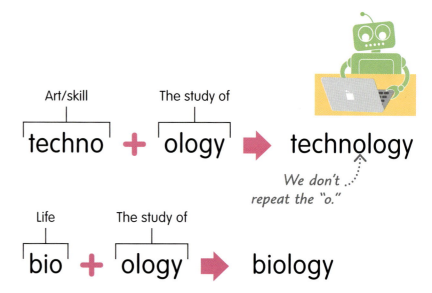

HOW WORDS WORK • BREAKING WORDS INTO PARTS   97

What are morphemes?

A morpheme is the smallest unit of a word that has its own meaning. A morpheme can be a stand-alone word, a root, or an affix. Splitting a word into morphemes helps with spelling, reading, and vocabulary. We can see in the example below how the word "play" changes meaning with every added morpheme.

A **morpheme** is the smallest unit of meaning in a word.

1 morpheme
play
to have fun

2 morphemes
playground
an outdoor area for children to play in

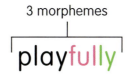

3 morphemes
playfully
done in a playful way

Bound and free morphemes

There are two types of morphemes: bound morphemes, which are always part of a word; and free morphemes, which can stand alone or join with other morphemes to form new words.

TRY IT OUT

Can you put together two words (free morphemes) to make a compound word? How many compound words can you think of?

1 Bound morphemes
A bound morpheme, such as a prefix or a suffix, can be attached to a word and add meaning to that word, but it doesn't make sense on its own.

Prefix
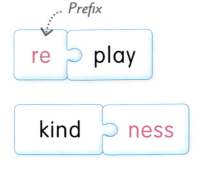

Suffix
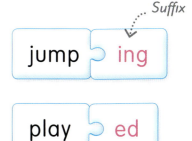

2 Free morphemes
A free morpheme is a word that can stand on its own. Joining two free morphemes together can form a new word called a compound word.

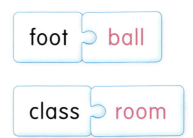

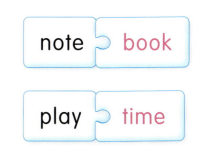

Prefixes

A group of letters added to the front of a root word is called a prefix. There are lots of different prefixes.

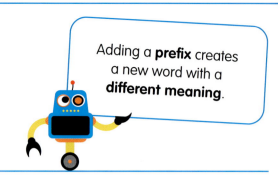

Adding a **prefix** creates a new word with a **different meaning**.

What is a prefix?

Prefixes are small groups of letters that can be added to the front of a root word to make a new word. Each prefix has its own meaning. Adding a prefix changes the meaning of the root word.

SEE ALSO	
Hyphens and dashes	88
Roots and root words	94
How to work out meaning	154

super- = above, great, big

superhero
prefix | root word

auto- = self

autograph

re- = again, back

return

sub- = under

submarine

Common prefixes

There are lots of prefixes we use regularly in everyday conversations and writing. Knowing the meaning of some of these prefixes can help you read, spell, and understand unfamiliar words. Here are some examples.

bi-	(two)	**bi**cycle	**bi**annual
com-	(with, together)	**com**panion	**com**press
mono-	(singular)	**mono**tone	**mono**logue
mid-	(middle)	**mid**night	**mid**day
inter-	(between, among)	**inter**act	**inter**national
over-	(too much)	**over**load	**over**do
semi-	(half)	**semi**circle	**semi**final

Using hyphens with prefixes

Hyphens are sometimes used between a prefix and root word to avoid confusion.

recover   re-cover

Hyphens are sometimes used if a prefix ends and the root word begins with the same letter. For example, "co-owner" and "de-escalate".

TRY IT OUT

How many different words can you think of with the prefix "re-"? Make a list.

What is a prefix with a negative meaning?

Some prefixes have a negative meaning such as "not," "no," or "against." These prefixes create a word that is the opposite of the root word.

dis- = not, opposite of

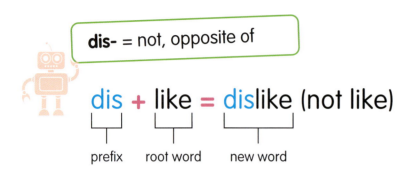

dis + like = dislike (not like)

prefix   root word   new word

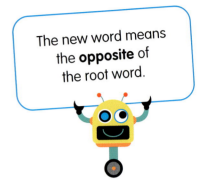

The new word means the **opposite** of the root word.

anti- = opposite, against

anti + social = antisocial (the opposite of social)

mis- = wrong, wrongly

mis + spell = misspell (spell wrongly)

non- = no

non + sense = nonsense (no sense)

The spelling of the root word does not normally change when a **prefix** is added.

in- = not

in + active = inactive (not active)

TRY IT OUT

How many different words can you think of with the prefix "**mis-**"? Make a list.

The prefix "un-"

The prefix "un-" can be added to adjectives and verbs. Usually "un-" means "not" when added to adjectives and "to do the opposite" when added to a verb. The spelling of the root word does not change.

un- + adjective = not

un + friendly

un + well

un + happy

un- + verb = do the opposite of

un + do

un + tie

un + wrap

The prefix "in-"

The prefix "in-" can change its form to "il-," "im-," or "ir-" depending on the first letter of the root word that it is added to. The prefix "in-" and its variations mean "not."

For root words beginning with "m"

in → im   im + mature

For root words beginning with "l"

in → il   il + legal

For root words beginning with "p"

in → im   im + possible

For root words beginning with "r"

in → ir   ir + regular

What is a suffix?

A suffix is a word ending that is made up of one or more letters. When placed at the end of a word, a suffix can change the word's meaning and its part of speech.

A **prefix** can only change a word's **meaning** …

… but a **suffix** can change its **meaning** and **part of speech**.

Common suffixes

Understanding the meaning of common suffixes can help you figure out the meaning of new words and their part of speech.

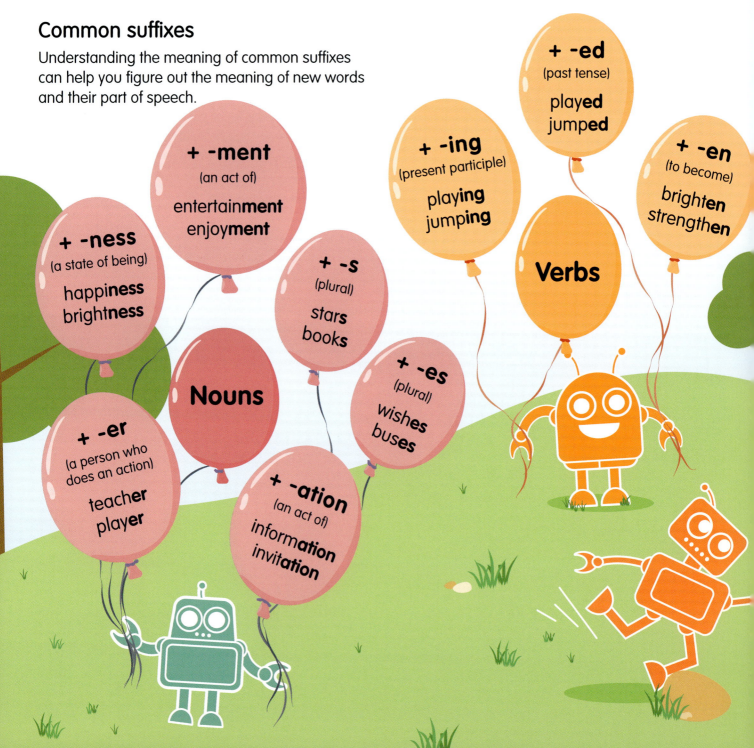

+ -ness (a state of being) happi**ness** bright**ness**

+ -ment (an act of) entertain**ment** enjoy**ment**

+ -er (a person who does an action) teach**er** play**er**

Nouns

+ -s (plural) star**s** book**s**

+ -es (plural) wish**es** bus**es**

+ -ation (an act of) inform**ation** invit**ation**

+ -ing (present participle) play**ing** jump**ing**

+ -ed (past tense) play**ed** jump**ed**

+ -en (to become) bright**en** streng**then**

Verbs

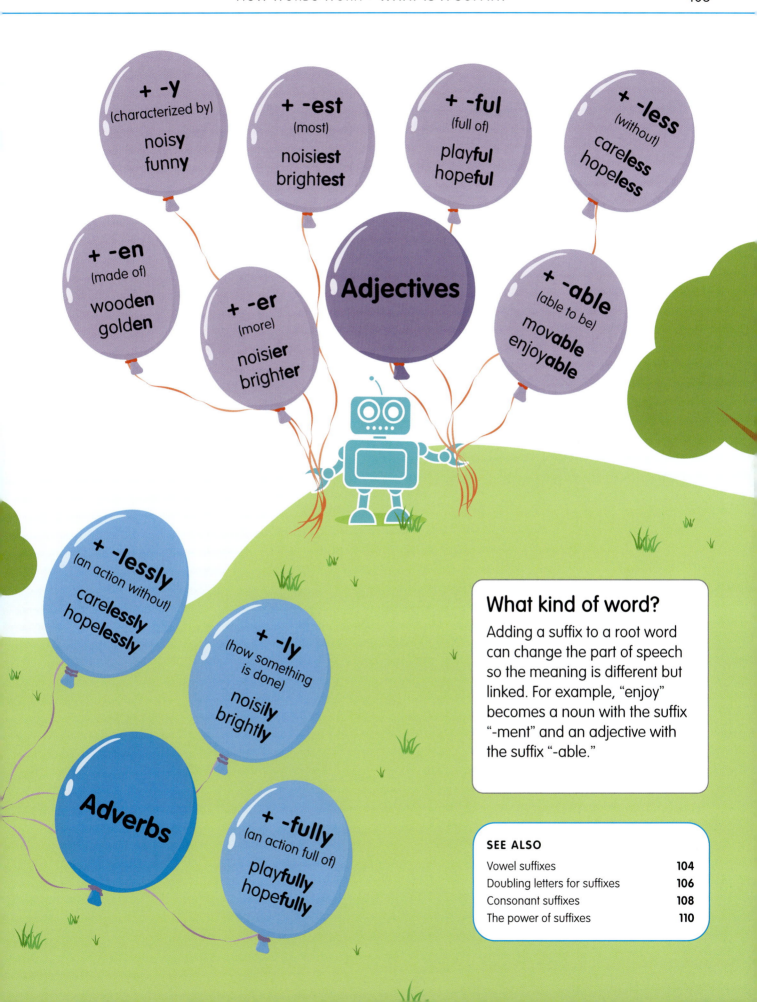

Vowel suffixes

Vowel suffixes are simply suffixes that start with a vowel. Different suffixes have different spelling rules, and the spelling rule often depends on whether the suffix is a vowel suffix or a consonant suffix.

SEE ALSO	
What is a suffix?	102
Doubling letters for suffixes	106
The power of suffixes	110
Plurals	112

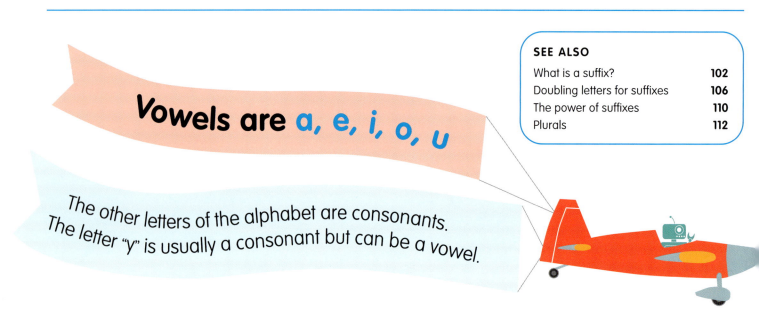

Vowels are a, e, i, o, u

The other letters of the alphabet are consonants. The letter "y" is usually a consonant but can be a vowel.

Keep the same spelling

When the root word ends with two consonants, you can add the vowel suffix without any change to spelling.

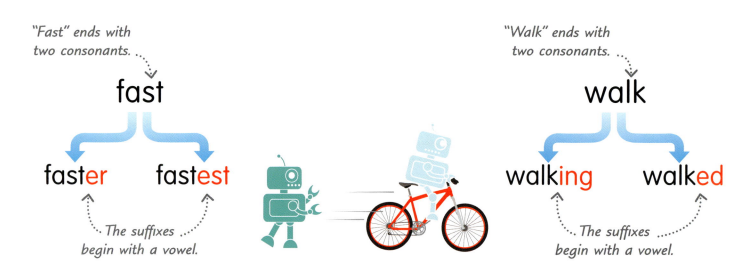

"Fast" ends with two consonants.

fast → faster, fastest

The suffixes begin with a vowel.

"Walk" ends with two consonants.

walk → walking, walked

The suffixes begin with a vowel.

Riding a bike is faster than walking.

HOW WORDS WORK • VOWEL SUFFIXES 105

Swap the "y" for an "i"

When the root word ends in a consonant followed by the letter "y," you usually swap the "y" for an "i" before adding the vowel suffix.

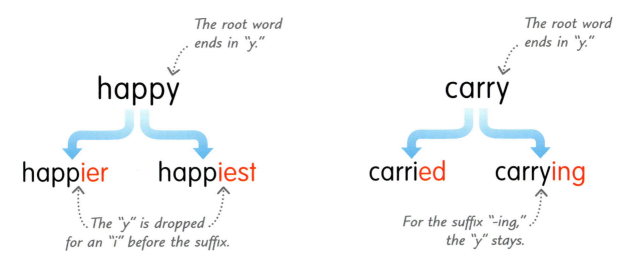

Drop the "e"

When the root word ends with the letter "e," you drop the "e" before adding the vowel suffix.

Doubling letters for suffixes

Sometimes you need to double the last letter of the root word before adding a suffix. Use your knowledge of vowels, consonants, and syllables to work out when to do this.

> A **syllable** is a beat in a word, usually with only one vowel sound.

1:1:1 rule

If a root word has **one** syllable, **one** vowel, and **one** final consonant, then the last consonant must be doubled before adding the suffix.

SEE ALSO

Roots and root words	94
What is a suffix?	102
Vowel suffixes	104
The power of suffixes	110

Root words with

 1 syllable — hop

 1 vowel — hop

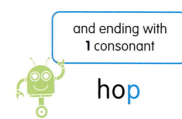 and ending with 1 consonant — hop

= Double the final consonant before adding the suffix.

1 syllable ending with 1 vowel followed by 1 consonant

hop → hopping   mud → muddy

The consonant is doubled before the suffix is added.

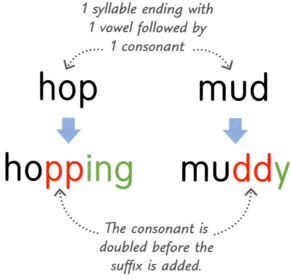
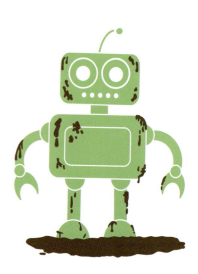

HOW WORDS WORK • **DOUBLING LETTERS FOR SUFFIXES** 107

2:1:1 rule

If a root word has **two** syllables, ends in **one** vowel followed by **one** consonant, and the stress is on the second syllable, then the last consonant must be doubled before adding the suffix.

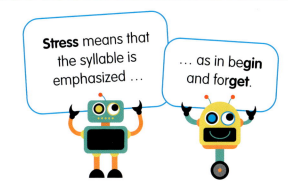

Stress means that the syllable is emphasized ...

... as in be**gin** and for**get**.

Root words with

| 2 syllables | ending with 1 vowel and 1 consonant | and the stress is on the second syllable | = Double the final consonant before adding the suffix. |

be gin   beg**in**   be**gin**

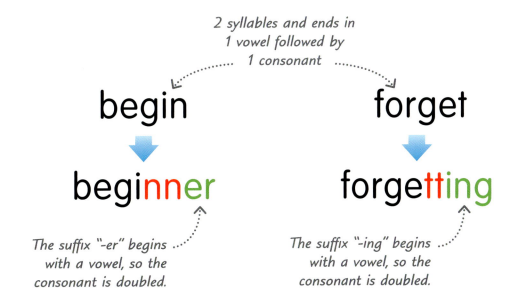

2 syllables and ends in 1 vowel followed by 1 consonant

begin   forget

begi**nn**er   forge**tt**ing

The suffix "-er" begins with a vowel, so the consonant is doubled.

The suffix "-ing" begins with a vowel, so the consonant is doubled.

Spelling exceptions

The rules don't apply for words that end in "w," "x," or "y." Notice how the suffixes are added to these words without doubling the last letter.

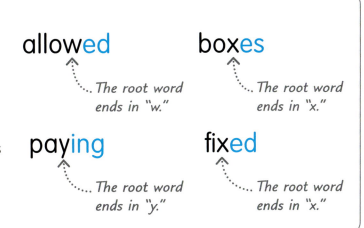

allow**ed**   box**es**

... The root word ends in "w."

... The root word ends in "x."

pay**ing**   fix**ed**

... The root word ends in "y."

... The root word ends in "x."

TRY IT OUT

Think of more words which need the last consonant doubled before adding the suffix.

Consonant suffixes

A suffix that starts with a consonant is known as a consonant suffix. Knowing consonant and vowel suffixes will help you with reading and spelling.

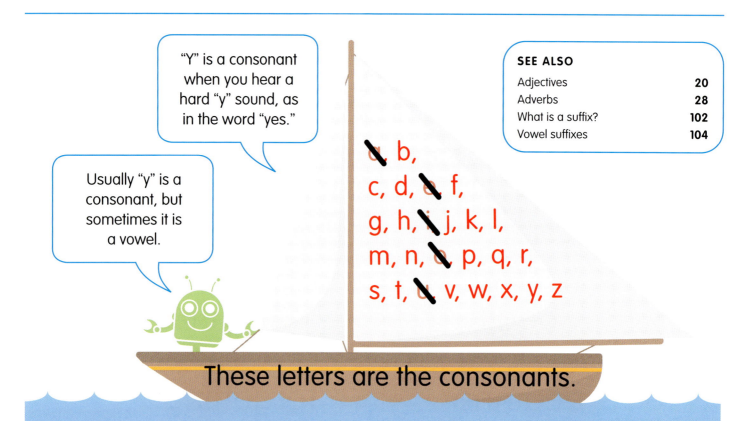

"Y" is a consonant when you hear a hard "y" sound, as in the word "yes."

Usually "y" is a consonant, but sometimes it is a vowel.

SEE ALSO	
Adjectives	20
Adverbs	28
What is a suffix?	102
Vowel suffixes	104

a, b, c, d, e, f, g, h, i, j, k, l, m, n, o, p, q, r, s, t, u, v, w, x, y, z

These letters are the consonants.

Consonant suffix spellings

If a suffix begins with a consonant, the spelling of the root word does not usually change. All we have to do is add the suffix onto the root word.

There are **no spelling changes** for most consonant suffixes.

nice + ly = nicely

hope + ful = hopeful

care + less = careless

state + ment = statement

bold + ness = boldness

child + hood = childhood

Adverbs with "-ly"

An adverb describes a verb, adjective, or even another adverb. We can often make an adjective into an adverb by adding the consonant suffix "-ly" to the end of the adjective.

> **TRY IT OUT**
> Try thinking of examples of root words where you can add "ly" or other consonant suffixes.

late + ly = lately

quick + ly = quickly

hopeful + ly = hopefully ← *The suffix "-ly" can be added to the end of the suffixes "-ful" and "-less."*

hopeless + ly = hopelessly ←

We'd better run **quickly** to catch the bus!

Spelling exceptions for the "-ly" suffix

There are some words where the spelling does change when adding the suffix "-ly."

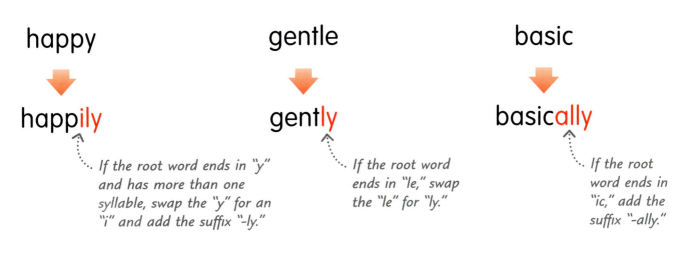

happy → happily
If the root word ends in "y" and has more than one syllable, swap the "y" for an "i" and add the suffix "-ly."

gentle → gently
If the root word ends in "le," swap the "le" for "ly."

basic → basically
If the root word ends in "ic," add the suffix "-ally."

The power of suffixes

A suffix can change both the meaning and the part of speech of a root word. The more you know about suffixes, the better your reading and spelling skills will be—and you'll increase your vocabulary, too!

Adjectives with the suffix "-ous"

When you add the suffix "-ous" to a word, you change the word to an adjective. The suffix "-ous" means "full of."

SEE ALSO	
What is a suffix?	102
Vowel suffixes	104
Doubling letters for suffixes	106
Consonant suffixes	108

Some snakes produce **venom**. — noun

Some snakes are **venomous**. — adjective

Sometimes the spelling of the root word changes. Here are some spelling rules for the "-ous" suffix.

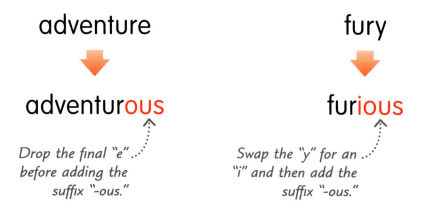

adventure → adventur**ous**
Drop the final "e" before adding the suffix "-ous."

fury → fur**ious**
Swap the "y" for an "i" and then add the suffix "-ous."

courage → courage**ous**
The "e" gives "courage" a soft "g" sound, so we need to keep the "e" and then add the suffix.

Nouns with the suffix "-ion" or "-ation"

When you add the suffixes "-ion" or "-ation" to a word, you change the word from a verb to a noun. Remember that "tion" sounds like "shun," as in the words "creation," "imagination," and "direction."

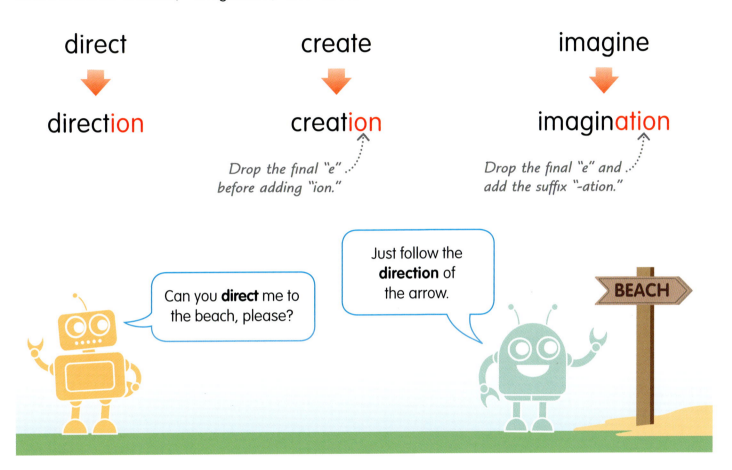

Being aware of suffixes

There are many different suffixes. Once you're aware of them, you'll notice that suffixes are very common. They have the power to make root words into lots of new words. Below are examples of some more suffixes. See how the suffixes change the meaning of the root words.

TRY IT OUT

Choose a suffix and write a list of words using that suffix. For example, how many words can you think of with the suffix "-able" (which means "able to")?

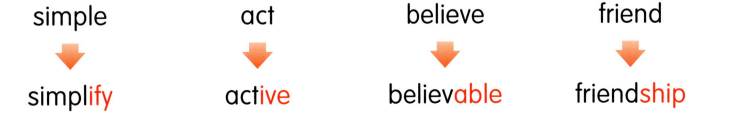

Plurals

Plural means there's more than one of something (whereas singular means just one). For most nouns, their endings show you if they're singular or plural.

Adding the suffix "-s"

To make a noun plural, we usually add the suffix "-s" to the end of the singular word.

> **SEE ALSO**
> Nouns   **12**
> Apostrophes to show possession   **74**
> What is a suffix?   **102**

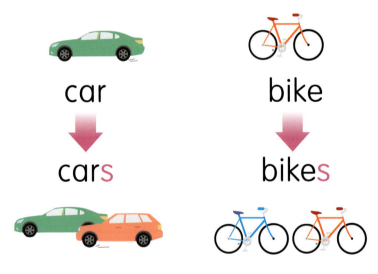

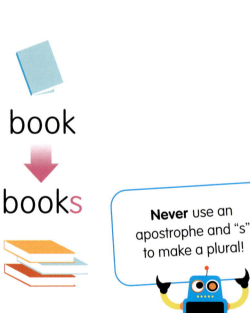

Never use an apostrophe and "s" to make a plural!

Adding the suffix "-es"

Some nouns take the suffix "-es" to make them plural. Add "es" if the noun ends in "ch," "s," "sh," "ss," "x," or "z."

Words ending in the letter "y"

When a singular word ends in a "y," we usually change the "y" to an "i" and add the suffix "-es" to make it plural.

Common mistakes

If a word has a vowel before its "y" ending, you just add the suffix "-s."

- ✔ toys
- ✘ toies
- ✔ days
- ✘ daies
- ✔ donkeys
- ✘ donkies

Irregular plurals

There are some words that, when changing from a singular to a plural, don't follow any of the rules! We just need to learn these individually.

   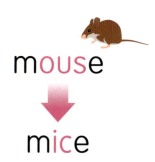

Some plurals stay the same

There are a few nouns that use the same word for both a singular item and the plural.

sheep   deer   species
moose   aircraft

We **don't change** these words to make them plural.

Homophones

Some words sound the same as others but have different meanings. These are called homophones. Sometimes they're spelled the same way and sometimes they aren't.

Some of these words may not always sound the same in **different accents**!

What is a homophone?

Homophones are words that are pronounced the same but have different meanings. As these examples show, you'll come across them quite often when reading and writing.

SEE ALSO	
Studying words	92
Silent and unstressed letters	116

see   sea

bare   bear

bored   board

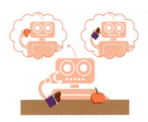   

whether   weather

What are near-homophones?

Near-homophones are words that sound almost the same but have different meanings and different spellings.

bowl   ball

HOW WORDS WORK • **HOMOPHONES**

Common homophones

It's important to recognize homophones so you understand the meaning of the text you are reading. Here are two of the most common homophones you will come across.

"to" means toward.

Debbie went to the park.

"too" means also.

Tom came too.

"two" is the number of cats.

Ali has two cats.

"they're" means they are.

They're going away.

"there" means a place.

He's there already.

"their" means belonging to them.

The group ate their lunch.

Identifying homophones

Context and visual clues can help you identify the correct meaning of homophones. Mixing up homophones can lead to misunderstandings!

Homonyms are words with the same sound and spelling but different meanings, like "break" (to snap) and "break" (time off school).

He lost his patience.

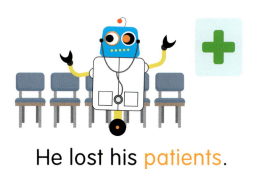

He lost his patients.

The sun shone.

The son shone.

Silent and unstressed letters

Silent letters are letters that can't be heard when we pronounce a word. Unstressed letters are vowels that are hard to hear when they are said out loud. Silent and unstressed letters can make spelling tricky.

Silent letters

We don't hear silent letters, but we do see them in words. Many different letters of the alphabet may sometimes be silent in words. Below are some examples.

Silent letters weren't always silent—long ago, they were pronounced in words.

Common silent letters

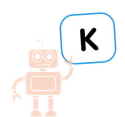

K
kneel
knight
know
knuckle

H
which
ghost
school
hour

L
should
calm
walk
half

B
lamb
subtle
comb
doubt

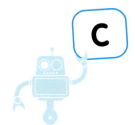

C
science
scissors
scene
ascend

W
write
two
answer
sword

Silent letters in homophones

In writing, silent letters can help you tell the difference between homophones (words that sound the same but are spelled differently).

knight

night

Unstressed letters

The most common vowel sound in English is an unstressed "uh" sound, called "schwa" (with a silent "c"). Try reading the words below with this unstressed sound in mind.

Words with **unstressed letters** may not sound the same in every accent!

zebr**a**

b**a**lloon

wat**e**r

carr**o**t

circ**u**s

foss**i**l

cam**e**l

lem**o**n

Depending on a person's accent, the unstressed letters in certain words may disappear altogether when spoken. This makes it sound like a whole syllable has gone.

libr**a**ry

fact**o**ry

deaf**e**ning

TRY IT OUT

There are no shortcuts for learning how to spell words that have silent or unstressed letters—you just need to memorize them. You can try emphasizing the silent or unstressed letters in words when writing them to help with the spellings.

SEE ALSO

Roots and root words	94
Breaking words into parts	96

Synonyms

You can replace common words in your writing with other words that have the same or a similar meaning. That way, you won't repeat yourself and your writing will be more lively and varied.

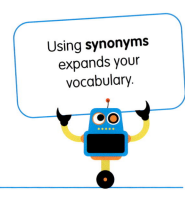

Using **synonyms** expands your vocabulary.

What is a synonym?

A synonym is a word whose meaning is identical or similar to the meaning of another word. For example, "simple" means the same as "easy," and "quiet" has a similar meaning to "silent." You can find synonyms in a reference book called a thesaurus.

SEE ALSO	
Adjectives	20
Verbs	26

I was happy to see my friends.

I was delighted to see my friends.

I was thrilled to see my friends.

I was overjoyed to see my friends.

Creating the effect you want

Make sure you choose the right word for what you want to say. There are many words for "big" that you can use with nouns to talk about size. They vary from words that mean "big" to "very big" to "extremely big." Are you talking about a big dog, a massive building, or an immense ice cap?

massive

huge

enormous

gigantic

big

large

HOW WORDS WORK • **SYNONYMS**   119

Why use synonyms?

Lots of words mean almost the same thing but with slight differences. You can use synonyms to describe exactly what you want to say. In this way, you add detail and make your writing more exciting and precise.

From under the cupboard scampered a *small* mouse, with a *small* cookie in its *small* paws.

Repeating "small" makes the text boring, and it is hard to know exactly how small the mouse is.

From under the cupboard scampered a *minuscule* mouse, with a *tiny* cookie in its *little* paws.

Verb synonyms

Like adjectives, verbs have synonyms. When you're writing, look at verbs you've used and see if you can replace them with powerful verbs—synonyms that are more specific and improve your writing.

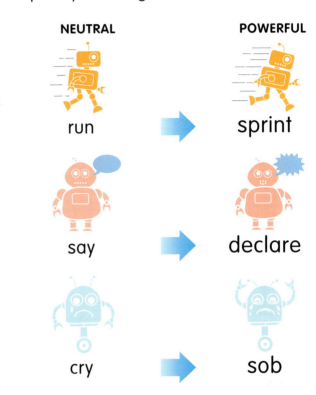

NEUTRAL	POWERFUL
run	sprint
say	declare
cry	sob

tremendous

immense

vast

TRY IT OUT

How many words can you think of that mean "hot" or "cold"? Make a list of synonyms to use when you're writing.

Losing yourself in a good book is the best feeling! It may take time to find your own reading "corner"— it could be short stories, epic adventures, poetry, or plays. Whether you want to explore our own world or escape into another one, reading stories, plays, and poems will help you learn new words and ideas. You'll also meet a huge range of characters!

READING STORIES, PLAYS, AND POEMS

Why read?

Reading is a fun and interesting hobby that will also help you expand your mind. Eager readers make high achievers—and happy ones, too!

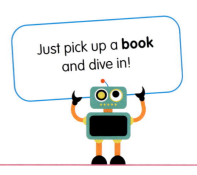

Just pick up a **book** and dive in!

Why read fiction?

Stories, plays, and poems are a gateway to exploring new places and ideas, meeting new characters, and taking a break from day-to-day life. Escape into different places or times on Earth, in space, or in fantasy worlds, all without leaving your chair.

1 Explore
Get to know exciting and diverse people, places, cultures, and time periods.

2 Learn
Let your brain soak up words, facts, opinions, and ideas from fiction and its characters.

3 Imagine
Experience impossible, fantastical adventures—no safety net required!

Choosing what to read

Now that you know why reading is so great, it's time to browse the shelves and choose your next book.

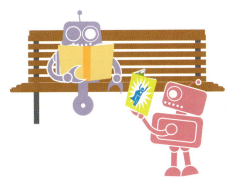
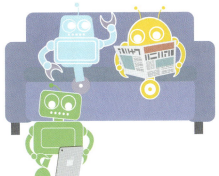

1 What type of fiction?
Scary, funny, or thrilling? Novels, poems, or comics? It's completely up to you!

2 How do you want to read?
Turn the pages of a book, read on a screen, or even have a book read to you.

3 Where to find it?
Browse your public library's shelves or website or look at school, at home, or in bookstores.

Amazing benefits of reading

Books are entertaining, but they also give your brain a workout. When you read, you follow clues in the language and plot to understand what's going on and predict what happens next. The skills you learn when reading can help you throughout your life.

✓ Discover exciting stories and explore new places.
✓ Find your own place in the world.
✓ Understand how other people see the world.
✓ Become a more confident reader.
✓ Learn how to write well by reading great writing.
✓ Get more out of all your school subjects.
✓ Enjoy a hobby that helps you unwind.

Reading before bed can help your brain relax into "sleep mode."

> **WORLD OF WORDS**
>
> ## The power of books
>
> Activist Malala Yousafzai has been passionate about reading since she was a child in Pakistan. She particularly enjoys stories that reflect real life. She's gone on to write several books, win the Nobel Peace Prize, and inspire other young people to achieve big dreams.

Features of stories, plays, and poems

Stories, plays, and poems cover many genres, including action, comedy, mystery, and romance. They allow the writer to express their imagination in countless ways.

What are the **differences** between stories, plays, and poems?

Stories

① **Subject** Invented characters in realistic or fantastic situations

② **Structure** Novels (often divided into chapters) or short stories

③ **Grammar** Usually in prose (full sentences and paragraphs)

④ **Narrator** Usually either an invisible observer (third person) or a main character (first person)

⑤ **Sounds** Mostly read silently, though they can be read aloud

SEE ALSO	
Why read?	122
Genres	126
Making sense of poetry	150

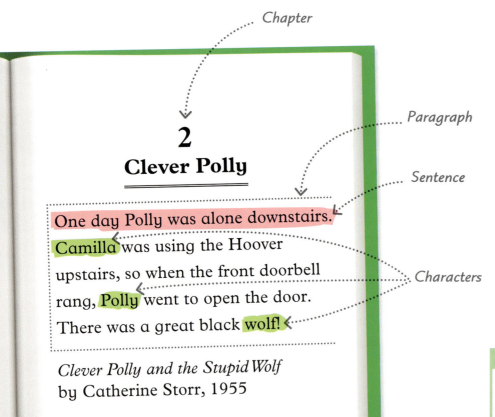

Clever Polly and the Stupid Wolf by Catherine Storr, 1955

SPEAK UP

Read each of these three text excerpts out loud. What differences can you hear, and what do they have in common?

READING STORIES, PLAYS, AND POEMS • FEATURES OF STORIES, PLAYS, AND POEMS

Plays

1. **Subject** Examples include comedy, tragedy, or musical
2. **Structure** Divided into scenes and acts (groups of scenes)
3. **Grammar** Written in dialogue (speech) with stage directions
4. **Narrator** Usually the characters, through their dialogue
5. **Sounds** Designed to be performed aloud by one or more actors to an audience

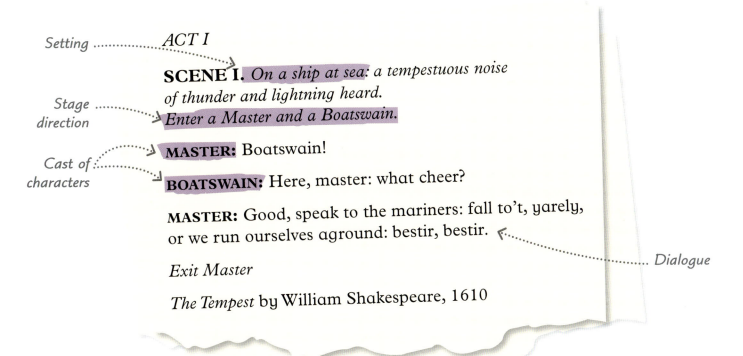

Setting — ACT I

Stage direction — SCENE I. *On a ship at sea: a tempestuous noise of thunder and lightning heard.*
Enter a Master and a Boatswain.

Cast of characters — **MASTER:** Boatswain!

BOATSWAIN: Here, master: what cheer?

MASTER: Good, speak to the mariners: fall to't, yarely, or we run ourselves aground: bestir, bestir. — *Dialogue*

Exit Master

The Tempest by William Shakespeare, 1610

Poems

1. **Subject** Fiction or fact, often from the poet's own experience
2. **Structure** Short or long, usually arranged in verses or stanzas
3. **Grammar** Lines of equal or different lengths, not always full sentences
4. **Narrator** Poems usually express the poet's own thoughts and ideas
5. **Sounds** Generally read aloud, so rhythm and rhyme add interest

I eat my peas with honey; — *Rhythm*
I've done it all my life. — *Rhyme*
It makes the peas taste funny,
But it keeps them on the knife.

Anonymous

126 READING STORIES, PLAYS, AND POEMS • GENRES

Genres

There are many different styles of fiction, called genres (French for "sorts" or "kinds"). Each genre has important elements that the reader expects, called conventions. Some genres, such as tragedy and myth, have been popular for thousands of years. Others, such as realism and science fiction, are much more modern.

Genre is the name for a particular **style of writing**, such as comedy. It is also known as "text type."

SEE ALSO
What is the setting? 130
Understanding characters 136
Identifying themes 172

Tragedy

A tragedy is a story that includes great suffering and a sad ending. The English playwright William Shakespeare is famous for his tragedies, such as *Hamlet* and *Macbeth*.

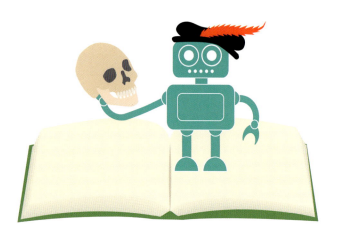

Tragedy conventions

1. **Fatal flaw** The main character has a fatal flaw, such as pride or jealousy.
2. **Self-discovery** The main character changes as they learn more about themselves.
3. **Shift** There is a shift—from good to bad—in the main character's fortunes.
4. **Suffering** The main character suffers due to the events in the story.

Romance

Romance has always been—and continues to be—one of the most popular genres of fiction. Whether it's a novel or a drama, romance always has a love story at its heart.

Romance conventions

1. **Rival** A rival to the main character adds a spark and a rise in tension.
2. **Secrets** The main characters keep secrets, which also add tension to the story.
3. **Help or harm** Other people either encourage or block the romance.
4. **Happy ending** In most cases, a romance finishes with a happy ending.

READING STORIES, PLAYS, AND POEMS • GENRES

Fairy tales

These timeless stories, full of magical events and bizarre plot twists, are especially popular with children. There are often many different versions of the same basic story.

Fairy tale conventions

1. **Magic** There are magical events and characters.
2. **Hero or heroine** This character faces an obvious villain.
3. **Resolution** The hero or heroine overcomes the villain.
4. **Moral** The story has a message we can learn from.

Comedy

This genre is light-hearted and makes fun of people and situations. There are various types of comedy (called subgenres), including satire, farce, and parody.

Comedy conventions

1. **Everyday life** Comedy often shows the frustrations of everyday life.
2. **Exaggeration** This genre often exaggerates an event or someone's actions.
3. **Fool** There may be a character in the story who acts very foolishly.
4. **Happy ending** Even if there's a serious edge, the story usually ends happily.

Realism

As its name suggests, this genre bases itself in reality. It tries to reflect the world around us by focusing on familiar situations and everyday—often seemingly boring—experiences.

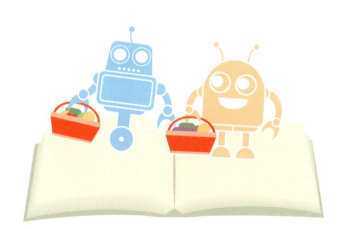

Realism conventions

1. **Real characters** The characters appear and sound like real people.
2. **Real settings** Settings are realistic and not out of the ordinary.
3. **Plot** The plot is believable, and the story is told in a truthful way.
4. **Language** Realism uses simple, clear language to tell the story.

Fantasy

This genre features worlds in which there is magic. The *Harry Potter* series is a famous modern-day children's fantasy about a school for wizards.

Adventure

These stories are exciting! The hero or heroine has a quest. But a villain—who seems to hold all the cards—stands in their way. The hero or heroine must be daring and smart to survive and triumph.

Fantasy conventions

1 Magic The key part of the story is magic or some supernatural element.

2 World-building The building of imaginary worlds is important in fantasy.

3 Cast Characters are well defined and are often "chosen" to carry out a mission.

4 Conflict The main character faces an inner struggle or a struggle with an enemy.

Adventure conventions

1 Thrills Adventure stories are jam-packed with thrills and excitement.

2 Tension The tension rises during the story as the stakes get higher.

3 Plot twists Adventure stories need plenty of twists and turns for interest.

4 Happy ending The story ends happily, after the hero or heroine succeeds.

Best of the rest

Horror and thriller
Tension builds to keep you on the edge of your seat in these scary genres.

Crime and mystery
A character, often a detective, solves a serious crime.

Historical
This genre of fiction takes place in the past and may include real historical people or events.

Young adult
These stories are written for teenagers and young adults.

Some stories may **combine** more than one genre.

READING STORIES, PLAYS, AND POEMS • GENRES 129

Myths and legends

Myths are ancient stories that were passed down through many generations. Eventually, they were written down. Legends are old stories in which historical fact has been exaggerated.

Science fiction

Closely related to fantasy and also called sci-fi, science fiction features alternative realities. Sci-fi stories often include aliens or center on how humans cope with challenges in the future.

Myths and legends conventions

1. **Big characters** Characters are much larger than life in myths and legends.
2. **Quests** Heroes and heroines face dangerous or thrilling tasks or challenges.
3. **Creatures** Often, mythical monsters or fantastic creatures have to be defeated.
4. **Strange things** Mythical stories often explain strange occurrences in nature.

Science fiction conventions

1. **Setting** Sci-fi is set in the future, space, or another world or universe.
2. **Science** Future technology and science will feature in the stories.
3. **Plot** However strange, the plot should be believable in its sci-fi setting.
4. **People** Sci-fi often focuses on how people live and survive in space or the future.

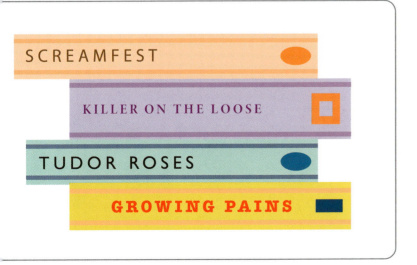

> **TRY IT OUT**
>
> Write an adventure story in which you have to go on a special mission. You'll need to escape danger. Don't forget to add a plot twist, too.

What is the setting?

The setting tells the reader where and when the story or play takes place, helping the reader imagine the story better. A setting can shift many times, jumping between different locations or time periods.

The **setting** is where and when the story happens.

Examples of settings

Where and when does the story take place? The author chooses the setting that helps tell the story in the best way.

SEE ALSO	
Adjectives	20
Why the setting matters	132
Creating a setting	270

1 **Where** does the story take place? A setting can be anywhere, such as:

In a haunted house

In outer space

In a jungle

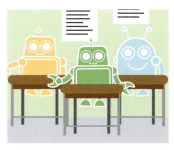
At school

2 **When** does the story take place? It can be set at any time, in any era, during any season, or in any conditions, such as:

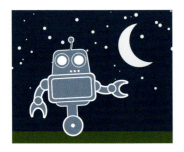
Day or night?

Past, present, or future?

What season is it?

What is the weather like?

What does the setting do?

A setting not only tells the reader where and when the story takes place, but also helps move the plot along, gives the story context, and offers clues to the story's theme and mood.

Each of these paragraphs begins with Sadia trembling. How does the setting help you work out why she is trembling?

> **TRY IT OUT**
>
> Describe the setting of a story. Maybe the story takes place in a park, or maybe it's on the moon!

Sadia trembled. All around her, a cold blanket of white sparkled in the winter sun. The *forest was covered in snow*.

The setting of the snowy forest tells us that Sadia is trembling from the cold.

Sadia trembled. She knew the audience was waiting for her. In a moment, the curtain would rise and she would be *on stage*.

The setting of the stage tells us that Sadia is trembling with nerves.

How the scene is set

The setting is sometimes described in a paragraph toward the beginning of a story, but often clues are mixed in with the action and revealed gradually. Look for places and things mentioned in the story to help identify the setting. Details add to the image formed in the reader's mind. In a play, the stage directions describe the "set"—made up of scenery and objects—that will be created on stage.

Sadia is by herself on stage.

Suddenly, the red curtain rose, and Sadia was **alone on stage**. For a moment, the spotlight blinded her. Then she saw the **familiar auditorium**, with its paneled walls and **double doors** at the back. **It was packed with students and parents**—and they were all looking right at her. **Poor Sadia felt like running out of the double doors.** Why on earth had she agreed to perform in the school talent show? But when she heard the music start, she clutched the microphone in her hand and began to sing.

She's been in the school auditorium many times.

There is a large audience.

The repetition of "double doors" shows that nervous Sadia wishes she could run away.

Why the setting matters

The author sets the scene for the reader, describing the details that matter most to the story, poem, or play. Imagining the setting helps the reader understand the story and how the characters feel.

The reader should be able to **imagine** the **setting**.

Settings in stories

In fiction, the setting is described as part of the story, often through the point of view of the characters. What would the characters see, hear, or feel in the setting?

In this paragraph from *Oliver Twist* by Charles Dickens, the setting is a street in Victorian London as seen through the eyes of Oliver. What image does this description create in your mind?

SEE ALSO
Adjectives — 20
What is the setting? — 130
Creating a setting — 270

The adjectives paint a vivid picture of the setting.

Describing sights, sounds, or smells brings the setting to life.

A dirtier or more wretched place he had never seen. The street was very narrow and muddy, and the air was impregnated with filthy odors. There were a good many small shops; but the only stock in trade appeared to be heaps of children, who, even at that time of night, were crawling in and out at the doors, or screaming from inside.

The children could be an important detail.

It's nighttime.

The reader can imagine the screaming children.

Oliver Twist by Charles Dickens, 1838

Settings in plays

In a play, the setting is usually described in stage directions that enable the play's director and set designer to create the set on stage. The set is made up of scenery and props that give the audience clues as to when and where the play takes place.

These opening stage directions from the musical play *The Pirates of Penzance* by Gilbert and Sullivan describe the setting for the first scene of the play. Imagine what the set might look like.

> **WORLD OF WORDS**
>
> William Shakespeare wrote his plays with the intention of directing them himself, so he only included brief notes on the settings.

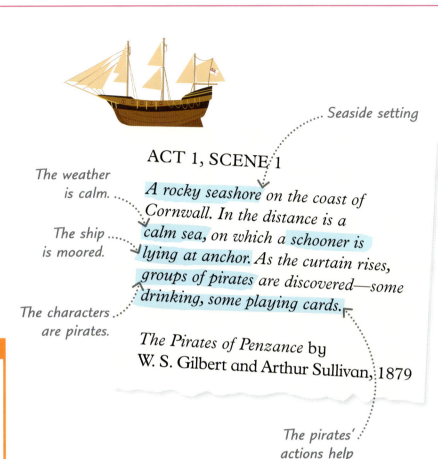

ACT 1, SCENE 1

A rocky seashore on the coast of Cornwall. In the distance is a calm sea, on which a schooner is lying at anchor. As the curtain rises, groups of pirates are discovered—some drinking, some playing cards.

The Pirates of Penzance by W. S. Gilbert and Arthur Sullivan, 1879

- Seaside setting
- The weather is calm.
- The ship is moored.
- The characters are pirates.
- The pirates' actions help set the scene.

Settings in poetry

In a poem, the setting can help establish the mood and the feeling that the poet is trying to convey to the reader or listener.

The first verse of the poem "The Pied Piper of Hamelin" describes the town before it is invaded by rats.

> Hamelin Town's in Brunswick,
>   By famous Hanover city;
> The river Weser, deep and wide,
> Washes its wall on the southern side;
> A pleasanter spot you never spied;
>   But, when begins my ditty,
> Almost five hundred years ago,
> To see the townsfolk suffer so
> From vermin, was a pity.

From "The Pied Piper of Hamelin" by Robert Browning, 1842

- The name of the setting
- Describes the town in the present day.
- Sets the scene of the rat problem.
- Goes back in time to when the action happens.

Characters

Authors create and write about fictional characters that have personality traits like people in real life. Stories include main characters and secondary characters.

The main character is sometimes called the **protagonist**.

What are characters?
A character is a person or another type of being in a story. Main characters play a major role. Other characters have supporting, or secondary, roles.

SEE ALSO
Understanding characters   136
Who's telling the story?   138
Creating characters   272

1 Main characters
A story needs to have a main character, or **protagonist**, who drives the plot. Stanley Yelnats in *Holes*, Bilbo Baggins in *The Hobbit*, and Katniss Everdeen in *The Hunger Games* are all main characters. Even Wilbur, the piglet in *Charlotte's Web*, is a main character.

2 Secondary characters
Hermione and Ron in the *Harry Potter* series are **secondary characters** and both play an important role in the story. They add depth and color to the narrative, but the story does not revolve around them—it revolves around the main character, Harry.

WORLD OF WORDS

Not all stories are told from the point of view of the main character. *Howl's Moving Castle* by Diana Wynne Jones is all about Sophie, but it has a third-person omniscient narrator—a storyteller who knows everything.

READING STORIES, PLAYS, AND POEMS • CHARACTERS   135

Antagonists

In a story, the main character, or protagonist, often has to face an enemy, or **antagonist**. Antagonists give stories their energy by providing tension and conflict. Usually villainous, they create obstacles for the main character to overcome. Unforgettable antagonists include Harry Potter's archenemy Lord Voldemort, Matilda's tyrannical headmistress Miss Trunchbull, and the Baudelaire orphans' scheming guardian Count Olaf.

An **antagonist** works against the goals of the main character.

> **TRY IT OUT**
>
> Think of some of your favorite stories. Who's the antagonist? What problems do they cause for the main character?

Character traits

The qualities that make up a character's personality are called **traits**. What is the character like? Do you sympathize with them or not? All the characters—especially the main character—should be believable, well-rounded people. They may be cheerful, sporty, artistic, or shy—yet sometimes they may say or do things that are the opposite of what you might expect. Especially when under pressure!

A **trait** is a characteristic that someone has.

CHEERFUL

SPORTY

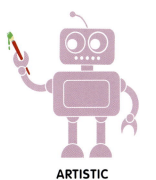
ARTISTIC

SHY

Understanding characters

We need to get to know characters in stories to understand their behavior. We can compare them, look at what they say, and analyze how they change during the story.

Characters can be complicated—just like people in real life!

Getting to know characters

When we read a story or watch a play, we follow a main character. In the fairy tale *Beauty and the Beast*, we may know what the Beast looks like, but we may also want to know what his feelings and motives are.

SEE ALSO
Characters — 134
Creating characters — 272

OUTSIDE
Furry face
Scary horns
Piercing eyes
Flaring nostrils
Fearsome fangs

INSIDE
Ruthlessness
Sadness
Shame
Anger
Love for Beauty
Longing to break the curse
Fear of losing Beauty

Looking at dialogue to understand characters

What characters say can tell us a lot about them and the way they think. In *Beauty and the Beast* from Logan Marshall's *Favourite Fairy Tales*, we know that the Beast is a terrifying monster, but we can find out more about his thoughts and feelings through his actual words.

Then Beauty begged him to let her go and visit her father. The Beast was very unwilling to grant her request.
"If I let you go, **I am afraid you will never come back to me,**" he said, "**and then I shall die of grief.**"

The Beast is scared of losing Beauty.

He loves Beauty and can't live without her.

Comparing characters

It's often useful to compare characters in a story. Here, we look at four key aspects of the two main characters in *Beauty and the Beast*.

KEY ASPECT	BEAST	BEAUTY
Home life	Lives in the castle alone—until he imprisons Beauty (as a deal after her father steals a rose)	At first at home with her family; later as a prisoner in the Beast's castle
Personality	Often kind, but unpredictable, too—for example, he's prone to fits of sudden anger	Happy, easygoing, and humble; kind-hearted nature; thoughtful to others
Appearance	Hideous appearance; scary; terrible to look at—for both Beauty and her father	Young and beautiful
Generosity	Generosity comes with conditions—for example, Beauty's father has to give up his daughter	Unconditional; courageously takes the place of her father in the castle to spare his life

Evolution of characters

Characters usually evolve (develop), such as changing from cowardly to brave, as the story progresses. A character may need to adapt to survive at key moments in the plot. In *Beauty and the Beast*, the Beast changes from a ruthless monster into a handsome prince and loving husband.

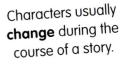

Characters usually **change** during the course of a story.

1 Our first impression of the Beast is a terrifying monster who threatens Beauty's father with his life.

2 When Beauty has to live with the Beast in his castle, we begin to see his kind and gentle side.

3 We see the Beast's vulnerability when he thinks Beauty has left him and he almost dies of heartbreak.

4 After Beauty has kissed the Beast, he transforms into his former self—a happy, handsome prince.

Who's telling the story?

Authors create the character of a "narrator" to tell their story. The narrator is part of the story, like any other character—remember, it's not the same as the author.

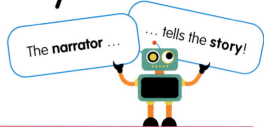
The **narrator**... ...tells the **story**!

I/we (first-person narrator)

In a story told in the first person, the reader sees what the narrator sees and can access their actions, thoughts, and feelings. In diaries, writers describe their daily lives.

> **SEE ALSO**
> What's the writer's purpose? **202**
> Audience **204**
> Choosing a narrator **274**

1 Uses "I" and "we" The reader sees the events and characters in the story through the narrator's eyes.

2 The story is told from the narrator's point of view. The reader only knows things that the narrator knows.

3 The narrator is a character in the story. They might be the main character or a witness to the central story.

I'm a dragon named Draco. My job is to protect the dragon eggs until they hatch.

Draco is the narrator of the story and writes as "I."

You (second-person narrator)

The second person is not common in fiction writing. It sounds personal—as if the narrator is talking directly to the reader.

1 Uses "you" The narrator addresses the reader directly using "you."

2 Includes the reader The reader is in the action of the story.

Look closely at the dragon nest and **you**'ll see five eggs waiting to hatch.

He/she/it/they (third-person narrator)

The narrator describes the actions, thoughts, and feelings of one or more of the characters and the reader may discover the narrator's opinions, too.

1 **Uses "he," "she," "it" or "they"** The narrator tells the story of one or more characters; the narrator is not in the story.

2 **The narrator may switch characters.** The story may change from one character's point of view to another's.

3 **The reader only knows what the characters know.** The narrator's view is limited, which can add suspense.

Draco was a dragon. His job was to protect the dragon eggs until they hatched. **He** often sang as he watched over them.

The narrator uses "he" to describe Draco, one of the characters in the story.

He/she/it/they (third-person omniscient narrator)

An omniscient narrator is a narrator who knows everything. This narrator can not only give their own opinions and all the characters' opinions, but also reveal information that none of the characters is aware of.

1 **Uses "he," "she," "it," or "they"** The reader is told the story of one or more characters.

2 **The narrator may switch characters.** The reader may hear different points of view in different chapters.

3 **Tells you what characters know and more** The narrator can move through time to talk about the past and future.

Draco was a dragon. His job was to protect the dragon eggs until they hatched. **He** often sang as he watched over them. **Little did he know that this time, one egg wasn't a dragon egg at all!**

The narrator knows things that Draco doesn't know.

Introducing plot

A good story has to have a strong structure that gives it shape—as well as an absorbing storyline, or plot. The plot will contain dramatic events and turning points and will move toward a resolution at the end.

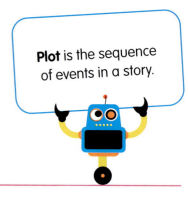

Plot is the sequence of events in a story.

What's the plot?

Many plots share similar features. In fact, almost every story features at least one of these classic plots: rebirth, the quest, overcoming a monster, rags to riches, and voyage and return. For example, *Peter Pan* is a voyage and return story, while *Beauty and the Beast* is about rebirth—the Beast is transformed from a terrifying monster into a kind, happy prince.

SEE ALSO	
Genres	126
The three-act structure	142
Identifying themes	172

A quest
Frodo takes the ring to the perilous land of Mordor in *The Lord of the Rings*.

Overcoming a monster
Jack finds gold and defeats a fearsome giant in *Jack and the Beanstalk*.

Rags to riches
With the help of a genie, Aladdin becomes a prince in *Aladdin*.

Voyage and return
Alice enters, then tries to return from Wonderland in *Alice in Wonderland*.

READING STORIES, PLAYS, AND POEMS • INTRODUCING PLOT 141

How plots are built

A playwright creates scenes and acts, while an author usually builds a structure out of chapters. The main events of the story build on each other and connect to form a plot line. The language or characters may vary from section to section, but the parts build a coherent whole.

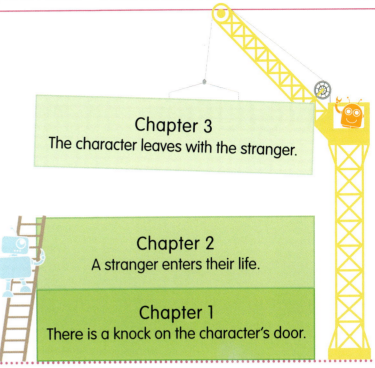

Chapter 3 The character leaves with the stranger.

Chapter 2 A stranger enters their life.

Chapter 1 There is a knock on the character's door.

Twists and turning points

The writer often increases pressure on the main character, so they are in danger of losing everything. There will also be one or more turning points, where the plot suddenly changes direction. This generates energy and surprise, as shown in the story of *Aladdin*.

1 Call to action The main character's life is turned upside down by a sudden event near the start of the story.

A poor city boy named Aladdin is befriended by a wealthy but untrustworthy wizard.

2 The goal is established The character realizes the dangers they must face and discovers their ultimate goal.

The wizard traps Aladdin in a cave. Inside, Aladdin finds a magic lamp that grants wishes.

3 Midpoint The character's goal becomes so important that they have to accept that they can't back away from it.

Back at home, Aladdin's mother cleans the lamp, releasing a genie who obeys the lamp's owner.

4 Darkest hour All hope seems lost. There's no way forward, is there …?

The wizard steals the now-rich Aladdin's lamp and uses its powers to take everything from him.

5 Climax The main character has a final, dramatic chance to achieve their goal.

Aladdin regains the lamp and his fortune after he finds the wizard and tricks him in return.

The three-act structure

Most stories have a beginning, middle, and ending, called a three-act structure. You can chart a plot using a story map.

All stories can be split into **acts**, even if the acts aren't labeled on the page!

The story map

Plays are often divided into three **acts**. Even stories that aren't split into chapters or acts contain a hidden **three-part structure** in which drama is introduced and resolved. This can be shown through a **story map**. Because of their shape, story maps are sometimes called **plot pyramids**. Here, a map of *Jack and the Beanstalk* shows how the tension in a story can change as the plot moves forward.

> **SEE ALSO**
> Introducing plot   140
> Identifying themes   172
> Plot and structure   266

Beginning
Jack and his widowed mother live together. They are so poor that Jack has to go to market to sell their only cow.

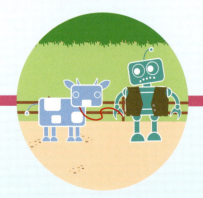

Initial incident
Jack trades the cow for some "magic" beans. Jack's mother throws the beans away. A huge beanstalk grows outside.

Early conflict
Jack remembers stories about clouds containing gold, so he climbs up the beanstalk and finds a scary giant and his riches.

Rising

Act 1
Settings and main characters are established. An event occurs, and the characters' world changes forever.

Act 2
Conflict and suspense rise. The main character has to face mounting problems and intrigue.

READING STORIES, PLAYS, AND POEMS • **THE THREE-ACT STRUCTURE**   143

> **TRY IT OUT**
>
> Reduce a well-known fairy-tale plot to three sentences: for beginning, middle, and end. Get used to looking for three parts (or a three-act structure) in stories you read. Afterward, try identifying key points using the story map, below.

Climax
Jack clambers down the beanstalk. He cuts it down with an ax. The giant falls off the beanstalk and dies.

Late conflict
Jack visits the giant again and steals his harp, but he wakes the giant up. The angry giant chases Jack out of his castle.

Some stories are **open-ended**. This means that not all the action is resolved at the end of the story.

Resolution
Jack and his mother are safe from the scary giant for good. They live happily ever after.

Act 3
Problems reach a peak as threats gather into a battle or crisis. Then all is resolved as the story ends.

Reading plays

Plays are written to be performed. The text of a play (the script) contains the characters' speech (their lines) and instructions (stage directions) for the actors to follow. Once you understand these, you'll have no problem reading plays.

A **playwright** is someone who writes plays.

What is a play?

Just like stories or poems, plays can be about anything, be written in different styles, and feature lots of characters or just one or two. Performance is what makes plays different. This can take place on stage (in a theater, in an auditorium, or even in the open air), on the radio, or on television.

SEE ALSO	
Features of stories, plays, and poems	124
Performance	146
Exploring dialogue	166

A **musical** is a play containing song and dance to help tell the story.

Reading between the lines

Most playwrights present their work in a standard way, as shown on the opposite page, to make it easy to follow. Styles can vary though. Tennessee Williams, for example, used very detailed stage directions, while Harold Pinter's plays are famous for their pauses and silences.

WORLD OF WORDS

The musical *Joseph and the Amazing Technicolor Dreamcoat* by Tim Rice and Andrew Lloyd Webber was originally created for school productions.

Understanding a script

Reading a script for the first time can be confusing. A good starting point is the cast list, which gives all the characters' names and often some notes about them. Here are some other conventions that playwrights use:

> "Stage left" or "stage right" means the left or right side according to the **actor** on the stage, not the audience.

Plays are divided into scenes. In some plays, scenes are grouped into acts.

Stage directions do not use italics for the characters' names.

SCENE: *The kitchen in the now-abandoned farmhouse of* **JOHN WRIGHT**, *a gloomy kitchen, and left without having been put in order … At the rear, the outer door opens and the* **SHERIFF** *comes in followed by the* **COUNTY ATTORNEY** *and … two women … The women have come in slowly and stand close together near the door.*

These stage directions set the scene as the action begins.

COUNTY ATTORNEY: *(rubbing his hands)* This feels good. Come up to the fire, ladies.

MRS. PETERS: *(after taking a step forward)* I'm not—cold.

SHERIFF: *(unbuttoning his overcoat and stepping away from the stove as if to mark the beginning of official business)* Now, Mr. Hale, before we move things about, you explain to Mr. Henderson just what you saw when you came here yesterday morning.

Stage directions are given in italics. When next to dialogue, they are also given in parentheses.

The characters' names are given in capital letters before their lines and any stage directions.

COUNTY ATTORNEY: By the way, has anything been moved? Are things just as you left them yesterday?

SHERIFF: *(looking about)* It's just the same. When it dropped below zero last night, I thought I'd better send Frank out this morning to make a fire for us—no use getting pneumonia with a big case on, but I told him not to touch anything except the stove—and you know Frank.

Dialogue in plays isn't in quotation marks.

COUNTY ATTORNEY: Somebody should have been left here yesterday.

Trifles, a one-act play by Susan Glaspell, 1916

Performance

Performance can bring a story to life, develop meaning, and aid comprehension. It can also be fun!

Reading aloud or acting in a play or movie are all kinds of **performance**.

Stories, poems, plays, and movies

There are many kinds of performances across different forms of writing. How something is performed can alter the theme, the tone, and even the meaning of the text.

> **SEE ALSO**
> Reading plays 144
> The effects of language 156
> Using language techniques 260

You might read a story aloud or listen to an audiobook.

The text might be a poem to be read aloud or alone.

The text could be written as a play to be acted out.

It might be a movie that's been performed to a camera.

Some stories are told in more than one way—*Charlotte's Web* is a **book**, a **play**, and a **movie**!

What makes a performance?

Some stories are specially written to be performed (such as a script for a play), whereas some aren't (such as a book). Both kinds of stories will be changed by the way they're acted out. Here's how performance can shape a text.

1 Silence Pauses can draw the audience in and add drama and tension to a performance.

2 Emphasis and tone You can stress certain words or syllables for effect and meaning.

Then …

Welcome to the **scariest** show on earth!

READING STORIES, PLAYS, AND POEMS • PERFORMANCE   147

Performing a play

A play is an example of a text that is written with performance in mind. How the set looks, the costumes, dialogue, and stage directions all contribute to meaning through performance. Below is an annotated example from *Macbeth*.

SPEAK UP

Try to repeat this sentence seven times, each time with emphasis on a different word. How does that change the meaning?

I didn't say he ate the chocolate.

Stage lights or sounds can mimic the weather.

Props or furnishings may be used to make the setting feel real.

ACT 1, SCENE 1: A desert place

[*Thunder and lightning. Enter three WITCHES.*]

FIRST WITCH: When shall we three meet again? In thunder, lightning, or in rain?

SECOND WITCH: When the hurlyburly's done, When the battle's lost and won.

THIRD WITCH: That will be ere the set of sun.

FIRST WITCH: Where the place?

SECOND WITCH: Upon the heath.

THIRD WITCH: There to meet with Macbeth.

Macbeth by William Shakespeare, 1606

If the play is being read aloud by one person, they might put on different voices.

Punctuation can show actors how to deliver a line.

Actors may put their own emphasis on words, but the writing's natural rhythm will help.

---

3 Movement Body language, such as facial expressions or dancing, can add emotion.

4 Sets A stage's furnishings may be designed to look dramatic or help understanding.

5 Costumes Clothes and accessories help describe a character and tell the story.

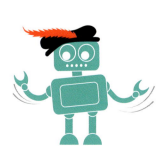
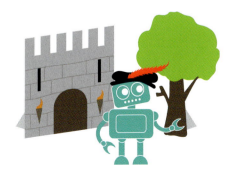

What is a poem?

Poetry is a flexible and imaginative way to express ideas and emotions in writing. Poets use a wide variety of structures, language, rhythm, or rhyme to connect with their readers.

Types of poem

Some types of poetry have a completely free form. Others follow strict rules that give writers a clear framework to work within.

> **SEE ALSO**
> The effects of language 156
> Figurative language 158
> Writing about poetry 282

Narrative
Narrative poems tell a story. They are usually long and divided into grouped sets of lines (called stanzas). They often have a regular rhyme scheme.

Ballad
A type of narrative poem, a ballad tells a traditional story or legend. In the past, ballads were often set to music.

Lyrical
Lyrical poetry explores a poet's feelings and emotions about a topic. This poetry often has a songlike quality.

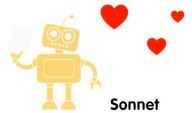

Limerick
A limerick is a funny, playful poem with a strict rhyme scheme. It usually starts "There was a …."

Ode
Odes are dedicated to a person, place, or thing admired by the poet. They express admiration, praise, or celebration.

Sonnet
A sonnet is usually about love. Sonnets follow strict rules: they always have 14 lines, a regular rhythm, and a rhyme scheme.

Haiku
A short Japanese poetry form, a haiku is traditionally about nature. Its three lines have five, seven, and five syllables.

Epic
An epic is a long narrative poem that usually describes a heroic adventure. Epics are central to many historical cultures.

Free verse
Free verse is a type of poetry that doesn't follow any rules. It's very flexible, with no specific rhythm, rhyme scheme, or line length.

Key features of poems

Most poems share some common features, even if they might look very different on the page. These features help the poet give the poem meaning and shape.

Structure
Lines of poetry are usually shorter than lines of prose and are often grouped into stanzas.

Sound
Poems are best read aloud. Poets use rhythm and rhyme to bring their words to life. A poem's rhythmic pattern is called its meter.

Form
Form describes the type of poem and the way it's laid out, including the length of its lines, its rhyme scheme, and its rhythm.

Writer's purpose
All poems have a purpose. A poet might use their poetry to express feelings of love or tell a story.

Language
Poets often use language features, such as imagery, repetition, and alliteration, to paint a vivid picture for their audience.

To describe the pattern of rhymes in a poem (called a rhyme scheme), we give each line a letter. Lines that rhyme are given the same letter. This poem's rhyme scheme is: ABABCDCDEFEFGG.

The poem describes the poet's joy when thinking about violets.

The lines are shorter than prose.

This poem is a sonnet. It uses 14 lines and a regular rhyme scheme.

For the first 12 lines of this poem, alternating lines rhyme in pairs.

Alliteration helps create a memorable image in the reader's mind.

The poem has a steady rhythm that carries it along.

The last two lines rhyme. They are called a rhyming couplet.

A	I had not thought of violets late,
B	The wild, shy kind that spring beneath your feet
A	In wistful April days, when lovers mate
B	And wander through the fields in raptures sweet.
C	The thought of violets meant florists' shops,
D	And bows and pins, and perfumed papers fine;
C	And garish lights, and mincing little fops
D	And cabarets and soaps, and deadening wines.
E	So far from sweet real things my thoughts had strayed,
F	I had forgot wide fields; and clear brown streams;
E	The perfect loveliness that God has made,—
F	Wild violets shy and Heaven-mounting dreams.
G	And now—unwittingly, you've made me dream
G	Of violets, and my soul's forgotten gleam.

"Sonnet" by Alice Moore Dunbar-Nelson, 1922

Making sense of poetry

A new poem can seem hard to understand when you first read it. Taking your time to read a poem carefully can help you make sense of it.

When reading a **poem**, think about how the poet gets their **ideas** across.

Where to start with a poem

Reading poetry is a personal experience, and each person will connect with a new poem in their own way. There's no right or wrong way to interpret a poem (as long as you can back up your ideas with evidence), but it can be useful to have tools to help you find a way in. Try following these steps to help you tackle any poem you come across.

SEE ALSO

The effects of language	156
Figurative language	158
Writing about poetry	282

SPEAK UP

Rhythm

Reading a poem aloud can help you hear its rhythm. This is because of the way you stress particular words or parts of words as you read. The poem "From a Railway Carriage" by Robert Louis Stevenson sounds like a steam train rattling along.

1 Reading for meaning
A good place to start is to slowly read through it. What do you think it is about? In "From a Railway Carriage," the author tries to convey the speed and excitement of a railway journey.

2 Form and structure
Once you understand the basic meaning, think about the overall shape of the poem. Can you see any patterns? Is there a regular rhythm or rhyme? Does the poem follow any rules?

READING STORIES, PLAYS, AND POEMS • **MAKING SENSE OF POETRY** 151

Repeating "and" tells us the view is constantly changing. The poet keeps adding things to the list.

Repeating the same letter sound (called alliteration) helps quickly establish the fast rhythm.

Similes help us picture the view from the train.

Faster than fairies, faster than witches,
Bridges and houses, hedges and ditches;
And charging along like troops in a battle
All through the meadows the horses and cattle:
All of the sights of the hill and the plain
Fly as thick as driving rain;
And ever again, in the wink of an eye,
Painted stations whistle by.

"From a Railway Carriage" by Robert Louis Stevenson, 1885

The poem has rhyming couplets. This means that adjacent pairs of lines rhyme. In many other poems, alternate lines like the first and third lines and the second and fourth lines rhyme.

The title suggests the poem will describe the view from a window of a train.

The poem has a strong and regular **rhythm**, like a train.

3 Language features
Poetry is often packed with rich and varied language. Take some time to find examples of figurative language in the poem and think about why the poet has used them.

4 What is the effect?
Finally, review your ideas about the poem's meaning, structure, and language. How has the poet brought together all these elements to create their chosen image or effect?

Asking about a story

When we read a story, asking questions can give us a better understanding of what we are reading; the setting; and the characters' thoughts, actions, and feelings.

Who? What? Why? Where? When? How?

Why ask questions?

Asking questions helps us focus on different elements of the story—like pieces of a jigsaw puzzle—that we can then put together to see the whole picture.

SEE ALSO
Understanding characters	136
What are inferences?	160
Using evidence from the text	182

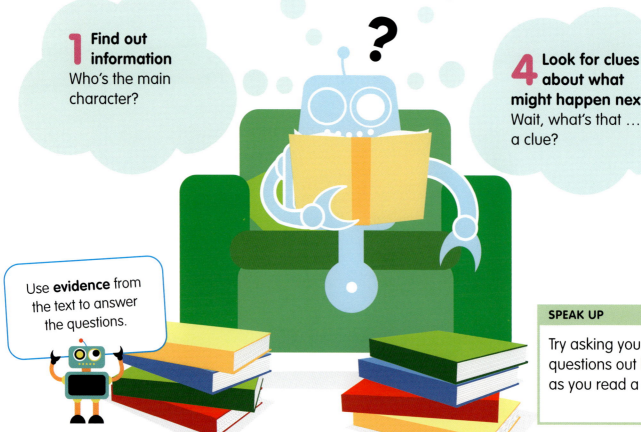

1 Find out information Who's the main character?

2 Check your understanding Did the character mean to do that?

3 Think more deeply about the story Why did the author say that?

4 Look for clues about what might happen next Wait, what's that ... a clue?

Use **evidence** from the text to answer the questions.

SPEAK UP

Try asking yourself questions out loud as you read a story.

READING STORIES, PLAYS, AND POEMS • ASKING ABOUT A STORY   153

Let's use questions!

When we start to read a story, or part of a story like this one, asking questions gives us a sense of what's important.

> **TRY IT OUT**
> What other questions can you ask about Jo and Meg?

Who?
The story is about Jo and Meg. They are sisters.

"What in the world are you going to do now, Jo?" asked Meg one snowy afternoon, as her sister came tramping through the hall, in rubber boots, old sack, and hood, with a broom in one hand and a shovel in the other.

"Going out for exercise," answered Jo with a mischievous twinkle in her eyes.

"I should think two long walks this morning would have been enough! It's cold and dull out, and I advise you to stay warm and dry by the fire, as I do," said Meg with a shiver.

"Never take advice! Can't keep still all day, and not being a pussycat, I don't like to doze by the fire. I like adventures, and I'm going to find some."

Little Women by Louisa May Alcott, 1869

When?
The story is probably set in winter, as it's snowy.

How?
Jo is talking mischievously, but Meg shivers when she talks.

What?
Jo is going outside to exercise. Meg prefers to stay by the fire.

Where?
The sisters' house has a hall and a warm fire.

Why?
Jo is going out because she wants to have an adventure.

Putting it all together

Asking questions helps us identify the main points in a story. Now we can put everything together to create a short summary of what we have read.

This story is about two sisters: Jo and Meg. They are at home. It's winter, and it has snowed. Jo wants to go outside and have fun, but Meg is cold and wants to stay by the fire. It's likely that Jo is the main character because she wants to have an adventure!

How to work out meaning

When you're reading stories, you'll come across words that are unfamiliar or new to you. To help you work out their meaning, you can often use clues, which may be in the surrounding words or even hidden in the words themselves.

Using context to understand

When you use context, you look at all the words together in a sentence or paragraph. This can help you work out the meaning of any new words.

SEE ALSO	
Roots and root words	94
Breaking words into parts	96
What are inferences?	160
New words and terms	216

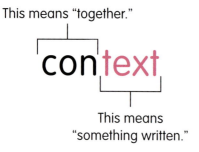

This means "together." / con / text / This means "something written."

Understanding words

After each paragraph or page, think about what you have read before moving on. Did you understand everything? Were there words you didn't recognize?

Dictionaries are very useful, but they can slow you down, interrupting your enjoyment of a story. Try using the methods on the opposite page first.

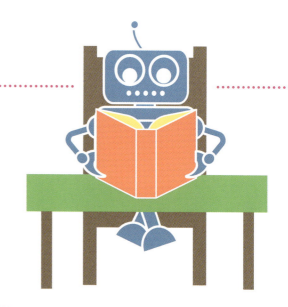

TRY IT OUT

Use the methods described opposite to help you figure out the meaning of the words in pink. Then use a dictionary to check if you're right.

Dorothy and her companions spent the night in an abandoned house with cracked windowpanes and an overgrown garden.

Working out new words

Try these methods for working out the meaning of new words. See how they are used in the extract below from the start of *The Wonderful Wizard of Oz*. In this extract, we meet Dorothy, who lives on a farm. To help us picture her home, the author tells us about it in more detail.

1 Root words
Common root words from other languages may help you work out the meaning of new words.

2 Long words
You can break long words into parts (called morphemes) and put their meanings together.

3 Context
You can use words you already know around a new word to help you work out its meaning.

The words "midst" and "middle" (below) are synonyms and share the same root—"mid."

The words after "lumber" tell you that it's something heavy that is used to build a house.

You might need a dictionary for words you can't work out using context clues.

Dorothy lived in the **midst** of the great Kansas **prairies**, with Uncle Henry, who was a farmer, and Aunt Em, who was the farmer's wife. Their house was small, for the **lumber** to build it had to be carried by wagon many miles. There were four walls, a floor and a roof, which made one room; and this room contained a rusty looking **cookstove**, a cupboard for the dishes, a table, three or four chairs, and the beds. Uncle Henry and Aunt Em had a big bed in one corner, and Dorothy a little bed in another corner. There was no **garret** at all, and no **cellar**—except a small hole dug in the ground, called a **cyclone** cellar, where the family could go in case one of those great **whirlwinds** arose, **mighty** enough to crush any building **in its path**. It was reached by a **trap door** in the **middle** of the floor, from which a ladder led down into the small, dark hole.

The Wonderful Wizard of Oz by L. Frank Baum, 1900

The words after "cellar" tell you it's a space under the house.

This word has the root "cycle" and is a synonym of whirlwind.

Breaking this word into two parts tells you that these are fast, twisting currents of air.

The words "crush any building" tell you "mighty" means "very strong."

This nonliteral use of the word "path" means "in its way."

The effects of language

Language is a very powerful tool. The author's choice of language can create different effects and influence how a reader responds to a text.

Authorial intent is the author's **purpose** in writing the text.

Ways that language affects the reader

An author carefully chooses their language depending on their intention. How does the author want the reader to respond? Readers form opinions and understanding of the text through the language that the author uses. The choice of language can affect how you imagine the setting, the traits of the characters, and even the themes of the text.

SEE ALSO

Figurative language	158
Understanding the tone	164
Using language techniques	260
Narrative techniques	276

1 Intellectual effect
Language can express ideas, impressions, and suggestions to the reader.

2 Imaginative effect
An author can use language to conjure up sights, sounds, or even smells for the reader.

3 Emotional effect
Language can create feelings within a reader, such as excitement, fear, sadness, or humor.

Language techniques

An author often uses language techniques to help convey their desired effect. The use of these techniques can bring a story to life and emphasize a theme, thought, or feeling.

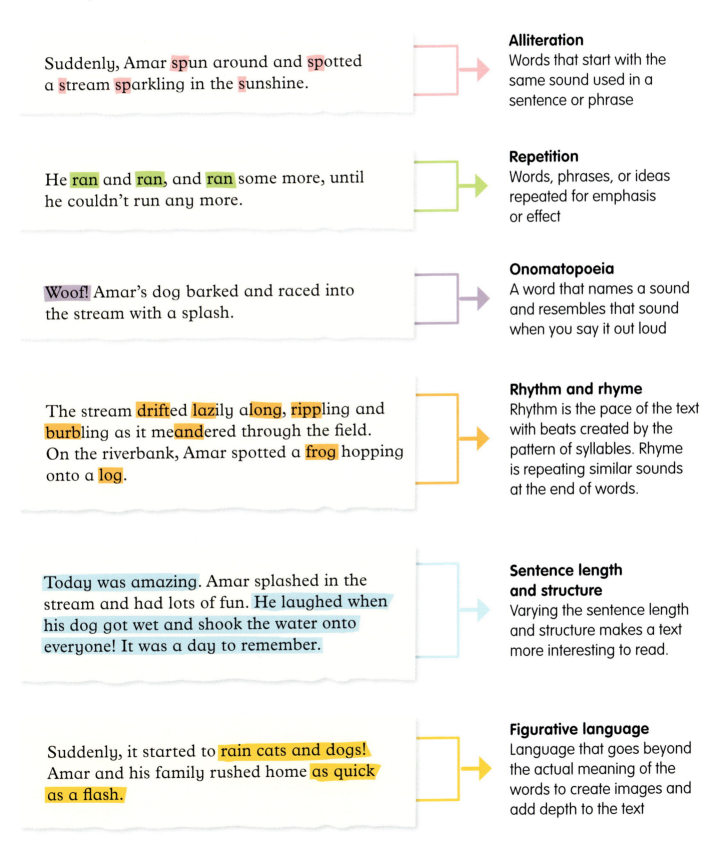

Alliteration
Words that start with the same sound used in a sentence or phrase

Suddenly, Amar spun around and spotted a stream sparkling in the sunshine.

Repetition
Words, phrases, or ideas repeated for emphasis or effect

He ran and ran, and ran some more, until he couldn't run any more.

Onomatopoeia
A word that names a sound and resembles that sound when you say it out loud

Woof! Amar's dog barked and raced into the stream with a splash.

Rhythm and rhyme
Rhythm is the pace of the text with beats created by the pattern of syllables. Rhyme is repeating similar sounds at the end of words.

The stream drifted lazily along, rippling and burbling as it meandered through the field. On the riverbank, Amar spotted a frog hopping onto a log.

Sentence length and structure
Varying the sentence length and structure makes a text more interesting to read.

Today was amazing. Amar splashed in the stream and had lots of fun. He laughed when his dog got wet and shook the water onto everyone! It was a day to remember.

Figurative language
Language that goes beyond the actual meaning of the words to create images and add depth to the text

Suddenly, it started to rain cats and dogs! Amar and his family rushed home as quick as a flash.

Figurative language

Language that conveys something other than its usual meaning is called figurative language. Writers use it to make their descriptive writing more effective.

Figurative language helps build an image for the reader.

Why use figurative language?

Effective use of figurative language can transform ordinary descriptions into vivid images in a reader's mind. It has the power to appeal to senses and emotions and can even help readers understand the deeper meaning or theme of a piece of writing. There are several different types of figurative language.

SEE ALSO
The effects of language	156
Analyzing poetry	168
Descriptive writing	262

1 Simile
A simile describes something by comparing it to something else, usually by using the words "like" or "as."

The snow sparkled like diamonds.

The simile helps you form a clearer picture of what the snow looked like.

2 Metaphor
A metaphor is like a simile but says something **is** something else rather than **like** something else.

The long journey was a roller-coaster.

The metaphor implies the journey had good and bad moments.

3 Personification
Giving a nonhuman thing, such as an object, human characteristics is called personification.

The mountain stood tall and proud.

READING STORIES, PLAYS, AND POEMS • FIGURATIVE LANGUAGE

WORLD OF WORDS

Find a novel or poem, and see if you can spot any figurative language techniques in the writing. What effect does the language have on you as a reader?

4 Alliteration
Repeating the same letter or sound at the start of two or more words is called alliteration.

The wind whipped past the climbers.

When you say this out loud, the repeated "w" sounds like the wind.

5 Allusion
An allusion refers to something familiar, such as a person, place, or literary work, to make the reader think of that thing.

The climb was a Herculean effort.

Alluding to the mythical hero Hercules shows that the climb was not easy.

6 Idiom
A well-known phrase that has a different meaning from its literal one is called an idiom.

The peak was a sight for sore eyes.

This tells readers that the tired climbers were happy to reach the peak.

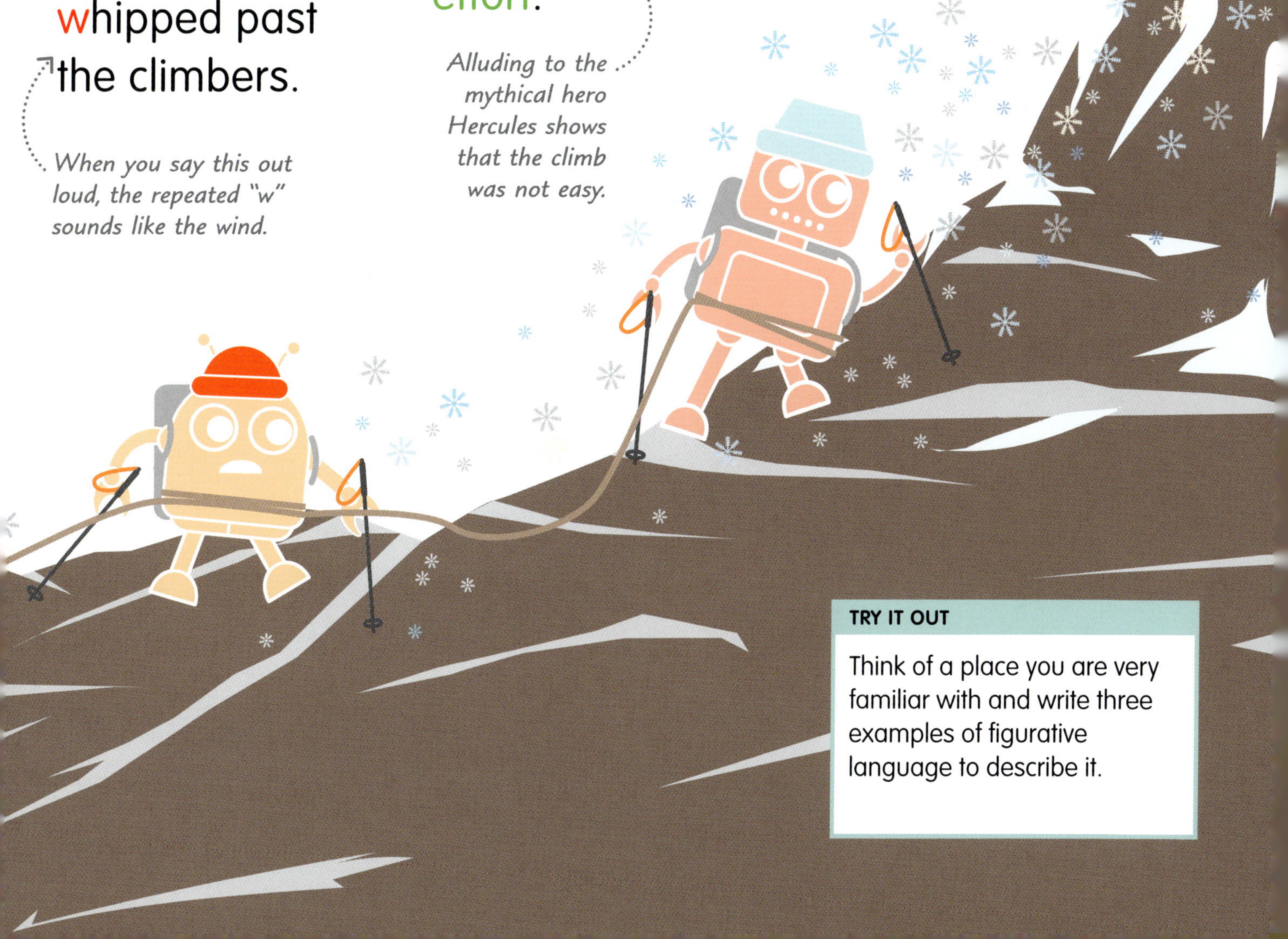

TRY IT OUT

Think of a place you are very familiar with and write three examples of figurative language to describe it.

What are inferences?

An inference is drawing a conclusion based on clues and evidence in a text. Sometimes you need to be a bit like a detective to find the evidence and draw your own conclusions.

Authors often leave **clues** that you will need to work out by **making inferences**.

Finding evidence in a text

Evidence in a text may be explicit or implicit. Explicit evidence is stated directly in the text. Implicit evidence isn't stated clearly—it's implied. You have to read between the lines to work it out. Pictures can give you clues about what's going on in a story, too. However, when a text isn't illustrated, you may have to work a little harder to make inferences.

> **SEE ALSO**
> How to make inferences 162
> Using evidence from the text 182
> Inferring meaning 220

EXPLICIT

José read the book.

IMPLICIT

José returned the book to the library and picked another by the same author.

You might infer that José read and enjoyed the book because he chose another by this author.

Maya entered the classroom.

Maya limped into the classroom holding her skateboard.

You might infer that Maya fell off her skateboard on the way to school.

It rained all through the night.

When I left early in the morning, there were deep puddles outside.

You might infer that it had rained heavily in the night.

Making inferences about characters

Characters often show what they're like and how they're feeling through their actions and words. You need to be on the lookout for these hints when reading stories.

> **TRY IT OUT**
> Listen for things that people imply in everyday speech. Can you infer what they really mean?

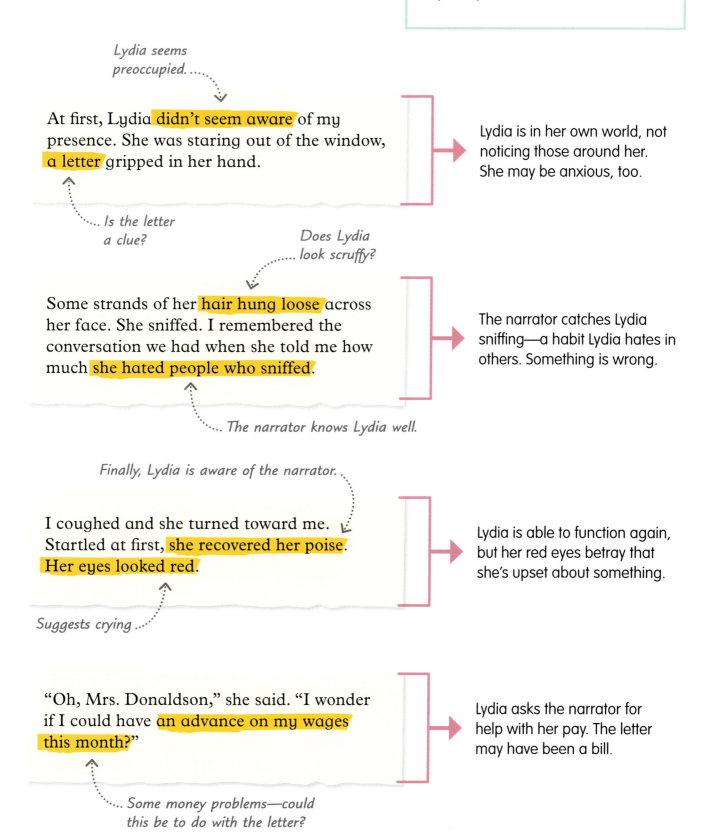

Lydia seems preoccupied.

At first, Lydia **didn't seem aware** of my presence. She was staring out of the window, **a letter** gripped in her hand.

→ Lydia is in her own world, not noticing those around her. She may be anxious, too.

Is the letter a clue?

Does Lydia look scruffy?

Some strands of her **hair hung loose** across her face. She sniffed. I remembered the conversation we had when she told me how much **she hated people who sniffed**.

→ The narrator catches Lydia sniffing—a habit Lydia hates in others. Something is wrong.

The narrator knows Lydia well.

Finally, Lydia is aware of the narrator.

I coughed and she turned toward me. Startled at first, **she recovered her poise**. **Her eyes looked red**.

→ Lydia is able to function again, but her red eyes betray that she's upset about something.

Suggests crying

"Oh, Mrs. Donaldson," she said. "I wonder if I could have **an advance on my wages this month?**"

→ Lydia asks the narrator for help with her pay. The letter may have been a bill.

Some money problems—could this be to do with the letter?

How to make inferences

You develop your inference skills by reading stories carefully—and applying what you know from your own experiences. The clues are all there in the text.

Making **inferences** is one of the ways you **analyze** text.

Looking at single words

You can draw inferences just by looking at specific word choices. What pictures are created in your mind by the words on the page? How does a character enter a room, for example?

SEE ALSO
What are inferences?	160
Using evidence from the text	182
Inferring meaning	220

Maybe Maya doesn't want to be noticed today.

Maya crept into the classroom.

You might infer that she likes having fun.

Maya slid into the classroom.

Perhaps Maya's in a hurry—or she's a witch!

Maya flew into the classroom.

Maya is unsteady. Is she ill or clumsy?

Maya stumbled into the classroom.

READING STORIES, PLAYS, AND POEMS • **HOW TO MAKE INFERENCES**

Looking at dialogue

You can infer a lot of information about situations and characters from what they say. Sometimes you can even pick up clues from what they don't say!

"Are you okay?" I asked Harry.
"I'm fine."
"Are you sure?"
"Yeah, totally."
"Really? It's just you look kinda green..."
"Look, I'm not bothered by spiders. Trust me."
"As long as you're..."

"Miss! Miss Wagner! Harry's just fainted!"

This is a clue that Harry may not be fine.

Harry knows that the narrator thinks he's scared of spiders.

Despite what Harry says, he doesn't look well.

This is a strong hint that Harry's afraid of spiders!

Making predictions

The more you read, the better you'll become at recognizing clues and making inferences. Based on what's stated or implied by the writer, you'll start to pick up skills in predicting what's going to happen.

In the novel *David Copperfield* by Charles Dickens, we're introduced to the character Uriah Heep. What can you predict about this person's influence in the book?

> I predict that Uriah Heep is going to cause trouble in the story.

This means thin and pale—with a deathly appearance.

Is he spying?

The boy seems older and looks creepy.

This echoes "cadaverous." His hand is like that of a corpse.

"I saw a cadaverous face appear at a small window on the ground floor ... and quickly disappear. The low arched door then opened, and the face came out ... It belonged to a red-haired person—a youth of fifteen, as I take it now, but looking much older ... He was high-shouldered and bony; dressed in decent black, with a white wisp of a neckcloth; buttoned up to the throat; and had a long, lank, skeleton hand ..."

David Copperfield by Charles Dickens, 1850

Understanding the tone

How does the author want the reader to feel? This mood is what we call the tone. The tone can change within a text, depending on what the author wants to convey.

What is tone?

The tone is the mood of the text. The author's choice of language sets the tone. Language can bring up feelings such as humor, suspense, or sadness that help the reader have a deeper understanding of the text.

SEE ALSO	
Who's telling the story?	138
The effects of language	156
Audience	204
Levels of formality	206

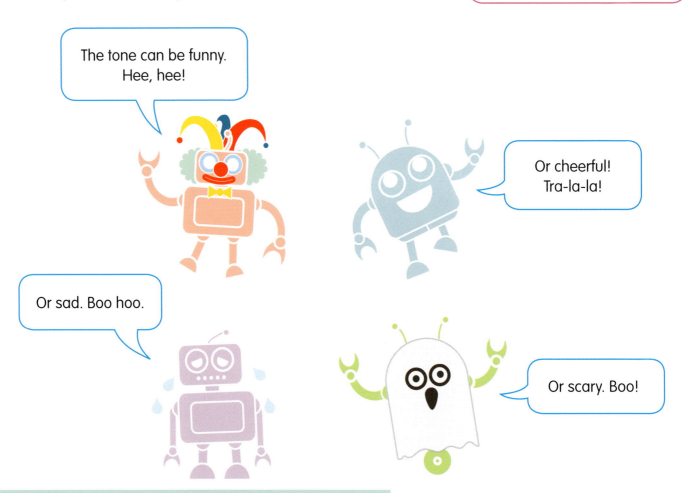

TRY IT OUT

Try writing a paragraph with a funny tone. Now write a paragraph with a spooky tone. Notice how you use different kinds of language for different tones.

READING STORIES, PLAYS, AND POEMS • UNDERSTANDING THE TONE

How to understand the tone

When thinking about tone, consider why the author chose certain words. How do those words make you feel? Compare the tone and the language in these extracts from *The Wind in the Willows* and *Black Beauty*.

> **SPEAK UP**
>
> Read the extracts below out loud. How does the tone of the writing affect the expression in your voice?

1 When Mole climbs out of his hole, it is the beginning of his adventures with new friends on the river.

Similar-sounding verbs are fun to read and show Mole's determination.

Positive language creates a cheerful scene.

So he scraped and scratched and scrabbled and scrooged and then he scrooged again and scrabbled and scratched and scraped, working busily with his little paws and muttering to himself, "Up we go! Up we go!" till at last, pop! his snout came out into the sunlight, and he found himself rolling in the warm grass of a great meadow.

"Pop" is fun use of onomatopoeia.

The Wind in the Willows by Kenneth Grahame, 1908

2 Black Beauty is a horse who tells the story of his life.

Short, direct sentences express Black Beauty's longing.

What more could I want? Why, liberty! For three years and a half of my life I had had all the liberty I could wish for; but now, week after week, month after month, and no doubt year after year, I must stand up in a stable night and day except when I am wanted, and then I must be just as steady and quiet as any old horse who has worked twenty years.

Repetition conveys how slowly time can pass.

Black Beauty by Anna Sewell, 1877

Language emphasizes boredom or hard work.

Exploring dialogue

Dialogue is a literary device in which characters speak to each other. It adds drama, color, and plot details to stories and plays and is used in some poems and nonfiction, too.

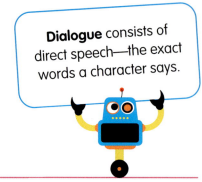

Dialogue consists of direct speech—the exact words a character says.

Purposes of dialogue

Dialogue is a vital part of many stories. It uses direct speech to help the reader develop a stronger understanding of the text, including its characters and plot.

SEE ALSO	
Punctuating direct speech	72
Performance	146
Choosing a narrator	274

1 Drives plot
Dialogue is carefully chosen by a writer. Every word helps push the story forward. Dialogue drives the plot and keeps readers engaged.

2 Develops character
Dialogue tells us more about a character's personality and how they're feeling. What they say and how they say it is vital to how the reader views them.

3 Helps understanding
Dialogue is an important part of a story. By showing a character's point of view and how they speak, it can help the reader understand the story.

Famous catchphrases

Effective dialogue can be memorable for readers—both the phrase itself and what it tells us about the character. Below are some famous examples.

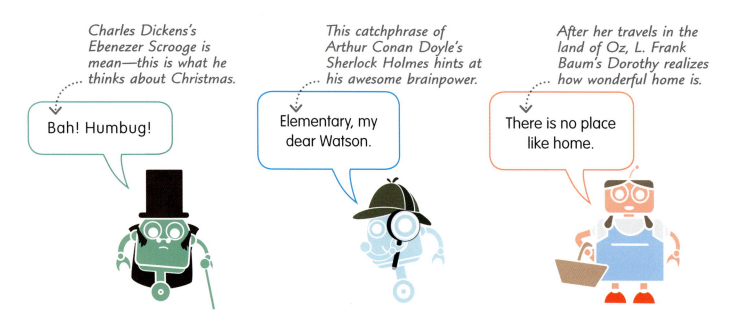

Charles Dickens's Ebenezer Scrooge is mean—this is what he thinks about Christmas.

Bah! Humbug!

This catchphrase of Arthur Conan Doyle's Sherlock Holmes hints at his awesome brainpower.

Elementary, my dear Watson.

After her travels in the land of Oz, L. Frank Baum's Dorothy realizes how wonderful home is.

There is no place like home.

READING STORIES, PLAYS, AND POEMS • EXPLORING DIALOGUE   167

Analyzing dialogue

We can use our knowledge of grammar and vocabulary to analyze the language and punctuation used in dialogue. Notice the effects that the narration and the direct speech have in the example below.

> **TRY IT OUT**
>
> What else does this extract show us about the characters of Mr. and Mrs. Bennet?

DIALOGUE

"My dear Mr. Bennet," said his lady to him one day, "have you heard that Netherfield Park is let at last?"

Mr. Bennet replied that he had not.

"But it is," returned she; "for Mrs. Long has just been here, and she told me all about it."

Mr. Bennet made no answer.

"Do you not want to know who has taken it?" cried his wife impatiently.

"*You* want to tell me, and I have no objection to hearing it."

This was invitation enough.

"Why, my dear, you must know, Mrs. Long says that Netherfield is taken by a young man of large fortune from the north of England; that he came down on Monday in a chaise and four to see the place, and was so much delighted with it that he agreed with Mr. Morris immediately; that he is to take possession before Michaelmas, and some of his servants are to be in the house by the end of next week."

Pride and Prejudice
by Jane Austen, 1813

Mr. Bennet's part of this conversation is mostly given through narration. This helps show that he is a quieter character than Mrs. Bennet.

The dialogue reveals part of the plot—that the young man is rich.

"impatiently" helps us know more about Mrs. Bennet's tone in the dialogue.

Here, we can see that Mr. Bennet does not share his wife's enthusiasm.

This is a long, unbroken piece of dialogue that's all one sentence! When read, it creates a rhythm that conveys Mrs. Bennet's excitement.

> When **reading dialogue**, the reader may change their voice for different characters.

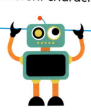

Analyzing poetry

Sometimes you need to look a little more closely at a poem. Think deeply and use all the skills you have learned to understand the meaning and effects of the poem.

Analyzing a poem can help you discover its **hidden meaning**.

Asking the right questions

Asking yourself some questions about a poem can help you unpack its meaning. Some useful questions are listed below, but you might find you come up with some of your own when you look at a poem.

> **SEE ALSO**
> Making sense of poetry 150
> The effects of language 156
> Writing about poetry 282

1 What is the form and structure of the poem? Is it divided into stanzas?

2 Does the poem have a regular rhythm or a rhyme scheme?

3 What does the title tell you about the poem? What might it be about?

4 Can you spot any language features in the poem?

5 What effects do the form, structure, and language techniques have on you as the reader?

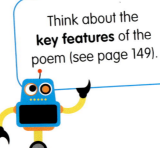

Think about the **key features** of the poem (see page 149).

Connecting with poems

A poem will mean something different to every reader because we all experience the world in different ways. Thinking about how a poem relates to your own life and experiences is an important and useful way of connecting with what you read.

READING STORIES, PLAYS, AND POEMS • ANALYZING POETRY

Studying a poem in detail

Read this poem through several times to understand its meaning, then think about its form, structure, and language use. What effect do these techniques create? What do you think the poet was trying to achieve? Have they been successful?

> **WORLD OF WORDS**
>
> For the 2021 American presidential inauguration, American poet Amanda Gorman touched the audience with her expressive reading of her poem "The Hill We Climb."

The poet uses a **metaphor** *to compare hope to a beautiful bird singing in your soul to comfort you.*

The poem is arranged into stanzas. The first compares hope to a bird. The second describes how only the worst storms can silence its song. The third tells us hope is always there.

Language, such as "perches," has been carefully chosen to emphasize the symbol of the bird.

"Hope" is the thing with feathers -
That perches in the soul -
And sings the tune without the words -
And never stops - at all -

And sweetest - in the Gale - is heard -
And sore must be the storm -
That could abash the little Bird
That kept so many warm -

I've heard it in the chillest land -
And on the strangest Sea -
Yet - never - in Extremity,
It asked a crumb - of me.

"'Hope' Is The Thing With Feathers"
by Emily Dickinson (1891)

Imagery of a storm is used to describe tough times and unfamiliar situations.

Repetition of words containing "s" or "sh" softens the sound of the poem.

The poem has an ABCB rhyme scheme—the second and fourth line of each stanza rhyme. This adds a musical quality.

A poem's title can give us a clue as to what it may be about.

> **SPEAK UP**
>
> Read the final stanza aloud. It has a pattern of stressed and unstressed syllables. The rhythm is unhurried and thoughtful, like the poet's ideas.

Finding the main idea

The main idea is the key to what a text is about. Working out the main idea can help with your understanding of a story, play, or poem.

The **main idea** is the most important point of the story, play, or poem.

What is a main idea?

The main idea involves the main characters and the overall plot of a story, play, or poem. The main idea often develops gradually, with each chapter or scene having its own main idea. These build up to create the main idea for the text as a whole. Some texts have more than one main idea.

SEE ALSO

Identifying themes	172
Summarizing	178
Using evidence from the text	182

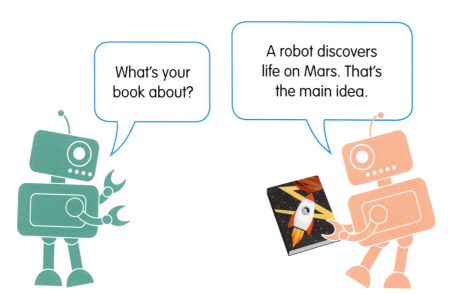

SPEAK UP

Take turns speaking and listening with a partner. The person listening needs to work out the main idea of what the other person is saying.

The difference between the main idea and the theme

The main idea is specific to what happens in a story, play, or poem. However, the theme has a broader message. The main idea can act as a brief summary, while the theme is a lesson or moral of the story.

Romeo and Juliet by William Shakespeare

Main idea: Romeo and Juliet defy a family feud and sacrifice their lives for love.
Theme: The power of love

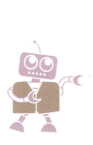

READING STORIES, PLAYS, AND POEMS • FINDING THE MAIN IDEA   171

Clues for finding the main idea

Read a story, play, or poem and see if you can find clues to help you work out the main idea.

> **TRY IT OUT**
>
> Use these steps to find the main idea in a text that you have read. Can you write the main idea in one or two sentences?

1 A story, play, or poem usually has one or more main characters. Identify who or what the text is about.

2 The main idea often involves a problem that needs to be solved. Work out what the problem is.

3 List the most important events in the text. Find connections between these events that tie the plot together.

Also check the **title** for clues to the main idea!

4 Reread the beginning and end of the text. This is where you'll often find clues to the main idea.

Icarus, a Greek myth

Main idea: Icarus flies too close to the sun and falls to his death.
Theme: Don't let pride lead to risky actions.

The Tortoise and the Hare, Aesop's fable

Main idea: The slow, steady tortoise wins a race against the boastful hare.
Theme: Steadfastness

Identifying themes

Themes are important ideas that run through stories. There may be one main theme or several, but they're always there, lurking beneath the surface.

Themes are the big issues behind the story.

How do themes work?

If the plot of a story is what happens, the theme is what the story is about. A theme is a topic that the writer explores and returns to again and again in the story. A short story may have a single theme, while a novel or a play might contain several.

Some classic themes are shown below.

SEE ALSO	
Genres	126
Asking about a story	152
Finding the main idea	170

- Good vs. evil
- Identity
- Friendship
- Justice vs. injustice
- Trust
- Family
- Jealousy
- Revenge
- Love

Short story

Novel

READING STORIES, PLAYS, AND POEMS • IDENTIFYING THEMES

Good vs. evil

Good vs. evil is a theme in many stories, including *Lord of the Flies* by William Golding. The book explores how a stranded group of schoolchildren struggle to survive on a remote island as good values (like teamwork) face evil ones (like violence).

This theme is visible in individual sentences and scenes and in the book as a whole.

1 "They looked at each other, baffled, in love and hate."

The words "love" and "hate" show the good and evil impulses in the group of boys.

2 In a key scene, a body floats down into the camp. Some of the boys think it must be the Beast, which represents evil.

3 Events cause the boys to choose between two groups. One group is led by an "evil" boy, and the other by two "good" boys.

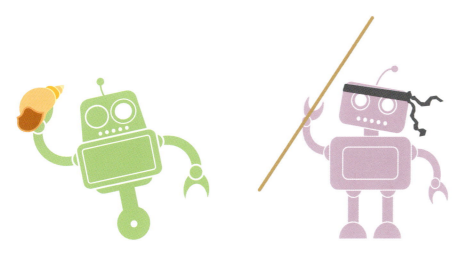

Friendship

The theme of friendship is key to many stories. The touching extract below from *Charlotte's Web* shows the importance of friendship. This key theme is explored and developed in the novel through Wilbur the pig's relationships with others.

> "You have been my friend," replied Charlotte. "That in itself is a tremendous thing."
>
> *Charlotte's Web* by E. B. White, 1952

TRY IT OUT

Can you think of a book or play with a more challenging theme to pin down, such as identity, responsibility, or appearance and reality?

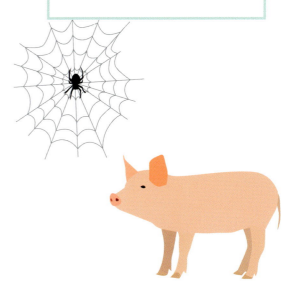

Stories can take different approaches to the same theme. For example, one might say friends will always be there, while another may suggest you have to work at friendship.

Comparing and contrasting fiction

When we compare and contrast fiction texts, we look for similarities and differences between aspects like the text's writing style, themes, characters, and language choices.

Why do we compare texts?

Comparing is looking for similarities and contrasting is looking for differences—either within one fiction text or across more than one text. This develops our understanding of an author's intentions.

> **SEE ALSO**
> Features of stories, plays, and poems — 124
> Asking about a story — 152

Comparing within a text

1 Comparing features within a text helps us get more out of the text. For example, by comparing different characters within the same text, we can better understand their personalities and circumstances.

Comparing across different texts

2 Comparing features across multiple texts can also reveal more about each of the texts. For example, comparing a modern and a historic setting can teach us how things have changed over time.

READING STORIES, PLAYS, AND POEMS • COMPARING AND CONTRASTING FICTION

Features to compare

There are lots of different aspects of a text that you can compare and contrast. It is important to think about how the author has approached a wide range of features and how the reader might respond to them. Here are some questions you can ask yourself about each one:

Form and genre
What purpose does the author's chosen form achieve? What impact does the genre have on the text?

Characterization
How has language or dialogue been used to reveal what the characters are like?

Narrative perspective
What type of narrator has been used? How has the narrative perspective enhanced the storytelling?

Setting
Where and when is the text set? What has been revealed about life in that place at that time?

Tone and theme
Has the writer used character, setting, or language to convey a certain tone or theme?

Language techniques
How has the writer used language techniques, such as imagery, for effect?

Narrative structure
How are the events in the text ordered or structured? How does this structure help draw the reader in?

Transition words

When you write a comparison of features within one or more texts, it is important to write about the features that you are comparing together, not separately. Using transition words like the ones given here will help you compare and contrast features more effectively.

However...   Just as...

In contrast...   On the other hand...

In the same way...   Similarly...

Comparing and contrasting fiction texts

When we compare and contrast two fiction texts, we look for similarities and differences in how the writers have approached a range of features and think about the effects of these features on the text and audience.

It's important to think about each of these key features of the texts one by one: narrative perspective, characterization, setting, tone, and language techniques. Other features that you can compare include the form, genre, themes, and narrative structure of the text. For each feature, make notes that you could use in your comparison.

Characterization
The writer uses descriptive language to convey Miss Crocker's unkind nature.

Narrative perspective
The text has a first-person narrator, Cassie Logan, so we get her perspective on the world around her.

Tone
The text has a negative tone with a sense of foreboding.

> Miss Daisy Crocker, yellow and buckeyed, glared down at me from the middle of the room with a look that said, "Sooooooooo, it's you, Cassie Logan." Then she pursed her lips and drew the curtain along the rusted iron rod and tucked it into a wide loop in the back wall. With the curtain drawn back, the first graders gazed quizzically at us. Little Man sat by a window, his hands folded, patiently waiting for Miss Crocker to speak.
>
> Mary Lou nudged me. "That's my seat, Cassie Logan."
>
> "Mary Lou Wellever," Miss Crocker called primly, "have a seat."
>
> "Yes, ma'am," said Mary Lou, eyeing me with a look of pure hate before turning away.
>
> Miss Crocker walked stiffly to her desk, which was set on a tiny platform and piled high with bulky objects covered by a tarpaulin.
>
> *Roll of Thunder, Hear My Cry*
> by Mildred D. Taylor, 1976

Setting
The old-fashioned address "ma'am" tells us that the extract is set in the past, and "first graders" reveals that it is set in an American school.

Language techniques
Vivid and detailed descriptions help set the negative tone of the scene.

READING STORIES, PLAYS, AND POEMS • COMPARING AND CONTRASTING FICTION

Narrative perspective
The third-person narrator tells the story from the point of view of more than one character.

Characterization
The writer describes Miss Stacy using positive language to convey her kind nature.

Language techniques
This simile tells us the teacher helps Anne grow as a person.

Tone
The text has a positive and hopeful tone throughout the extract.

Setting
References to "schoolwork" and "recitations" tell us the text is probably set in a school around the time it was written in 1908.

> In the new teacher she found another true and helpful friend. Miss Stacy was a bright, sympathetic young woman with the happy gift of winning and holding the affections of her pupils and bringing out the best that was in them mentally and morally. Anne expanded like a flower under this wholesome influence and carried home to the admiring Matthew and the critical Marilla glowing accounts of schoolwork and aims.
>
> "I love Miss Stacy with my whole heart, Marilla. She is so ladylike and she has such a sweet voice. When she pronounces my name, I feel *instinctively* that she's spelling it with an E. We had recitations this afternoon."
>
> *Anne of Green Gables*
> by Lucy Maud Montgomery, 1908

Writing the comparison

When writing your comparison, you should use transition words to introduce your points about how each feature is approached in the texts. Use evidence and examples from the texts to support your ideas, and try to explain the effects on the reader.

> Miss Crocker is portrayed as a forbidding character, with adjectives such as "yellow" and "buckeyed" to describe her appearance. In contrast, Miss Stacy is described using adjectives such as "bright" and "sympathetic." This language gives the reader a positive impression of her.

Summarizing

A summary is a brief retelling of a text that explains the main ideas and the most important points of the text. Being able to summarize shows that you have a good understanding of what you have read.

Summarizing means briefly retelling the story.

How to summarize

To summarize a text, retell it in your own words so that it is shorter but still includes the main ideas and some supporting details.

SEE ALSO
Characters 134
Introducing plot 140
Finding the main idea 170

1. Give the title and author of the text.
2. Use verbs to outline the main ideas.
3. Put the main ideas in a logical order.
4. Choose supporting details.
5. Paraphrase so the summary is in your own words.

Supporting details help describe or explain the main ideas.

Paraphrasing means putting an idea into your own words.

SPEAK UP

Tell someone about your day or about a recent event. Summarize what happened, giving the main points plus a few supporting details.

What is an objective summary?

An objective summary is not influenced by your own personal opinions or feelings. This example shows the difference between an objective summary and an opinion.

"In the play, Romeo compares Juliet's eyes to the stars in heaven." — *Objective summary*

"Yuck! When Romeo admires Juliet's eyes, it's so sappy!" — *Opinion*

Writing an objective summary

When writing an objective summary, it's important not to let your view of the text influence the summary. As you read the text, look for points that are essential to your understanding. Remember, when writing your objective summary, always stick to the facts! Here is an objective summary of *The Tortoise and the Hare*.

One day, the hare was mocking the tortoise for being slow. This annoyed the tortoise, who challenged the hare to a race. Soon the hare was so far ahead of the tortoise that he thought he would lie down for a nap. Slowly and steadily, the tortoise kept going. He passed the sleeping hare and won the race!

The Tortoise and the Hare by Aesop

Aesop's fable The Tortoise and the Hare tells the story of a boastful hare and a determined tortoise who run a race. The hare quickly takes the lead, but then decides to have a nap. The tortoise carries on and wins the race.

- Title and author
- Main characters
- Main idea
- Supporting details
- Conclusion

TRY IT OUT

Try summarizing your favorite book or a book you have recently read.

Proving your point

When you analyze writing—whether looking at tone, character, or description—you'll need to show how you arrived at your viewpoint using evidence from the text.

Prove your point using **evidence** from the text.

Explicit evidence

We can find evidence in the written text. Sometimes it is clearly stated and this type of information is treated as explicit evidence.

SEE ALSO
How to make inferences 162
Using evidence from the text 182

> As soon as you opened our front door, there was our living room with its fifth-hand threadbare nylon carpet and its seventh-hand cloth sofa.
>
> *Noughts & Crosses* by Malorie Blackman, 2001

In this extract from *Noughts and Crosses*, author Malorie Blackman gives explicit evidence about the narrator's home, describing his run-down living room.

Explicit evidence is stated directly in the text.

The evidence in Shakespeare's *King Lear* is explicit: the old King will give the biggest reward to the daughter who says she loves him the most.

> Tell me, my daughters,—
> Since now we will divest us, both of rule,
> Interest of territory, cares of state,—
> Which of you shall we say doth love us most?
> That we our largest bounty may extend
> Where nature doth with merit challenge?
>
> *King Lear* by William Shakespeare, 1606

READING STORIES, PLAYS, AND POEMS • **PROVING YOUR POINT**

Implicit evidence

As a reader, you often have to do some work—reading between the lines—to figure out exactly what a character really means. You can use these hints and clues—known as implicit evidence—to understand meaning and draw your own conclusions or inferences.

Implicit evidence is not stated directly; you have to find the clues.

This hints that the narrator is hardworking and was angry because the man he lived with was lazy.

This implies that the narrator is no longer angry.

I lived with a man once who **used to make me mad** that way. He would **loll on the sofa** and watch me doing things by the hour, following me round the room with his eyes, wherever I went. He said it did him real good to look on at me, **messing about.** He said it made him feel that life was not an idle dream to be gaped and yawned through, but a noble task, full of duty and stern work. He said he often wondered now **how he could have gone on before he met me,** never having anybody to look at while they worked.

Three Men in a Boat by Jerome K. Jerome, 1889

The narrator gives us a clue about the way the lazy man spoke.

This implies that the lazy man has learned something or that he's being sarcastic—it is up to the reader to decide!

> **TRY IT OUT**
>
> Find examples of explicit evidence in a novel. Then read between the lines to see if you can find any implicit meanings, too.

Using evidence from the text

Make a point effectively by citing evidence from the written piece of work you are studying. Show the reader how well you have understood the writer's text!

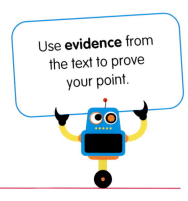

Use **evidence** from the text to prove your point.

Analyzing and interpreting

Fiction writers describe all sorts of things in their text. When they present dialogue or descriptions, they will rely on their readers to understand them. So we may need to analyze and interpret an author's words and phrases to find out what they intended. Analyzing and interpreting the haiku below reveals several key points about the author's intentions.

SEE ALSO
How to make inferences ... 162
Proving your point ... 180

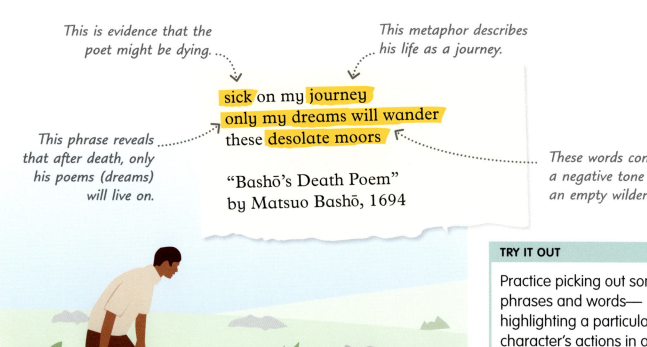

This is evidence that the poet might be dying.

This metaphor describes his life as a journey.

sick on my journey
only my dreams will wander
these desolate moors

"Bashō's Death Poem"
by Matsuo Bashō, 1694

This phrase reveals that after death, only his poems (dreams) will live on.

These words convey a negative tone and an empty wilderness.

TRY IT OUT

Practice picking out some phrases and words—highlighting a particular character's actions in a text that you are reading—to prove a point. Make sure you are using quotation marks correctly.

Using quotations

Citing evidence is when you use quotations from the text to support your own ideas. Pull out particular words and phrases from the text and justify your reasons for selecting these quotations.

When you quote the exact words from the original writer, it is called a **direct quotation**.

When FutureMouse escapes from its cage, scientist Marcus Chalfen is distraught. Archie, on the other hand, is relieved and makes no attempt to catch the mouse: "He watched it dash along the table, and through the hands of those who wished to pin it down."
White Teeth by Zadie Smith, 2000

Put quotation marks around quotes to show they are not your own words.

It is important to give the source of the quotation.

Developing your point

Once you have proved your point using evidence, you will need to find further evidence from the text that helps you build on your point and develop it thoroughly.

The rain eased a little, but was still steadily dripping from the dirty grey-green skies. That color made my head feel strange. The Umbrella Man was standing there, a lanky figure, as if he'd sprouted out of the broken tarmac like some ugly weed.

The Umbrella Man by G. Barker, unpublished

This phrase creates an ominous atmosphere.

The description and comparison to an "ugly weed" build on the ominous atmosphere by emphasizing the Umbrella Man as a villain.

Nonfiction covers everything that's not made up. A book about a space mission; an interview with an explorer; a school history book; even leaflets, posters, and advertisements—these all give you facts and information about different subjects and people. Nonfiction text surrounds us, and by reading it, we can learn more about the world.

READING NONFICTION

Types of nonfiction

Nonfiction texts are about real life. They tell you facts and details about a topic or a person. Nonfiction includes books, articles, letters, websites, and advertisements.

Nonfiction tells a true story using facts.

Electronic media
This includes online media, plus apps, TV, and radio.

Narrative nonfiction
The author tells the story of a real event or person.

Printed media
Newspapers and magazines report the news, explore topics, and offer opinions.

Informative texts
Guides, instructions, or reference books give facts about a particular subject.

READING NONFICTION • TYPES OF NONFICTION

> **TRY IT OUT**
>
> Pick out a few books from the nonfiction section of your local library. Can you spot if they are narrative nonfiction or reference books?

Key types of nonfiction

Narrative nonfiction, reference texts, and advertising are key types of nonfiction. Narrative nonfiction gives information through a story. Reference texts are organized in topics so you can dip into the part that interests you. Advertising materials tell you positive things about the products they want you to buy.

Narrative nonfiction Here, the writer uses dialogue to tell the exciting story of a young skateboarder who made it to the Olympic Games in 2021.

> Teenage skateboarder Sky Brown was desperate to represent Great Britain at the Olympics: "My parents thought it would be too much pressure," she said. "But I begged and begged."

Reference texts This reference text explores topics about skateboarding, such as when, where, and how the sport developed.

> Skateboarding was invented in the 1950s, and athletes first made a living from it in the 1980s. But it was not until 2016 that skateboarding became an Olympic sport.

Advertising An advertisement tries to persuade the reader to take up skateboarding and buy products by saying that the sport is cheap, easy, and fun.

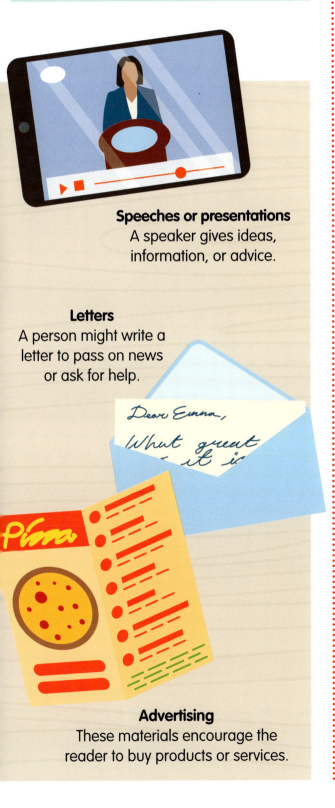

Speeches or presentations
A speaker gives ideas, information, or advice.

Letters
A person might write a letter to pass on news or ask for help.

Advertising
These materials encourage the reader to buy products or services.

GETTING FIT IS FUN!
50% OFF
ENTRY LEVEL
SKATEBOARDS

Reading informative texts

Informative texts give you facts, advice, or instructions. They cover many different subjects and have features to help you find and understand information.

Informative texts give you **facts** and **background** about a topic.

Types of informative texts

Informative texts can be short, like a poster or web page, or long, like a reference book, an encyclopedia, or an e-book. Their style can vary depending on the subject, audience, and purpose. Here are some examples of informative texts:

SEE ALSO
Reading online media 192
Layout and structure 214
Finding information 218

1 Reference
A children's book about bees explains in clear, simple words about types of bees and how they live.

2 Advice
A leaflet giving advice for people with sports injuries tells them how to exercise safely and get fit again.

3 Instructions
A website for filmmakers explains step by step how to make a good video and what equipment is needed.

Finding information

Some texts have step-by-step instructions showing how to do activities. Others are arranged alphabetically or by theme. In longer texts, tools can help you find what you need. See these examples from *DKfindout! Volcanoes* (2016).

1 Contents
At the start of a book, the contents page lists the headings of each section and chapter. It may list any images or maps, too.

2 Index
At the back of the book, the index lists the key topics in alphabetical order and gives the pages where you will find them.

3 Glossary
Near the back of the book, the glossary lists important words in the book in alphabetical order. It tells you what they mean.

Features

Pages may have headings, an introduction, pictures, maps, and captions to help you understand the topic.

WORLD OF WORDS

If you don't know what a word means, the text on the rest of the page may help you work it out. The images can help, too.

The main heading tells you what the pages are about.

The subheading tells you the topic of the paragraph.

The introduction sums up the content.

The caption explains what you see in the pictures.

The illustration helps you understand the text. You might not know the word "eruption," but you can see from the picture that it is lava pouring out of a volcano.

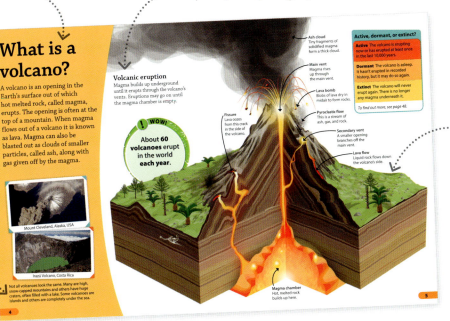

Magazines and newspapers

Printed publications, such as magazines and newspapers, are a means of communication known as printed media. These publications use a wide variety of features to inform and entertain their readers.

Online magazines and newspapers are a part of **digital media**.

Articles

Magazines and newspapers are both made up of articles. An article is a piece of writing designed for a wide audience. Magazine and newspaper articles share many similarities; however, magazine articles such as the one below tend to use more images.

SEE ALSO
Reading informative texts	188
Reading online media	192
Facts and opinions	222

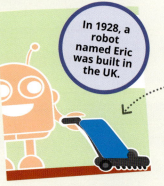

The **deck** or **standfirst** sums up the article.

Images are used to show you what the text is talking about.

The **main body** of the article contains the details of the story and is split into paragraphs.

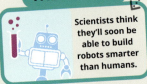

Articles often include separate panels of text with extra information.

Numbers or bullet points can be used to summarize key information.

READING NONFICTION • MAGAZINES AND NEWSPAPERS 191

Newspapers are one of the oldest forms of printed media.

Reliable and unreliable sources
Not all printed or digital media is reliable. You may come across articles that you suspect don't give you trustworthy information. These sources may be unreliable because they are out of date, written by authors with poor reputations, or full of opinions rather than facts.

Monkey festival for Thai town's furry friends

Macaques treated to a feast of fresh fruit and vegetables

By Simeon Gibbons

On Saturday, the people of Lopburi, in Thailand, got together, as they do every November, to honor their 2,000-strong population of macaques, which roam the town and its temples.

First held in 1989, the Monkey Banquet Festival is a way of saying thank you to the macaques, which the people of Lopburi believe bring them good luck. The festival now attracts tourists from far and wide.

One macaque started its feast with a ripe persimmon.

Dancers dressed in monkey costumes amused the crowd before the real monkeys got to feast on towers of vibrant fruit, vegetables, and other foods. As usual, it all ended in a messy food fight!

Alliteration grabs the reader's attention.

The byline tells you who wrote the article.

The lead, or opening, paragraph gives you a quick overview of the article.

The headline sums up the story in a few, often snappy, words.

The caption explains what the picture is about.

Reading online media

You can find information through websites, blogs, or social media on a computer, tablet, or phone using a web browser or other apps. Remember, anyone can post online, so the material that you find may not always be reliable.

If you're **unsure** about anything you see online, ask an adult.

Features of online media

Online content is arranged in different ways to help you find and understand information.

> **SEE ALSO**
> Types of nonfiction — 186
> What's the writer's purpose? — 202
> Facts and opinions — 222

URLs
The URL is the address where you can find the website.

Videos
Videos can help explain how things work and what places are like.

Interactive features
These include links to games, animations, or more information.

Pictures
These make the website more appealing and show things that are hard to put into words.

A red panda family

Charts and maps
Charts or diagrams give facts and figures. Maps show where places are in the world.

Bamboo is the red panda's main food.

www.red-panda-facts.org/endangered

Red pandas

These reddish-brown, cat-sized mammals were once thought to be related to giant pandas.

Red pandas live in the foothills of the Himalayas. Great climbers, they spend most of their time high in the trees.

Like giant pandas, red pandas eat bamboo, but just the tender shoots and leaves.

Red panda numbers

2001 — 14,500
2016 — 10,000

READING NONFICTION • **READING ONLINE MEDIA**   193

How reliable is online content?

Not all information online is reliable. Here are some things to think about:

✔ What's the URL? If it contains .gov, .edu, or .org, it is more likely to be factual.
✔ How up-to-date is the site?
✔ Who wrote the site—are they an expert?
✔ Information can be checked against books and websites you trust—ask your teacher for tips.

Social media
Posts can be read in apps or displayed on web pages.

Red pandas are endangered. ☹

That's terrible. They're so cute.

Comments and forums
Some sites have forums where people can comment and reply to others' posts.

Advertisements
Websites make money from advertisements placed by companies.

Finding content online

Find content by using a browser to search websites. Your computer's "find" command will search for words on the page.

🔍 www.red-panda-facts.org

1 URLs This address also shows the type of website: .com is a business, .gov means government, .edu means education, and .org is an organization.

🔍 Red pandas

2 Search bars Use the search bar on a browser to look for a topic. Once on a website, use the search bar to find the exact information you want.

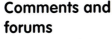

Read about <u>giant pandas</u>.

3 Hyperlinks Click on a hyperlink to find out more about that topic.

4 Tabs You can click on these small labels to go to different web pages.

TRY IT OUT

Enter your favorite animal into a search engine. Look at the top three search results. Use the checklist at the top of this page to check if you can trust the sites that come up.

Narrative nonfiction

Narrative nonfiction uses the structure of a story to tell you about real events or people. It is usually written to entertain, too, with a setting, plot, and sometimes dialogue.

Narrative nonfiction tells a **true story**.

How does it work?

Narrative nonfiction usually has the following features:

> **SEE ALSO**
> Who's telling the story?   138
> Language for different purposes   208
> Narrative techniques   276

1 The author either writes their story in the first person or tells of others' experiences in the third person.

2 You normally read narrative nonfiction like fiction—from start to finish to find out what happens.

3 It moves through time. The story might run from start to end or begin with a dramatic event, then rewind to show how it came about.

Biography

A biography is another person's life story. In an autobiography, the person tells the tale of their own life. Here, a 19th-century civil rights activist recalls, in the third person, being enslaved as a child.

An ellipsis means some words have been left out.

Truth is informing the reader. She doesn't know her exact date of birth.

Truth explains that the colonel was less brutal than some enslavers.

Sojourner Truth ... was born, as near as she can calculate, between the years of 1797 and 1800. She was the daughter of James and Betsey, slaves of one Colonel Ardinburgh.

She distinctly remembers hearing her father and mother say, that their lot was a fortunate one, as Master Charles was the best of the family ... comparatively speaking, a kind master to his slaves.

Excerpt from the *Narrative of Sojourner Truth*, 1850

Narrative history

This recounts an event in the past so the reader can imagine it. It often features the voices and feelings of people who lived through the event.

Apollo 11's launch day dawned on July 16, 1969. More than one million **excited** people lined the beaches in Florida near the launch site…

At **nine seconds** before launch, Saturn V's five engines ignited. They reached full power at the moment of liftoff—time zero. The huge rocket began to rise, with its **roar** being heard for hundreds of miles.

Excerpt from *Moon Landings* by Shoshana Weider, 2019

This note helps the reader get an idea of what it was like to be there.

To build drama, the writer slows the pace, giving details of the moments before liftoff.

Describing the sound as well as the sight brings the scene to life.

Travel narratives

These often describe a quest to visit a place or discover something. In the 14th century, Moroccan explorer Ibn Battuta traveled for nearly 30 years across Africa, Asia, and Europe.

We traveled to Siwasitan **[Sehwan, in what is now Pakistan]** …There is a plentiful supply of fish and buffalo milk, and **they eat also a kind of small lizard** stuffed with *curcuma* [turmeric].

When I saw this small animal and them eating it, I took a **loathing** … [to] it and would not eat it.

Excerpt from *The Travels of Ibn Battuta*, 1350s

The text in square brackets is extra explanation, added by the editor.

Travel writing informs readers about different places and ways of life.

This means "great dislike." Travelers sometimes find unfamiliar food difficult to eat.

Letters

Letters are a type of nonfiction text. They can be formal or informal, depending on who they are written to and what they are trying to achieve.

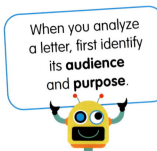

When you analyze a letter, first identify its **audience** and **purpose**.

Informal letters

Letters to friends or family are usually informal, with a chatty and casual style (see page 291). The purpose might be to entertain or inform, like in this letter about a family vacation.

SEE ALSO
How to write a formal letter — 288
How to write an informal email and letter — 290

Informal letters use an informal greeting and use first names. They are written to someone the author knows.

The writer uses double exclamation marks for emphasis.

Hi Jared,

How are you doing? I'd love to say "wish you were here," but this trip has turned into a total nightmare!! The apartment was double booked, so they shoved our whole family into one super-small room. My brothers and I are sleeping on lumpy mattresses on the floor and my parents snore like bulldozers. Still, beach is beautiful, so could be worse.

Miss you

Lots of love,
Mina

Jared Dwyer
4679 Barton Drive
Santa Ana, CA 90272

Informal letters might include exaggeration and express strong emotion.

Informal sign-off

A relaxed, informal style is used, such as this incomplete sentence.

Formal letters

A letter to someone a writer doesn't know well or at all is usually formal (see pages 288–89). Formal letters may have the purpose of advising, informing, arguing, or complaining, like in the example below.

> **TRY IT OUT**
>
> Look at a letter you have received, or ask a grown-up to let you borrow one. What is the audience and purpose of the letter? What is the tone? How could you tell?

The purpose of this formal letter is to complain about a problem on vacation and ask for money back.

The sender's address and the date are written at the top.

14 Linden Avenue
Los Angeles, CA 90013

August 20, 2022

This is the address of the person receiving the letter.

Beach Apartments
46 Rio Verde
48330 Puerto Vallarta
Mexico

A formal greeting uses "Dear" and the recipient's title and surname.

Dear Ms. Serrano,

I am writing to complain about poor service from your company.

The letter has a clear structure. It starts by stating the problem.

We booked a two-bedroom apartment for our family of five. When we arrived, we were told that the apartment was double-booked and were offered a one-bedroom apartment instead.

The writer explains the details of the problem.

Our three children had to sleep on the floor on uncomfortable mattresses and none of us had any privacy. The apartment was completely unsuitable and we will not be returning.

Formal language and correct grammar is used.

We would like you to refund the full cost of our vacation. We look forward to your response.

Yours sincerely,
Mr. and Mrs. Patel

The writer finishes by outlining what they want to happen.

The writer has ended the letter with a formal sign-off.

Reading speeches

A speech is a formal talk to an audience to inform, persuade, advise, or entertain them. The speaker structures their talk so it's easy to follow, and they use language techniques to express their views.

Giving speeches is also called **public speaking** or **oration**.

Speech structure

A good speech is made up of four parts, and there should be a smooth transition between the parts.

1 Opening
A speech needs an exciting opening to grab attention. It might be a strong opinion, a joke, or a surprising fact.

2 Key message
Speakers bring in their main idea or message near the start, so it's clear what the talk will be about.

3 Main content
This includes facts, figures, and quotes from experts. The speaker may include a few anecdotes—short, entertaining stories.

4 Ending
The speaker sums up their key points and final message. They may finish with an important idea or a call to action.

Speech techniques

Speakers can make their points in different ways. An informative speech will have many facts, and an entertaining speech will have funny stories.

1 Facts and figures
A speaker who aims to persuade people may use facts and figures as evidence to back up their point of view.

2 Quoting experts
The speaker might bring in quotes from experts that support their view.

3 Anecdotes
Entertaining stories from the speaker's experience or things they've heard help listeners understand the key message.

On my first day at the Robot Academy …

Language techniques

An effective speech uses several different language techniques.

Engaging the audience
Addressing the audience as "we" or "you" makes the speech feel personal.

Figurative language
A simile or metaphor can be entertaining and memorable.

Repetition
Speakers may repeat a point—often three times—so listeners remember it.

Emotive language
The speaker can make the audience feel sad, happy, or angry.

Rhetorical questions
These questions have an obvious answer that the speaker wants the audience to agree with.

Putting language techniques together

See how the language techniques described above are put to use in this speech about phasing out plastic.

A good speech gets the **audience** on the speaker's side.

The audience is addressed directly.

Repetition is used for effect.

A rhetorical question makes the reader think.

Dear people of Earth,

We all live on this planet and need to protect it. We all know that plastic bags are a problem, and we can all help rid the world of them. Plastic bags kill wildlife: a stork suffocates in a bag on a landfill site; a baby fish dies from eating plastic.

Can you make a difference? Just do one thing. Find an eco-friendly bag with strong handles and carry it every time you shop. Together, we can cure the world of the plague of plastic.

Emotive language makes the audience feel sad.

This metaphor describes plastic as a plague.

SEE ALSO
Identifying your audience and purpose — 246
Using language techniques — 260
Writing a speech — 298

Sales materials

The purpose of brochures, leaflets, and other sales or marketing materials is to sell or advertise a product or service. Although sales materials are a form of nonfiction, it's important to read any claims made in them with care.

Sales materials use **persuasive language**.

Convincing the reader

Sales text is an example of persuasive writing. It aims to convince you that a particular product or service will improve your life. Sales materials often use the strategies below to promote their products.

SEE ALSO
What's the writer's purpose?	202
Audience	204
Language for different purposes	208
Writing persuasively	292

1 Introducing
If you've never heard of the product or service, the text will introduce it to you.

2 Informing
The text tells you about the product or service, usually using persuasive language.

3 Giving details
Further information tells you more of what you need to know about the product or service.

4 Consistency
The text is consistent in tone—positive, sometimes urgent—throughout.

READING NONFICTION • **SALES MATERIALS**

Facts and opinions

Facts are statements that can be proved, whereas opinions are personal views that can't be backed up with evidence. Sales materials use both facts and opinions as marketing tools to persuade you to buy their products.

This is a fact because it can be proved by analyzing sales.

THE **MOST POPULAR SHAMPOO** IN CANADA*

*In terms of products sold

EVERYONE LOVES OUR SHAMPOO!

This is an opinion that can't be proved.

Always read sales material with a **critical eye**—the information may not be trustworthy.

Sales features

Brochures and leaflets contain various features aimed at persuading you to buy something, visit somewhere, or sign up for an activity. These features include snappy headings, persuasive writing, and enticing images.

The heading grabs your attention.

A visually appealing image entices the reader.

Visit Fairview!

The most picturesque town in the county

Nestled in scenic hills, Fairview is a town that's most definitely worth a visit. When you come here, you'll never want to leave!

Lose yourself in picturesque Fairview.

Throughout your visit, you'll be entertained. Call in at our top-rated museum, eat at our glorious cake shop, or stop by our new art gallery.

Sales materials include persuasive writing, such as exaggeration.

What's the writer's purpose?

Knowing why a text has been written can help you understand it. Writers might aim to inform, persuade, give different viewpoints, or entertain the reader.

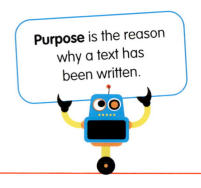

Purpose is the reason why a text has been written.

To inform and explain

Some nonfiction texts tell you facts about a topic or show you how things work. They may not give a particular viewpoint.

1 in 250 cars in the world is electric.

To persuade

The author may try to persuade the reader to agree with them, choosing facts and arguments that support their opinions. Advertisements say positive things about the goods and services they describe.

Electric cars are enormous fun—they get up to speed super-fast. You can drive up to 300 miles (483 km) before recharging them. What's more, electric cars look great and are comfortable inside. You can test-drive one today!

To give different viewpoints

Nonfiction texts may give different viewpoints, inviting the reader to make up their own mind. One paragraph below argues that electric cars are good for our world. The next one explains some problems with them.

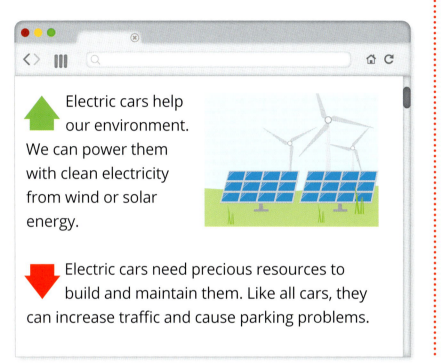

⬆ Electric cars help our environment. We can power them with clean electricity from wind or solar energy.

⬇ Electric cars need precious resources to build and maintain them. Like all cars, they can increase traffic and cause parking problems.

To entertain

Some texts are written for the reader to enjoy and might be entertaining true stories or observations. Texts that educate may use fun words or a playful style to make learning easier.

Electric cars are so **quiet** they had to make them **noisier**! Added sounds mean they don't surprise cyclists and pedestrians. Some electric cars have **dog mode**, which keeps your pets cool when your car is parked.

> **SEE ALSO**
> Audience 204
> Language for different purposes 208
> Facts and opinions 222

Audience

The audience is whoever the writer is aiming their text at. A text may have been written for adults or children, for people who know the topic or those who are new to it.

Knowing the intended **audience** helps you **understand** a text.

Identifying the audience

Look for clues in the text to discover who it is written for.

1 How old are they?
Nonfiction books for adults are usually different from those for children. You can work out who the intended audience is from the features of the text.

Adults:
- ✔ More complex language
- ✔ Long sentences and paragraphs
- ✔ Lots of detail
- ✔ Few or no illustrations

Young children:
- ✔ Simpler words
- ✔ Shorter sentences and paragraphs
- ✔ Focuses on the main ideas
- ✔ Includes several illustrations

2 What do they know?
A text aimed at readers who are new to the subject will generally explain everything from the start. A book for an audience that already knows the topic may not cover the basics in as much detail.

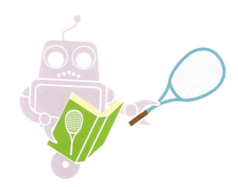

3 How is the text written?
If a text is packed with facts and instructions, it's probably been written to provide information. If a text is full of jokes, it's aimed at a lighthearted audience and is probably about a less serious subject.

READING NONFICTION • AUDIENCE   205

The audience and the text

The same topic can be covered in different ways, depending on the audience. A description aimed at children will usually be livelier and more fun than one aimed at adults, while an advertisement will use persuasive language to appeal to people who are likely to buy the product.

> Clues in the text can help you identify the **audience** and see the book in a different light.

Stories say that young Arthur easily pulled the magical sword Excalibur out of a stone and won the right to become king.

With simple words and a picture, this text is for children.

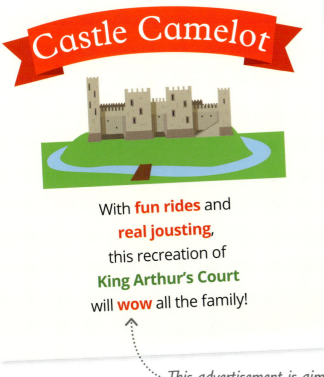

Castle Camelot

With **fun rides** and **real jousting**, this recreation of **King Arthur's Court** will **wow** all the family!

This advertisement is aimed at parents and children who like activities and history.

According to legends, in the 5th or 6th century, Arthur claimed the British throne after drawing the sword Excalibur from a stone. Yet modern scholars see Arthur as a myth, not a real historical figure.

With complex words and no pictures, this text is for adults.

SEE ALSO

What's the writer's purpose?	**202**
Levels of formality	**206**
Language for different purposes	**208**
Identifying your audience and purpose	**246**

Levels of formality

Nonfiction text can be formal or informal. The word "register" describes how formal or informal a writer's choice of language is. Formal register uses correct grammar and precise vocabulary. Informal register is chatty, like a conversation.

Register can be **formal** or **informal**, depending on the tone, choice of words, and writing structure of a text.

GLEN SCHOOL WINS TOP ECO AWARD

Environmental champion Glen School reuses and recycles more waste than any other primary school, and it has won this year's Council Eco Gold Award.

Millie, 11, helped run the project. "Wow, it's amazing," she said. "We worked incredibly hard, but I can't believe we actually won!"

Formal register
This nonfiction writing uses correct grammar and vocabulary. The writer does not use slang or contractions.

Informal register
This text includes slang and contractions and expresses strong feelings. Millie is excited about the award.

READING NONFICTION • LEVELS OF FORMALITY 207

WORLD OF WORDS

Rude and polite tones

You will find different tones in direct speech in nonfiction texts. Think about the tone of these examples. One person is rude, and the other uses polite phrases:

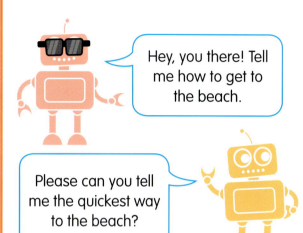

Hey, you there! Tell me how to get to the beach.

Please can you tell me the quickest way to the beach?

Principal Mrs. Amin explained, "**I am delighted** we have won this award. The children ran the project themselves. A group set up bins in every classroom for trash to reuse, recycle, or throw away. **They truly deserve praise** for their work."

The principal's tone

Mrs. Amin shows she's pleased and proud of the children. In her role as principal, she uses a less emotional tone than Millie.

▯ **HAPPY TONE**   ▯ **PROUD TONE**

Council member Shona Clark added, "**We are pleased to recognize** that our young people are taking the lead in making their school more eco-friendly."

The city council's tone

Shona Clark uses formal expressions to show that she approves of the children's actions. She does not use an emotional tone.

▯ **APPROVING TONE**

SEE ALSO

Understanding the tone	164
Audience	204

Language for different purposes

Writers choose their words carefully to have the right effect on their readers. The language that writers choose depends on the purpose of the writing. The text might be written to inform, persuade, or entertain the reader.

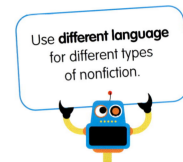

Use **different language** for different types of nonfiction.

Language and effects

Writers write to suit their purpose and their audience. If writers want to inform their readers, they may use a serious tone. To persuade readers, writers use words to try and make readers agree with a certain point of view. To entertain their readers, writers use language that readers will enjoy.

SEE ALSO	
The effects of language	156
Understanding the tone	164
What's the writer's purpose?	202
Using language techniques	260

INFORM	PERSUADE	ENTERTAIN
LANGUAGE		
The writer normally uses a neutral, formal tone to give facts and information.	The writer uses words that persuade readers to agree with their view or buy something.	The text may be funny to make the reader laugh or frightening to scare them.
⬇	⬇	⬇
EFFECT		
The reader is likely to take the text seriously and believe what the writer says.	The reader may agree with the writer or be tempted to buy something.	The reader enjoys the writing and may find it funny or exciting.
⬇	⬇	⬇
EXAMPLE		
How to Play Tennis	*Why Basketball Is Best*	*Epic Sports Failures*

Ways to use language techniques

Writers use language techniques for effect. To help the reader remember what they say, they might use repetition, figurative language, or short sentences. Using exaggeration or emotive words can affect readers' feelings.

> **TRY IT OUT**
>
> Write your own examples for each of these language techniques.

1 Technical language Words and phrases that are specific to a topic help inform readers.

She threw a straight karate punch called a choku zuki.
Technical phrase in karate

2 Figurative language Writers use similes and metaphors to describe what something is like.

Swimming outdoors is like being a fish in the sea.
Simile

3 Repetition The most important topic is repeated, often three times.

"This game is so much fun, fun, fun," she said.

4 Exaggeration Making something seem much more or much less than it really is can help make a point.

The batter hit the ball all the way into the next town!

5 Emotive words These words make a reader feel a certain way.

Racing on my bike, I feel free. Nothing can stop me.
The reader can sense the writer's feelings.

6 Sentence length Long sentences give more information, while short sentences stress the point.

Zumba is a fitness program using Latin American dance movements. It's an awesome workout.

›› Language to inform

When reading an informative text, you'll see that it uses a neutral, formal tone to provide facts and information. Informative texts are sometimes broken into short sections to make them easier to read.

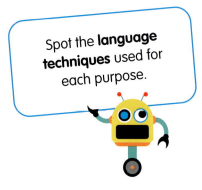

Spot the **language techniques** used for each purpose.

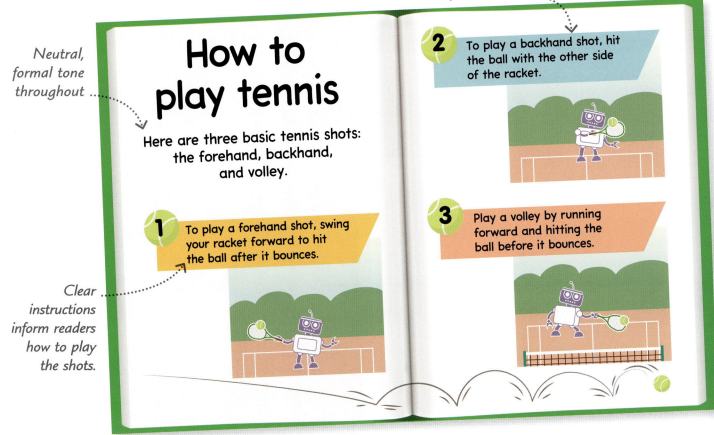

Technical language, such as names of tennis shots

Neutral, formal tone throughout

How to play tennis

Here are three basic tennis shots: the forehand, backhand, and volley.

1 To play a forehand shot, swing your racket forward to hit the ball after it bounces.

2 To play a backhand shot, hit the ball with the other side of the racket.

3 Play a volley by running forward and hitting the ball before it bounces.

Clear instructions inform readers how to play the shots.

What **effect** do different language techniques have on you?

TRY IT OUT

Different language techniques are used in nonfiction all around you in both writing and speaking. Watch an informative news report or a persuasive advertisement. See which language techniques you can spot!

Language to persuade

To persuade readers that their point of view is right, a writer might bring in evidence from experts. In an advertisement, a writer might use words to show how fantastic you will feel if you buy a particular product or service.

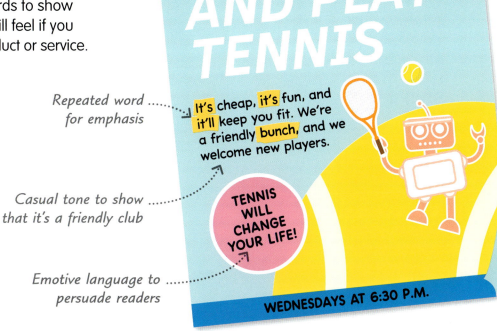

Language to entertain

This text tells a funny story, so the reader enjoys reading it. The author uses language to make the text lively. A scary story might use language that keeps the reader in suspense.

Different viewpoints

Some authors only tell you one viewpoint, while others provide more than one viewpoint. Always look for evidence in the text to see if the author backs up their viewpoint.

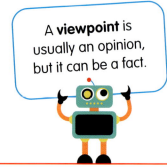

A **viewpoint** is usually an opinion, but it can be a fact.

One clear viewpoint

The author may describe one clear viewpoint in a text rather than discussing different ideas. For example, here, the author informs us that the Earth is round.

SEE ALSO
What's the writer's purpose? 202
Audience 204
Facts and opinions 222

The author states a fact.

==The shape of the Earth is almost completely round.== It bulges a little at the equator, the imaginary line around the middle of our planet. ==All planets are round like the Earth.==

….The author adds a new fact related to the first one.

Weighing viewpoints

Informative text should give a balanced viewpoint and provide arguments to support more than one opinion.

✔ Informs and explains
✔ Allows readers to consider different viewpoints
✔ Readers can decide for themselves.

The author encourages readers to answer this question themselves.

==Which meal is better: pizza or pasta?== You can pick the toppings for your pizza, but pasta comes with a wide range of delicious sauces.

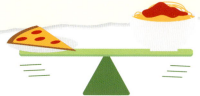

READING NONFICTION • DIFFERENT VIEWPOINTS

Clashing viewpoints

The text may cover opposite viewpoints so the reader can make up their own mind. For example, some people hate graffiti, while others love it.

SPEAK UP

What time do you like to go to bed? Do your parents agree with you? If not, can you discuss your different viewpoints and come to an agreement?

SUPPORTING VIEWPOINT

Graffiti artists liven up plain, dull walls with brightly colored designs. Their artwork makes our cities more welcoming.

OPPOSING VIEWPOINT

Spraying graffiti on walls in public places or others' property is a crime. People who graffiti should go to prison.

.... The author strongly opposes graffiti artists.

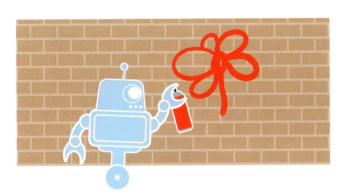

Looking for evidence

Check if the author gives evidence for their viewpoint. Here, the author backs up their opinion that having a cat is good for your health.

.... The author gives their opinion.

Owning a cat helps you live a longer, healthier life. Stroking a cat is relaxing, and studies show that living with a furry friend can lower stress levels and cut the owner's risk of heart disease by 30 percent.

The author provides a statistic ....
to back up their opinion.

TRY IT OUT

Think of a topic you feel strongly about. Look for evidence from a book or official website to back up your viewpoint. Write a paragraph giving your opinion and supporting it with evidence.

Layout and structure

Nonfiction includes newspaper articles and reference books, which often contain double-page spreads. Articles and spreads are laid out and structured in a way to help the reader find information easily.

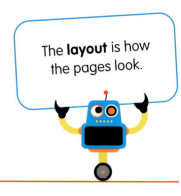

The **layout** is how the pages look.

Headings

Newspaper articles and reference-book spreads have headings to tell you about the content. Headings—especially those in newspapers—are often large, bold, and in capital letters to stand out. There may be subheadings, too, to break up the text.

Images and charts

To show you what the text talks about, nonfiction usually includes images, such as photographs, illustrations, and diagrams. Most images have captions to explain what you see. Charts and tables may be used to display information visually, too.

The headings of newspaper articles are called headlines.

News stories are laid out in columns of short paragraphs.

Subheadings break up the text, making it easier to follow.

DELHI TO BECOME THE LARGEST CITY IN THE WORLD

December 2021

The Indian capital is poised to overtake Tokyo, Japan, as the most populated city.

THE UNITED NATIONS predicts that within a decade Tokyo will lose its crown to Delhi, India, as the city with the world's largest population. Tokyo's population appears to have reached its peak at about 37 million. This is now likely to fall each year due to a declining birth rate and an aging population.

GROWING CITY
Delhi, however, continues to attract millions of young workers from all over India and outside, too—drawn to the megacity for jobs and money. More than 30 million people now live in Delhi, and this number is due to rise as Tokyo's population falls.

Urban areas are now home to more than half of the world's population.

TOP FIVE MOST POPULATED CITIES IN THE WORLD (2021)

TOKYO	37 million
DELHI	31 million
SHANGHAI	27 million
SÃO PAULO	22 million
MEXICO CITY	22 million

Captions tell you about the images.

Charts show information in an easy-to-understand way.

READING NONFICTION • LAYOUT AND STRUCTURE 215

Sections

Nonfiction text is often broken up into sections with subheadings to tell you what the text is about. In addition, spreads and articles usually have an introductory paragraph to sum up the content.

Lists

Bullet points are useful for lists. They break up the text and make each point easy to read. Numbered lists or sections are used if there are steps to follow or if the text needs to be read in a certain order.

The introduction summarizes the spread.

The sections shown here are the steps to follow.

How to make a strawberry smoothie

Zinging with fruity flavor and healthy nutrients, this smoothie takes very little time to prepare. It's an absolutely delicious treat for any time of the day. Just follow these four easy-peasy steps.

 10 MINUTES

INGREDIENTS
- 7 oz (200 g) strawberries
- 1 banana
- 7 fl oz (200 ml) milk
- 3½ fl oz (100 ml) natural yogurt
- 1 tbsp honey

EQUIPMENT
- Sharp knife
- Chopping board
- Measuring spoons
- Blender
- Glasses

1. Rinse the strawberries in cold water and drain them. Remove the green leafy part of the fruit by slicing off the top.

2. Cut the strawberries in half and put them to one side. Peel and slice the banana so it will blend easily in step 4.

3. Put the strawberries and banana into the blender. Add the milk, yogurt, and honey and secure the lid.

4. Blend the mixture until it's smooth. Then carefully pour it into glasses and enjoy with your friends!

Bullet points make lists easy to read.

Numbers show you the order to follow.

TRY IT OUT

Read the headings on a spread in a reference book without looking at the rest of the text. Can you work out what the text will be about?

SEE ALSO

Writing to inform and explain 284
How to present information clearly 286

New words and terms

There are different ways to work out the meanings of new words and terms that you come across in your reading of nonfiction.

Nonfiction often contains words that are specific to the **topic**.

Understanding words from context

Context is the text around the word. If you don't know what a word means, read some of the text before and after the word. Can you guess what the new word means from understanding the text around it? Use the words you do know to try and work out the meaning of the words that you don't know.

In this paragraph about dinosaurs, you can use the context to work out the meaning of the words **carnivores**, **herbivores**, and **extinct**.

> **SEE ALSO**
> Roots and root words   94
> Breaking words into parts   96
> What is a suffix?   102
> How to work out meaning   154

Knowing whether a word is a **noun**, **verb**, **adjective**, or another **part of speech** can help you work out the definition.

> The word "dinosaur" means "terrible lizard." It comes from the Greek "deinos" for terrible and "sauros" for lizard. Some dinosaurs were fierce **carnivores** who hunted for their food. Other dinosaurs were peaceful **herbivores** who ate plants. Dinosaurs are now **extinct**. They died out a long time ago.

Recognizing part of the word

Recognizing part of a word can help you understand the meaning of the whole word. For example, knowing the adjective "extinct" helps you understand the noun "extinction."

See page 94 to find out about **root words**.

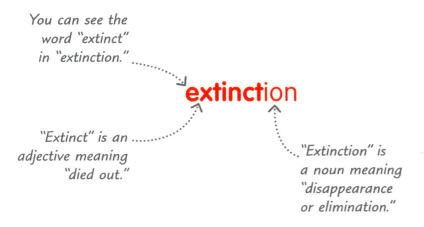

You can see the word "extinct" in "extinction."

"Extinct" is an adjective meaning "died out."

"Extinction" is a noun meaning "disappearance or elimination."

Dinosaurs are extinct. The extinction of the dinosaurs happened millions of years ago.

Using a dictionary

A dictionary can help us understand new vocabulary. Follow these steps to find a word in the dictionary.

TRY IT OUT

Open a dictionary to a random page. Find a word that you don't know. Try to memorize the word and its definition.

1 What letter does the word begin with? Turn to that letter's section in the dictionary.

2 What is the second letter of the word? Scan through the pages until you find the first and second letter together. Use the guide words at the top of each page to help.

3 Keep scanning the page for the remaining letters of the word.

4 The word entry will have the definition and any different forms of the word. Some words have more than one definition.

Guide words tell you the first and last words on the page.

This section contains words beginning with "d."

Dinner

dinner
NOUN dinner, dinners
Dinner is the main meal of the day.

Dd

dinosaur
NOUN dinosaur, dinosaurs
Dinosaurs were reptiles that lived on Earth for more than 150 million years. The last dinosaurs died 65 million years ago.

dip
VERB dip, dips, dipping, dipped
If you dip something into a liquid, you put it in and then take it out again.

Finding information

We often need to find specific information in a text, especially in nonfiction. Finding, or retrieving, information helps us answer questions about the text. This is also known as "finding evidence."

Finding information is a skill we use in everyday life.

Key features of nonfiction

When you're trying to find specific information in a nonfiction text, it helps to look at some key features, which can include headings; subheadings; pictures and captions; and diagrams, tables, charts, or graphs.

> **SEE ALSO**
> Using evidence from the text — 182
> Reading informative texts — 188
> Layout and structure — 214
> Inferring meaning — 220

A main heading gives the overall topic.

A subheading tells you what a specific section is about.

PLANET EARTH

There are eight planets in our solar system. Earth is the third planet from the Sun.

Life on Earth
Earth is the only planet known to support life. It has two things that are vital for living creatures: an atmosphere rich in oxygen and a large supply of liquid water on its surface.

An ideal distance
If Earth was closer to the Sun, it would be so hot, the water on the surface would boil away. If it was farther from the Sun, the water would freeze.

Orbiting the Sun

The **contents**, **glossary**, and **index** also help you find information.

Beneath Earth's surface, there are four distinct layers.

A caption gives more information about the picture it accompanies.

A diagram, chart, or table is a visual way of showing information.

READING NONFICTION • FINDING INFORMATION

Steps for finding information

You may need to find information to answer questions about a text. Use these steps to help you.

1 First, read the entire text. This will give you a general idea of what the text is about.

2 Read the questions. Make sure you understand them. What kind of information do you need to find? Where in the text are you most likely to find it?

3 Skim and scan the text to find the information needed to answer the questions. You may want to highlight the information in the text.

4 Now write the answer to each question in a full sentence.

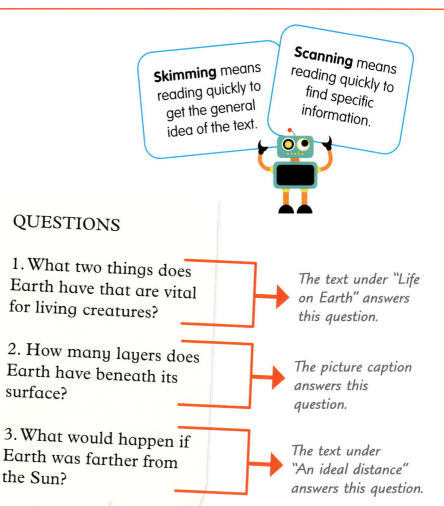

Skimming means reading quickly to get the general idea of the text.

Scanning means reading quickly to find specific information.

QUESTIONS

1. What two things does Earth have that are vital for living creatures? — *The text under "Life on Earth" answers this question.*

2. How many layers does Earth have beneath its surface? — *The picture caption answers this question.*

3. What would happen if Earth was farther from the Sun? — *The text under "An ideal distance" answers this question.*

ANSWERS

1. The two things Earth has that are vital for living creatures are an atmosphere rich in oxygen and lots of liquid water on its surface.

2. Earth has four distinct layers beneath its surface.

3. If Earth was farther from the Sun, the water on its surface would freeze.

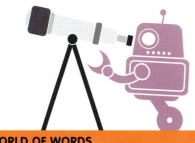

WORLD OF WORDS

We need to find specific information in lots of different kinds of nonfiction, such as instructions, lists, timetables, websites, and more.

Inferring meaning

To infer meaning means to work out things the writer does not say directly. Nonfiction is often more straightforward than fiction, but you still may need to do some detective work.

You can **use clues** from the text to work out its meaning.

Looking for evidence

If text is explicit, the writer says what they mean directly. If text is implicit, we have to look for evidence to work out what they mean.

EXPLICIT

The lizard lay under a rock to cool down.

The sentence is clear and easy to follow.

IMPLICIT

After the lizard crawled under a cold stone, its temperature rapidly dropped.

The sentence implies that the lizard was hot and moved under a stone to cool down.

Inferring information

To infer information, you can use your own knowledge and experience to make sense of the text. Look for key words that give you clues.

Who is doing what, why, and how?

With so many people watching the event, it seems that Zina is famous internationally.

When do people wheel themselves? Zina is probably a wheelchair user.

The star of the show wheels herself onto the stage. Watched by millions of viewers around the globe, she greets the audience, to the enthusiastic cheers of the crowd. This is no celebrity singer or Olympian. Zina has invented an Earth-saving solution to the problem of plastic waste.

The text implies that the person is not from the world of entertainment or sports.

Inferring feelings

To work out how someone in a text feels, check what they are doing and how. Does it show that they are happy, sad, angry, or worried?

The parents are feeling relaxed.

At Cally's Campsite, parents rest easy, knowing that a secure fence surrounds the site. Children squeal with delight in the shallow paddling pool, race through the fields, and dare each other to climb trees in the soft, springy meadow.

The children are happy, and they are having fun.

In this safe place, the children feel brave.

I conclude that families feel safe and enjoy themselves!

Inferring opinion

We can infer the writer's opinions from the words and expressions they use to show agreement or disagreement, approval or disapproval.

This expression shows Stephen has self-respect.

Stephen is elderly, but he walks tall like a man decades younger. His friendliness is infectious. People smile, laugh, and relax when they speak with him.

The writer tells us Stephen has a positive influence on people.

We can infer that the writer approves of him.

SEE ALSO

What are inferences?	160
How to make inferences	162

Facts and opinions

A fact is something you can prove is true. An opinion is a person's belief or feeling, which you cannot prove is true or false. Nonfiction can contain both facts and opinions—here's how you can tell the difference.

What's the difference?
You can find evidence to prove a fact, for example, by looking it up in an encyclopedia. But you cannot prove an opinion is true.

> **SEE ALSO**
> Facts, questions, and instructions   **60**
> What's the writer's purpose?   **202**
> Inferring meaning   **220**

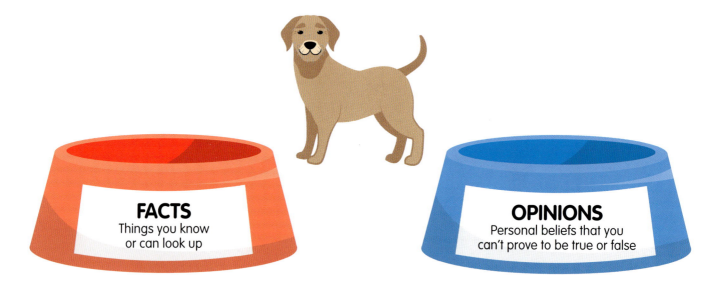

FACTS
Things you know or can look up

OPINIONS
Personal beliefs that you can't prove to be true or false

- This is a dog.
- Dogs have four legs.
- Dogs are mammals.

- Dogs are beautiful.
- All families should have a dog.
- Dogs make the best pets.

Distinguish between facts and opinions

Language can help you identify facts and opinions. Texts with facts tend to use verbs that state something. Texts giving opinions often use words to do with thinking.

FACTS

> The graph shows/demonstrates/confirms …

OPINIONS

> The politician thinks/argues/claims …

TRY IT OUT

Fact or opinion?

Which of these two sentences gives a fact, and which gives an opinion?

> A 2020–2021 survey showed that dogs are the most popular pets. Sara Deen, head of the Canine Trust, says, "Dogs are the best companions for people who live alone."

Be careful!

A text may use the language of facts but not give any evidence to back up the information.

> A survey of dog owners confirmed that dogs make the best pets.

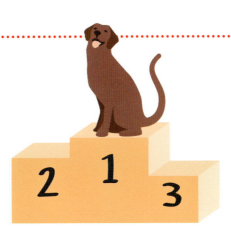

The survey says that dogs make the best pets. Dog owners are likely to give this opinion because they love dogs. However, there is no evidence that the statement is true.

Implicit and explicit evidence

Evidence in nonfiction may be explicit (stated clearly) or implicit (implied by the text).

1 Explicit evidence
"Josh enjoyed a long run around the park with his lively dog, Mustard."

You know that Josh went to the park with his dog.

2 Implicit evidence
"They arrived home exhausted. Mustard dropped his stick and shook his wet, muddy coat."

Mustard is muddy and has a stick. They've probably been to the park.

Comparing and contrasting nonfiction

Sometimes you might be asked to compare nonfiction texts, such as two pieces of writing about the same event. This involves looking at the similarities and differences between a range of features in the texts.

Form, purpose, and audience

When looking at nonfiction texts, a good way to start is to identify the form, purpose, and audience. Understanding these elements will help you identify how other features of the text, such as language and structure, are used for effect.

> **SEE ALSO**
> What's the writer's purpose? 202
> Audience 204
> Language for different purposes 208

1 **Form** is the type of text, such as a newspaper article, advertisement, website, or leaflet.

2 **Purpose** is the reason for writing a text, such as to entertain, persuade, or advise.

3 **Audience** is who the writing is for—for example, children, nature enthusiasts, or musicians.

A flyer advertising a new attraction aims to persuade children and families to attend.

An online news article informs adults in the local community about the same tourist attraction.

OPENING THIS FALL!
Wilson's WATER PARK
Make a splash at Riverton's brand new indoor water park, featuring a whopping 32 attractions for little kids and big kids alike!
BOOK NOW!

TOURISM DRIVE
A local businesswoman has bought land at the edge of town that has been unused for 12 years. She has vowed to use the site for a new indoor water park. Some locals are unhappy about the news, but others say it will not only provide much-needed jobs for the area, but also boost tourism.

Features to compare

Writers use a range of techniques to achieve their purpose and communicate with their audience. When you're planning a comparison of nonfiction texts, you should think about how the writer has used each of the following features for effect:

Tone What is the tone of the writing? Is it funny or serious? Is it formal or informal? Does it suit the audience and purpose?

Structure How is the writing organized? Is it in the past or present tense? Is it written in the first, second, or third person?

Language What language features and vocabulary have been used? How do they suit the form, purpose, and audience?

Presentation Have images been used? Is there any clever use of color? Is the text all the same size or does it vary?

Formal address and language are used, as the letter has been written on behalf of the Queen of England.

Dear Mr. Jones,

I am writing to express my gratitude for the lovely card you sent the family to congratulate us on the wedding of our son Arthur.

We were so touched by your kind words and thank you for taking the time to write.

Yours sincerely,
Anna Hoffman
Lady-in-Waiting

The tone is formal but warm.

The large headline draws attention to the subject matter of the piece.

Scott of the Antarctic

Robert Falcon Scott, born June 6, 1868, became a naval cadet at the age of thirteen. Between the years 1901 and 1904, Scott commanded the National Antarctic Expedition and had a hero's welcome back to Britain having reached the farthest South. This spurred Scott on, and his desire to be the first to reach the South Pole was born.

The text is written in the third person, as it is a biographical account.

Context

When you are comparing texts, it is important to consider their context (when and where they were written). Context can affect the features of a text and the way these features appeal to the audience.

Comparing and contrasting nonfiction texts

When we compare and contrast two pieces of nonfiction writing, we think about how features like their form, structure, and language are used and the effect that these features have on the reader.

As you plan your comparison, think about each of these features in turn: form, purpose, audience, language, structure, and presentation. Write down your observations about each feature as you read through the texts.

Look at both **language** and **layout** when comparing nonfiction texts.

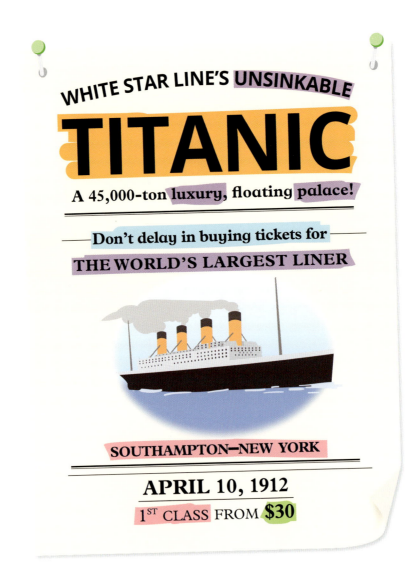

Form
An advertisement promoting tickets for the Titanic

Purpose
To persuade the audience to buy tickets for the Titanic

Audience
Wealthy people who want to travel to New York

Language
The language exaggerates and emphasizes the ship's positive features.

Presentation
Images and enlarged key information grab the reader's attention.

Structure
The advertisement first tries to impress and persuade the audience before telling them the ticket price.

READING NONFICTION • COMPARING AND CONTRASTING NONFICTION   227

Form
A newspaper article about the sinking of the Titanic

Purpose
To persuade readers to buy and read the newspaper and to inform them of the important facts surrounding the ship's sinking

Audience
Readers of the newspaper and those interested in the Titanic

TITANIC SINKS

Tragedy as "unsinkable" ship strikes iceberg

Monday, April 15, 1912

The maiden voyage of the Titanic, the White Star Line ship that was deemed unsinkable, has ended in disaster as it struck an iceberg and sank in the early hours of this morning.

The ship's voyage from Southampton to New York ended after it hit the iceberg late last night before sinking in the North Atlantic. Distress calls made via wireless technology were too late, leading to catastrophic loss of life.

Reports indicate that first- and second-class passengers—women and children first, followed by the men—were rescued before any third-class passengers. Over 1,500 people are believed to have died during the sinking.

Presentation
The dramatic heading and subheading are in bold and enlarged to add impact.

Structure
Key dramatic facts are prioritized before other details to shock the reader and draw them in so they keep reading.

Language
The writer has used dramatic language and statistics to keep the audience's attention.

Writing the comparison

When writing a comparison of nonfiction texts, use transition words to move from one point to the next clearly and effectively. Strengthen your writing by including evidence and examples from the texts, and try to explain how the texts are suited to their audience and purpose.

The advertisement uses exaggerated language to create a positive and optimistic tone that will persuade the audience to buy a ticket. In contrast, the newspaper's language is much more dramatic and negative, which makes the audience feel sad and shocked.

Summarizing multiple paragraphs

A summary can take a text that is several paragraphs long and turn it into a concise statement that conveys the text's most important ideas.

What's the main idea?

The main idea is the author's key message. When you're planning a summary, it's important to find the main idea of the text and the details that support it.

> **SEE ALSO**
> Finding the main idea **170**
> Summarizing **178**
> Finding information **218**

1 Often, the very first sentence of a paragraph or section explains the main idea of the text that follows.

2 The final sentence of a paragraph may summarize the key information and can help consolidate the main idea.

3 Combine your thoughts from each of the paragraphs you have read and ask yourself the following questions:

Objective summaries

An objective summary is one that doesn't include any personal opinions about what's written. When summarizing nonfiction, it is important that you are objective and focus on the facts in the text in order to produce an accurate summary.

1 Look for the key information within the paragraphs. What facts are essential?

2 Write a sentence that identifies the main topic and the key information.

3 Write one or two main ideas. Use your own words, but don't give your opinions.

4 Find the most important supporting details and include them.

Writing a summary

When you are writing, it is important that you use evidence from the text to support your summary. The text below shows how a summary can work.

> **TRY IT OUT**
>
> Read multiple paragraphs from a piece of nonfiction and write a summary. Give it a short headline—four or five words long.

The first sentence explains the text's main idea—that a historic coin has been found.

The main details of the original text have been included in this summary.

> A local man has found an ancient coin on the beach. Vincent made the discovery after being given a metal detector for his birthday.
>
> Vincent was surprised to find the coin during a family visit to the beach in July and is not sure what he'll do with it yet.

> An ancient coin has been found during a local family's visit to the beach in July. Vincent found the coin by using a metal detector.

The rest of the text gives key supporting details.

> When you're summarizing, it's important to **use your own words** so you're not plagiarizing.

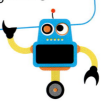

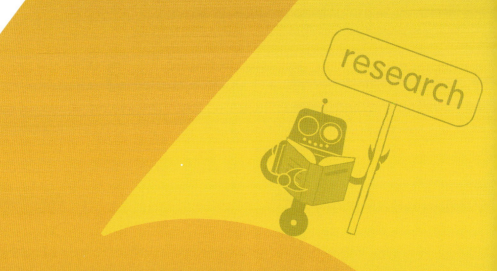

Writing well is not just about good handwriting, although that's important, too! In fact, putting pen to paper, or fingertips to keyboard, is just one part of a complex process. There are other key stages—from coming up with ideas to choosing the most suitable vocabulary—and the more you understand about these stages, the better your writing will be.

WRITING

How to write well

Whether you're writing stories, poems, letters, or diaries, good writing involves using your imagination, thinking about the audience and purpose of your text, choosing your words carefully, and revising and editing your work.

Writing doesn't always come easily. But with practice, we can all **improve**.

As simple as ABC

From our alphabet of 26 letters, we form words. What we do next is fascinating: we use our imagination to mold those words into stories (narratives); create descriptions; write explanations, guides, and summaries; or draft letters.

Who and what is it for?

We must think about who is going to read our writing: the audience. Also, what is the purpose of the piece? The style and type of writing depend on what we want to achieve or the desired effect.

WORLD OF WORDS

A haiku is a short poem with three lines and 17 syllables, or beats, in a 5-7-5 pattern (see page 182). The first haikus were Japanese poems about changing seasons. When writing a haiku, a poet has to choose their words very carefully because the poem is so short!

From start to finish

First, write down your thoughts, then arrange them so the order makes sense and the text flows how you want it to. To make your text as good as possible, revise and edit your writing by checking grammar, punctuation, and spelling and making sure the text is easy for your reader to understand. After one final check, known as proofreading, you're done!

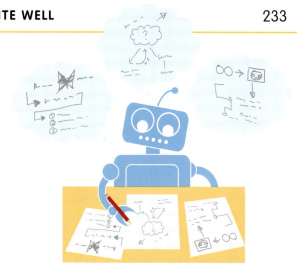

Practice makes perfect

Like practicing with a musical instrument, the more you write, the better you get. Not only is it useful to write often, but it is also helpful to try out a variety of styles and formats. Experiment. Try summarizing a movie you've seen or writing a haiku.

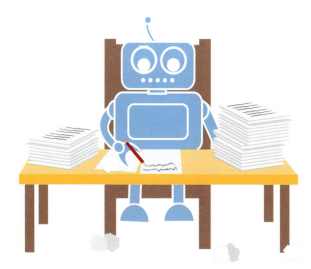

TRY IT OUT

Take a passage from a book you love as a starting point. Think about the effect the passage has on you and the words that the writer chose to achieve that effect. Then try writing a text of your own in a similar style.

The stages of writing

Writing is a step-by-step process, from the very first seeds of a story to the final check for errors in a finished proof. Once you break a task down into smaller steps, or stages, it immediately becomes much more manageable.

Proofread your work, or get someone else to help you.

The writing process

Preparing to write involves thinking and reading about your topic or story and planning and sorting your ideas. Next comes the writing stage—getting thoughts down on the page or screen. You will then reread and edit your work.

> **SEE ALSO**
> Adjectives 20
> Using language techniques 260
> Revision, editing, and proofreading 304

Recording ideas using mind-maps, flowcharts, bulleted lists, and visuals

Shaping ideas into a logical order and researching any extra information

Preparation

Planning
What type of writing is it? Sit down and get your thoughts on the topic or story together. Write down anything that pops into your mind; read and learn from other writers, too. It's the ideas that are important here—let them flow without criticism or judgment and be creative in your planning.

Organizing ideas
Next, work on those ideas. Which are you throwing away? Which are you keeping? Start digging deeper. Maybe you want to research a topic. Or you've thought of a setting for a story but need to find out what the weather is like there in June. Extra background will help you.

WRITING • **THE STAGES OF WRITING** 235

Proofreading

Checking your final written work carefully is called proofreading. This is a vital stage that helps you spot any mistakes—such as spelling and grammatical errors—you might have made. Consider getting someone else to proofread your work as they won't be familiar with the text, so are more likely to spot any issues.

> **TRY IT OUT**
>
> It's a fascinating process to collaborate: working with others can increase your skills and creativity. Think of a project you can work on together, such as a newsletter or magazine. You can all contribute articles, and one person may want to collate or edit them.

It's important to get even the smallest details right.

Writing thoughts and ideas down in an early version of the text called a first draft

Editing and proofreading the text or asking someone else to help

Writing

Editing

Get writing
Write a first draft. Don't overthink this—just write. The key thing is to start writing and to go with the flow. Resist the urge to fix little things as you go—you may interrupt a really important thought and lose it. You will get the chance to go back and fix things later.

Rereading
We spot errors and improve our writing by rereading it over and over again. Reading it aloud can help, too. The process of revising our work—and editing our own words, sentences, and paragraphs—is a stage that needs plenty of time. Always do a thorough final check, or proofread.

Coming up with ideas

We may not always realize it, but we all have ideas. It is crucial to record them so we can use them as a starting point for our writing.

Start small. All writing—even a big idea—begins that way.

Creative thinking

Generating ideas—also known as "brainstorming" or "thought showers"—is a fun process. Think creatively and write down as many ideas as you can. This process can work well as a group activity.

SEE ALSO	
Research	238
Organizing ideas	244
Planning a story	264

1 Let the ideas flow—jot down every single idea.

2 Encourage wild, different ideas.

3 Build on your own ideas and the ideas of others.

4 Think in pictures—images really help bring ideas to life.

5 Afterward, sift through for the best ideas.

SPEAK UP

When you're coming up with ideas in a group, make space for everyone's voice. Just write them all down without judging and discuss what works best.

Ideas for stories

Making notes, rereading favorite books, and using real-life stories can be a good starting point for coming up with new ideas for your own story.

1 Work out what your character is like.

2 Use writing prompts—topics to get you started.

3 Think about other books and authors that you admire. The more you read, the more sources of information you will have.

4 Think about real-life stories or people for inspiration.

Jotting down your thoughts is important for **nonfiction writing**, too—and, as you research the topic, you can also add other people's ideas.

Writing prompt

Recording your ideas

It is easy to forget even the best ideas—especially if you're working in a big group—so it's crucial to record them! There are all sorts of ways of doing this.

TRY IT OUT

Try planning your next written homework task using a list with bullet points and a mind-map. Which one works best?

MIND-MAPS

STICKY NOTES

FLOWCHARTS

LISTS WITH BULLET POINTS

COLOR-CODING

SKETCHING IMAGES

Research

An easy way to improve your writing is to investigate the topic before you get started. Examine lots of sources to build up your knowledge and broaden your perspective.

Researching a subject will help you to write about it.

What is a source?

A source is something that provides information—it could be a book, a website, or even a person. When writing fiction, you might research the time or place in which your writing is set; for nonfiction, you might look for evidence to back up your ideas.

SEE ALSO	
Reading online media	192
Learning from other writers	240

1 Primary sources
First-hand accounts, such as letters, photos, sound recordings, or videos, are primary sources. They are usually nonfiction.

2 Secondary sources
Second-hand accounts, like online articles or encyclopedias, are secondary sources. They often analyze primary sources.

Never pass someone else's words or ideas off as your own—it is called **plagiarism** and it is seen as cheating.

Photos and letters are primary sources: they are recorded first hand.

A person's notes about a primary source are a secondary source.

WRITING • RESEARCH 239

How to conduct research

Whether you are writing nonfiction or fiction, your research should be thorough and reliable. Make sure you give accurate references for your sources.

Try to use **several sources** in your work to give a wide **perspective**.

1 Find good sources
Think of questions to guide your research. What are you trying to find out? Can you find any sources with any interesting ideas?

2 Sort information
When you're ready, start sorting the information you found. Group similar ideas together to make your writing task easier.

3 Quote or paraphrase
Include your research in your writing by quoting a source or describing the ideas in your own words (called paraphrasing).

4 Acknowledge your sources
Always give references for the sources you use. These are details of who wrote each source and where you found it.

Reliable sources

It's important your source is reliable, with ideas that are unbiased (fair) and backed up with evidence. Out-of-date books or articles and many internet sources are unreliable. Ask yourself these questions to check if a source is reliable.

Is the source from a respectable publication you recognize and can trust?

When was it written? Is it up to date?

Does the information agree with other sources you have found, and are those sources reliable?

Are the claims backed up with evidence?

Does the writing use factual language and a serious tone?

megamonstersspotted.com

12/07/2019

SEA DEVIL ATTACKS BOAT

Three fishermen lost in latest attack of giant kraken

Hamnoy, the oldest fishing village in Norway's Lofoten Islands, has been hit by tragedy this week. A small fishing boat carrying three experienced fishermen left the village on Sunday morning at 5:55 a.m. but failed to return. Conditions on Sunday had been fair, but local inhabitants spoke of bright green lights illuminating the skies and otherworldly wails emanating from beyond the mountains. The boat was discovered destroyed, with its three fishermen missing. Early evidence suggests the kraken, the region's most feared predator, is back.

King Sverre of Norway first witnessed the giant sea creature in 1180. Sightings have been rare since, but it seems the mammoth cephalopod has returned—and now has a taste for human blood. The Mayor of Lotofen, Odd Bohinen, was eager to play down the growing threat.

Learning from other writers

If you're looking for ways to improve your writing, why not start by reading the work of other writers? You can learn so much by studying how others make their work great.

Read the work of lots of other writers to find **inspiration** for your own writing.

Where to find inspiration

There's no simple recipe to follow when looking for inspiration—it can come from anywhere. In writing, you can get ideas from a whole range of fiction or nonfiction. Try to read books that are similar to the type of writing you wish to try, from poems, novels, and plays to movies, newspapers, and magazines.

SEE ALSO

What is the setting?	130
Understanding characters	136
Asking about a story	152

Questions to ask yourself

When you're reading another writer's work, it can really help to ask yourself some of these simple questions to help you identify what you like—or dislike—about their work.

- ✓ What do you like about their style?
- ✓ Does anything stand out in a good or bad way?
- ✓ How has the writer used form, structure, and language effectively?
- ✓ What could you take away from your reading to apply to your own writing?

WORLD OF WORDS

Shakespeare was inspired by lots of other stories. For example, *Hamlet* comes from a Scandinavian saga. In the same way, some modern movies use ideas from Shakespeare: *The Lion King* is based on *Hamlet*.

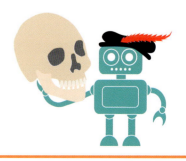

What to look out for

Keep a notebook handy when you are studying a piece of writing and pay close attention to how the writer has approached different elements. Think about how you can let these things inspire your own writing.

> **TRY IT OUT**
>
> Now go and find inspiration from the world around you. Think about your favorite book—if you were writing a story of your own, what inspiration would you take from your favorite story and why?

1 Form What form did the writer choose for their writing? Was it a speech, novel, poem, or play? Why was it effective?

2 Structure How did the writing begin and end? Did it jump straight into the action? Did the writer use a cliffhanger?

3 Language Did the writer use language techniques like metaphor or alliteration? Were they effective? If so, why?

4 Genre What was the genre of the writing? Did the writer follow any typical conventions that you found effective? What did you like about them?

5 Characterization and narration Were characters described in detail or were their traits revealed through dialogue? Who was the storyteller?

Avoiding plagiarism

When you are looking at another writer's style, remember you're trying to learn new skills and find inspiration—you can't just steal someone else's ideas or copy the text word for word! That's called plagiarism and it's considered cheating.

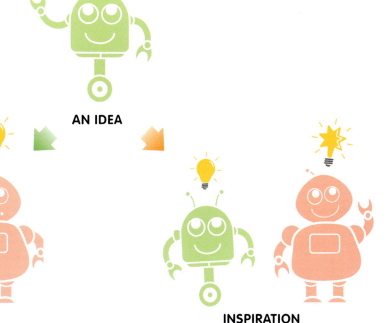

AN IDEA

A COPY

INSPIRATION

Collaboration and synthesis

When you collaborate, you work on a project with other people. When you synthesize, you merge information gathered from several different sources into your own writing.

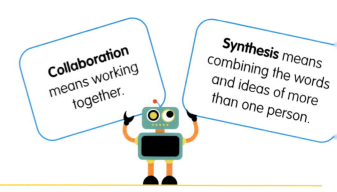

Collaboration means working together.

Synthesis means combining the words and ideas of more than one person.

How do you collaborate?

Collaboration involves listening carefully to others and discussing and debating ideas to deepen your learning and produce a better project. It can make a task less daunting and more enjoyable. It's also a useful tool for later in life, when collaboration may be a key part of your college work or job.

SEE ALSO
The stages of writing	234
Coming up with ideas	236
Research	238

Let's do our project on the light bulb.

Good idea! Didn't Thomas Edison invent it?

A few people came up with the same idea—but they didn't collaborate!

Constructive criticism

A collaboration should include constructive, or useful, criticism. Effective collaborators listen closely, ask helpful questions, and offer suggestions. They give other group members positive and constructive feedback in the form of helpful and polite comments.

TRY IT OUT

Work with a group of friends. Choose a topic that interests all of you. Ask everyone to do a search on the internet and write down five facts about the topic. Then work together to create a presentation on the topic using the most interesting facts.

What is synthesis?

Synthesis is part of the research process—you explore different sources of information and take notes on what experts say. Then you can review your notes and choose what to include to support your own ideas. You can use quotes (the writer's exact words in quotation marks) or paraphrase (put the writer's words into your own words).

Organizing ideas

Once you've come up with some interesting ideas for a piece of writing, whether it's a story, book review, or article, the next stage is to start sorting them out.

Writing **lists** and **notes** will help **order** your ideas.

Making lists and taking notes

Some people like to make a list. Others may write each point as a separate note. (This can also be done digitally.) Keep adding, examining, and refining your ideas as you go, referring back to any research you have done.

SEE ALSO	
Coming up with ideas	236
Research	238
Planning a story	264
Planning a poem	278

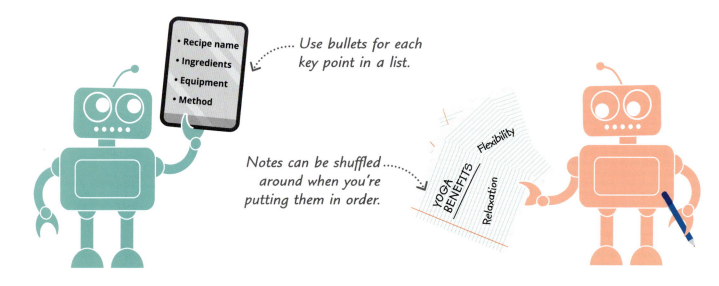

Use bullets for each key point in a list.

Notes can be shuffled around when you're putting them in order.

Ordering points

If you're writing fiction, you should follow a narrative sequence or loosely order the events by time. In nonfiction, your points should be strung together in a logical way that is easy to understand. To argue a case, you will write your points down in a certain order to persuade your reader.

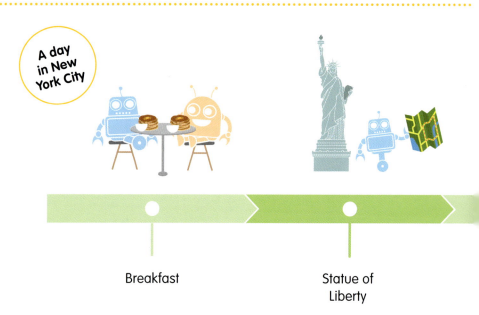

WRITING • ORGANIZING IDEAS   245

Writing it down

Writing each separate point on a piece of paper makes it simple to organize your ideas. Find similar ideas—a bit like putting the same colors together. If they match, you may be able to write about them close together in the text. Throw away ideas that don't fit in logically for this piece of writing.

- Empire State Building
- Statue of Liberty
- Fifth Avenue
- Central Park
- Ride the subway
- Ride the ferry
- Pancakes
- New York cheesecake
- Pizza

TRY IT OUT

Worrying about the perfect first sentence can stop you in your tracks. Next time you're stuck staring at a blank page or screen, try writing your introduction at the end—when you know all about your subject—along with your summary, or conclusion. This will help you write more freely.

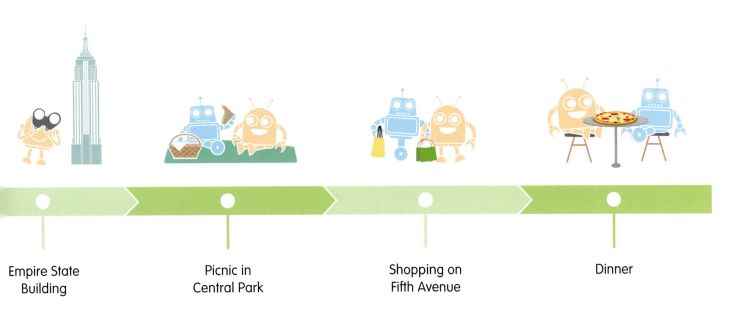

Empire State Building — Picnic in Central Park — Shopping on Fifth Avenue — Dinner

Identifying your audience and purpose

When planning your writing, remember who and why: you need to think about who the text is intended for, as well as why you are writing it.

What are you writing?

A text can be written in very different ways, depending on the effect you want it to have on the reader. The idea of discovering some ancient remains could be turned into an essay, a funny poem to read aloud, or a private diary entry.

Thinking about who you're writing for and why can help you decide what to write and how to present it.

Who is it for?

Start thinking of your reader as your audience. You have your own voice, but you should adapt your writing to suit your audience.

1 What do they know?
If your audience is younger or doesn't know much about the topic, you might need to give more explanations and use simpler words.

2 What do they think?
If they don't feel the same way about the topic as you do, you may need to persuade them to support your viewpoint.

3 What do they expect?
Do you think they want to learn, laugh, or enjoy a thrilling story? An approach they don't expect could confuse them.

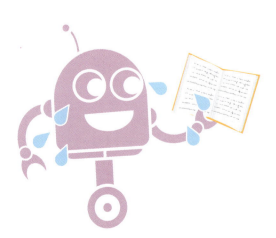

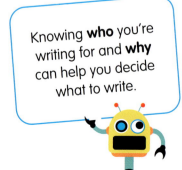

Knowing **who** you're writing for and **why** can help you decide what to write.

Why are you writing it?

Your approach to a writing task will change based on your purpose.

1 If you're analyzing a topic, you might include a lot of facts in a neatly structured essay with a clear conclusion.

2 If you're looking to entertain, you might write a funny poem that rhymes or a short story with witty dialogue.

3 If you need to tell people about an event, you might produce a poster with a few words and a picture.

Thinking about your **purpose** will help you decide the best approach.

Finding the right approach

These three texts all describe some mysterious bones that were found in China over a hundred years ago. Each passage has a different "who" and "why" and takes a different approach to the same subject.

> Someone found strange carved bones in a field in China and sold them as "dragon bones." They had signs scratched onto their surface.

...... Using simpler words, this is for younger readers.

> At the end of the 19th century, animal bones were found in a field in Hsiao-t'un, China. Sold as "dragon bones" to chemists, these fragments had pictographs carved on their surface.

...... With more detail and complex vocabulary, this writing is intended for older readers.

> I flop to the ground, exhausted. But something's poking up out of the earth. I grab an edge and pull. A flat bone emerges from the soil. It's covered in tiny, mysterious symbols!

This text aims ..... to entertain; it is an exciting story.

TRY IT OUT

Think about whether you want to write nonfiction or a story about these "dragon bones" and decide who you are writing it for. How will this change what you write?

SEE ALSO

What's the writer's purpose? 202
Audience 204

Choosing the form

Before you start a piece of writing, you need to decide on the form—the type of writing. There are many different types of forms, and you should choose the one that best suits the purpose of your writing task and your audience.

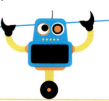

Your teacher might tell you to use a particular **form**, such as a poem.

Narratives and articles

Narratives are texts in the form of stories. They can be fiction or nonfiction and, like articles, are often longer than other writing forms. You'll need storytelling or research skills for these forms.

SEE ALSO

Features of stories, plays, and poems	124
Types of nonfiction	186
What's the writer's purpose?	202

Fiction
Write from your imagination. If you are fascinated by space, you could write a story about a community of humans surviving on another planet in the future.

Articles
You might write a magazine or newspaper article, including facts and opinions, about the plan to send human beings to Mars.

Nonfiction
Tell a true story. For example, you might write about astronaut Mae Jemison, the first Black woman to travel into space.

Stories based on real events
You could take a true story, such as an account about astronauts who fixed a problem with their spacecraft before returning safely to Earth, and change some of the details to make the story more dramatic.

WRITING • **CHOOSING THE FORM**   249

Plays, poetry, and speeches

If you are writing a piece to be read out or performed, you could choose the form of a play, speech, or poem.

1 Plays A play tells a story that's intended to be performed on stage, screen, or radio. You can write about real or imaginary people.

2 Poetry Either fun or serious, poems express the writer's feelings. The words are carefully chosen and arranged for their meaning, sound, and rhythm.

3 Speeches You speak aloud to inform, advise, persuade, or entertain your audience. Use language techniques to make your talk lively.

Texts that give information

If you are giving factual information, advertising goods or services, or explaining how to do something, try writing reference nonfiction, leaflets, or instructions.

1 Reference This form gives you the facts about a subject, such as the solar system, or explains something, such as how planets orbit the Sun.

2 Leaflets A leaflet advertises, gives advice, or tells you about something. Your local park may have a leaflet about the activities there and how to join in.

3 Instructions This form of writing tells you how to do something. A recipe book might tell you which ingredients to use for cheap, healthy meals.

Writing in the right style

Writing style is the way you write rather than the topic or the content. You can write about the same topic in different ways. The style you choose depends on why you're writing and who you're writing for.

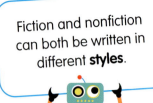

Fiction and nonfiction can both be written in different **styles**.

Types of writing styles

Consider the purpose of your writing and your audience so you can decide which style will work best.

> **SEE ALSO**
> The effects of language — 156
> What's the writer's purpose? — 202
> Audience — 204

1 Formal or informal Formal style uses correct English, while informal style allows casual language, slang, and contractions.

2 Neutral or personal Neutral style sticks to the facts of the matter, while personal style aims to affect the reader's feelings.

Tips for a good writing style

Think about these points before you write. When you edit your piece, check you've followed them.

Use full sentences. Some can be short, others long—but not too long.

Use the right structure for the form of writing. For example, narrative text flows from paragraph to paragraph, while topic-based text has subheadings and sections.

Your style should be consistent. For example, make sure you stick to formal or informal style throughout.

Use repetition occasionally to stress an idea.

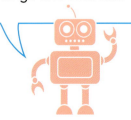

Examples of different writing styles

Here are three different styles of text, all about crossing the road safely.

1 School newsletter
This newsletter is both neutral and formal in style. It gives instructions to parents and children in a clear way.

> 1 Look for a safe place to cross the road. Use a pedestrian crossing if you can.
>
> 2 Look and listen for traffic.
>
> 3 Cross when there is no traffic—keep looking and listening.

The text is formal and neutral and uses correct English.

2 Message to a friend
This message is in an informal, chatty style. It's similar to having a conversation with a friend.

> Yay! My little sister learned to cross the road alone!

The writer uses casual language and exclamation marks.

3 Story for children
This extract from a story has a personal style. It draws in the reader and affects their feelings.

> Dad goes on and on: "Don't look at your phone while crossing the road!"
> Last week, I watched this girl step off the curb, head down over her screen. A cyclist screeched to a halt, just missing her feet. I guess Dad's right.

This expression shows that Dad annoys the writer.

Tone

The tone is the mood of the writing—it shows how the writer feels. Word choice, sentence structure, or punctuation vary the tone. For example, compare "Hey, what are you doing?" (friendly) with "Hey! What on earth do you think you're doing?" (angry).

SPEAK UP

We speak differently from how we write—we often don't use full sentences and we may interrupt each other.

Writing sentences

When you write sentences, you should always make them grammatically correct and use the right punctuation. But they should also be intriguing and exciting to read!

Building a sentence

In order to be correct, a sentence should be a complete thought that makes sense on its own. It must also include a capital letter, a verb, and closing punctuation.

> **SEE ALSO**
> What is a sentence? — 36
> Types of sentences — 38
> Starting and ending sentences — 70

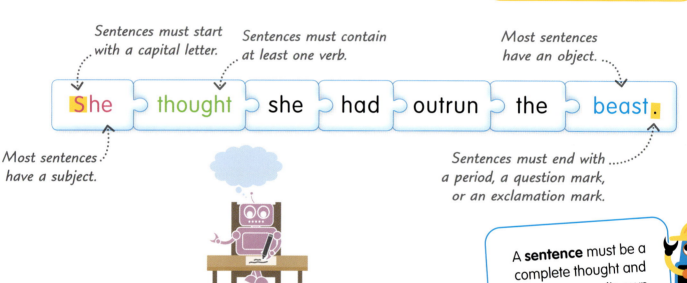

Sentences must start with a capital letter.

Sentences must contain at least one verb.

Most sentences have an object.

Most sentences have a subject.

Sentences must end with a period, a question mark, or an exclamation mark.

A **sentence** must be a complete thought and make sense on its own.

Joining sentences

You can use conjunctions to make sentences longer and more interesting. Conjunctions like "but," "and," "so," or "because" can join two sentences together.

Two short sentences

She thought she had outrun the beast. — She was wrong.

She thought she had outrun the beast, — but — she was wrong.

Add "but" to join the sentences.

Keeping it interesting

While they should always be accurate, your sentences should also be fun to read. Try to keep your reader's attention by carefully choosing your words and varying punctuation.

1 Vocabulary There are thousands of words to choose from, so take the time to pick ones that will paint a clear picture in your reader's mind.

> She was **absolutely convinced** she had outrun the **enormous, slimy** beast, but she was **mistaken.**

...Try to use interesting words.

2 Punctuation Those little marks and dots are very important! Vary the punctuation you use, and use it to create tension and surprise.

> She thought she had outrun the beast **...** but she was wrong!

...Ellipses can be used for suspense.

Common mistakes

Always be on the lookout for these common mistakes when you're writing sentences.

1 Check that the subject and the verb in a sentence agree. A singular subject needs a singular verb; a plural subject requires a plural verb.

✗ These players was the winners.
✓ These players were the winners.

2 An incomplete sentence is called a fragment: it doesn't form a complete thought. Check your writing for fragments and add the missing information.

✗ The next soccer game.
✓ The next soccer game is soon.

3 It is a mistake to join two sentences (or main clauses) with a comma—it is simply not strong enough for the job. Instead, separate the two sentences with a period.

✗ The team won the game, they were thrilled.
✓ The team won the game. They were thrilled.

4 In this example, who is waving the flags? Always read your sentences back to make sure they make sense—you might need to change the word order.

✗ The fans ran toward the players waving flags.
✓ Waving flags, the fans ran toward the players.

Using sentences effectively

When you write, it's best to use a range of sentences to keep your reader's interest. Using a mixture of short, medium, and long sentences creates rhythm and varies the pace.

Varying sentence length

Sentences can range from very short to very long. They can be built up from a number of smaller sentences and clauses. Using just one length of sentence in your writing can make it clunky or boring, so it is best to use a variety.

> **SEE ALSO**
> What is a sentence? **36**
> Multiclause sentences **44**
> Writing sentences **252**

SINGLE-CLAUSE SENTENCES

Lucia was a fearless girl.

MULTICLAUSE SENTENCES WITH TWO MAIN CLAUSES

She had the fastest feet this side of Fairview, but she had an even quicker brain.

MULTICLAUSE SENTENCES WITH A SUBORDINATE CLAUSE

When the local bank was robbed by a band of thieves, Lucia was the person to call.

Building detail

Long sentences are great for building detail or creating tension, for example, when you describe a vivid scene or a scary event. As more and more detail is added, the picture gets clearer and the tension builds.

All the fans were whirring like crazy, a baby was crying, and tempers were fraying when four intimidating figures burst in through the bank doors wearing bizarre animal masks.

This long sentence shows how you can build up the detail or tension in a scene.

Creating tension and excitement

Sometimes it's okay to break the rules! Using a series of short sentences or sentence fragments can be effective for building excitement and tension in your writing. Following a very long sentence with a very short one can also add impact.

> **SPEAK UP**
>
> Write a story using a range of different sentence lengths, then read it out loud. How effective does it sound?

Using lots of short sentences and fragments builds the tension.

Where was Lucia? Silence. Just a clock was ticking. The fans had stopped blowing. Hot. Hot. Hot. Where was she?

We sat huddled on the floor, trying not to catch any of the thieves' eyes, then someone gasped. Lucia had arrived.

Using a short sentence after a long one can ease a tense scene.

Varying voice

Using both the active and passive voice (not in the same sentence though) can also be effective.

1 **The active voice** (see page 64) focuses on who is performing the action in a sentence.

Lucia is the focus of the sentence.

Lucia caught the thieves.

2 **The passive voice** tells us something is happening to the subject of the sentence.

The thieves were caught by Lucia.

The passive voice uses a form of the verb "to be" with the main verb.

3 **Which should you use?** It depends on what part of a sentence you want to draw attention to. The active voice stresses the subject of a sentence; the passive voice emphasizes the action.

Writing paragraphs

Paragraphs break up a passage of text, making it easier to read. All the sentences in a paragraph should be about the same person or people, place, topic, or time.

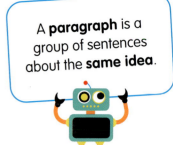

A **paragraph** is a group of sentences about the **same idea**.

How to start and end a paragraph

To start a new paragraph, leave a space (indent) at the start of your first line and begin writing. If your paragraph finishes before the end of a line, leave the rest of the line blank.

SEE ALSO
Layout and structure 214
Transition words 258

Indent at the start of the paragraph

near the equator.
　　Tropical rainforests are warm and damp. Temperatures can reach 38°C (100.4°F) and it rains all year round. The hot, steamy forests are home to many plants and animals.
　　Beneath the dense canopy, you'll find plants climbing to reach the sunlight,

The paragraph finishes before the end of the line.

Structuring a paragraph

Paragraphs often have three parts: a topic sentence, supporting sentences with more information, and a final or concluding sentence.

1 Topic sentence This sentence gives the reader the main idea of the paragraph.

2 Supporting sentences These sentences provide more information—facts, examples, or description.

3 Final or concluding sentence This sums up the topic or links to the next paragraph.

Tropical rainforests are warm and damp. Temperatures can reach 100.4°F (38°C) and it rains all year round. The hot, steamy forests are home to many plants and animals.

Why do we use paragraphs?

Writers use paragraphs to introduce a change of subject or a change of scene or to report a conversation.

Start a new paragraph to show:

✔ A change of topic
✔ A change of place
✔ A jump in time
✔ When a new speaker begins talking

TRY IT OUT

Look at a newspaper article or a page of a fiction or nonfiction book. Can you tell why a new paragraph has been started?

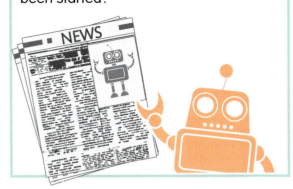

When he was four, Leon learned to feed his family's pigs. He went out early every morning to gather acorns from the woods. It was tiring.

→ A chapter or section starts with one time, place, topic, or speaker.

Two years later, Leon and his family moved far away into the mountains. There, Leon made friends with an elderly goatherd.

→ There has been a jump in time.

The goatherd taught Leon how to care for his goats. The boy learned how to milk the goats and trim their hooves. He soon adapted to his new life.

→ This is a new topic.

"We're going to town to sell the goats' wool," said the goatherd one day. Off they walked, leaving the goats alone.

→ A person starts speaking.

Leon heard the town before he saw it: the clattering of carts, loud chatter from the marketplace, and the sound of children playing with friends.

→ There is a change of place.

Transition words

We use transition words to link sentences and paragraphs so our writing flows from one topic to the next and our ideas and arguments are clearly explained—this is known as cohesion.

How to use transition words

You can repeat words, phrases, and ideas so your writing flows well and your reader remembers what you're talking about. Use pronouns, too, such as "he" or "she." Transition words help link to the next topic.

SEE ALSO
Conjunctions 48
Writing paragraphs 256
Narrative techniques 276

KEY
- REPEATED WORDS
- REPEATED PHRASES
- REPEATED IDEAS
- PRONOUNS
- TRANSITION WORDS

Kweku Tsin peered down the hole. It looked dark and scary. But the pangs of hunger were sharper than his fear, so he jumped down. He landed at the bottom, a little sore and bruised.

To his surprise, Kweku Tsin had fallen down the hole into an underground town. Spotting an elderly woman, he asked, "Hello, have you any food?"

What are transition words?

We use transition words to continue with a similar idea (addition), change to a different idea (contrast), show the order of events (order), or finish what we're saying (summing up).

Addition: in addition, also, furthermore, likewise, similarly, besides

Contrast: but, yet, however, even so, on the other hand, unlike

Order: first, second, before, meanwhile, after

Summing up: to sum up, overall, in conclusion, in summary, to conclude

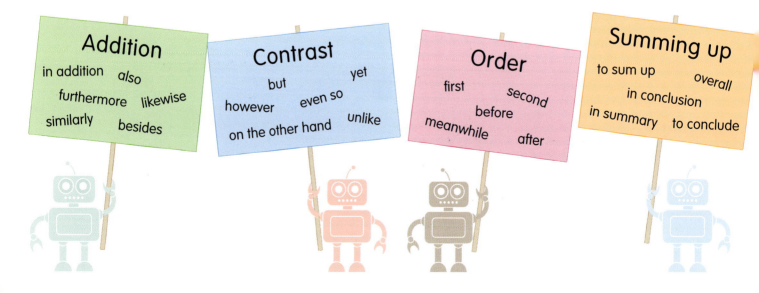

Linking one idea to another

Transition words are used to connect sentences within and between paragraphs. They prepare the reader for what is coming next and help them follow the flow of the text.

1 Following the same idea
The writer follows the idea that polar regions are cold by explaining that deserts can also be cold.

2 Giving a contrasting view
The text introduces a main difference between polar regions and deserts: deserts can also be extremely hot.

3 Ordering events or ideas
The first idea was about the extreme temperatures in polar regions and deserts. The second is about how animals survive these extreme climates.

4 In conclusion
The final paragraph sums up the two ideas.

First, polar regions and deserts are extreme climates because of their temperatures. Polar regions are bitterly cold.

Similarly, deserts can also be freezing cold. In the Gobi Desert in northern China and Mongolia, winter temperatures plunge to -40°F (-40°C). In frozen Antarctica, they plummet to an extraordinary -135.8°F (-93.2°C).

However, deserts can also be baking hot. Most hot deserts are close to the equator. Afternoon temperatures may reach a scorching 122°F (50°C), or higher.

Second, both regions make challenging habitats for animals. Some polar animals live in caves or burrows to shelter from the cold. Many desert animals also stay underground in holes or burrows to avoid the daytime heat.

In conclusion, polar regions and deserts are harsh environments, but some animals are specially adapted to live in them.

Transition words are used as cohesive devices both within and between paragraphs.

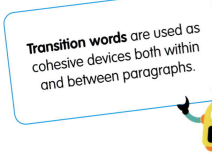

Using language techniques

We write to suit our purpose and with our readers in mind. Do you want to inform, persuade, or entertain them? The language techniques you choose will affect how readers react to what you have written.

Use **language techniques** to suit your purpose.

Ways to use language

You can use different techniques in the same text, but don't use too many together or they can lose their impact. You should always have a good reason for using a language technique. Here are some to try.

> **SEE ALSO**
> The effects of language 156
> Identifying your audience and purpose 246
> Writing in the right style 250

Figurative language
This builds an image: for example, "walking into a storm without a raincoat" is a visual way of describing taking foolish risks.

Using effective word choices
For instance, sensory language can be used to describe a storm: windows clattering, wind howling, sky darkening.

Sentence length
A short sentence at the end of a paragraph gives emphasis or creates suspense. A long sentence explains what happens in detail.

Punctuation
For example, replacing some words with an ellipsis builds suspense, leaving readers to guess what happens. An exclamation mark shows excitement.

Onomatopoeia
A word that sounds like what it is describing, such as the hiss of a snake or clang of the cymbals, helps the reader imagine the noise.

Repetition
Repeating words emphasizes them, as in "Stop. Stop right now!" Alliteration is repeating initial sounds and can be fun to read, such as "frosty freezing fog."

WRITING • USING LANGUAGE TECHNIQUES   261

Language techniques in action

This story is written to entertain, but it also has a message about not being selfish. It uses different language techniques to deliver its message.

Sentence length
A short sentence provides emphasis.

Figurative language
The language describes wisdom as a weight that is too heavy for Anansi alone.

Effective word choices
Sensory language creates images in the reader's mind.

Long ago, people didn't know how to farm or make clothes. Up in the sky, Nyame kept all the world's wisdom in a clay pot. One day, Nyame gave the pot to Anansi the spider.

Anansi was delighted! But he refused to share the gift. Tying the pot in front of him, he started to climb a tree. Climbing with the weight of wisdom was tough.

Anansi's son was watching him. "Tie the pot to your back," he suggested. Anansi tried, and climbing became easier.

Suddenly, Anansi thought, "I'm supposed to be the one with all the wisdom!" Angrily, he threw down the pot, and it smashed to smithereens. All the world's wisdom flew across the earth, and everyone learned to farm and make clothes.

Anansi and the Pot of Wisdom
A tale from Ghana, West Africa

Punctuation
The exclamation mark shows Anansi's excitement.

Onomatopoeia
This helps readers imagine the sound of the pot hitting the ground.

Repetition
The main topic of the story is repeated for emphasis. It also uses alliteration.

> **SPEAK UP**
>
> Read the first paragraph of a story aloud. What language techniques does the writer use and how do they make you feel? Try creating that mood and effect in your writing.

Descriptive writing

With practice, a writer can improve their descriptions by using the right words. Writing a great description will create a powerful, lasting picture in the reader's mind.

Descriptive writing is used to describe people, places, or things.

How to write a great description

Good descriptive writing involves paying close attention to details. Using expressive language and all of your five senses—sight, hearing, touch, smell, and taste—makes writing more interesting and engaging to read.

> **SEE ALSO**
> Using language techniques   **260**
> Narrative techniques   **276**

Smash! The sound of pots and pans hitting the floor. I race down the passageway, as quick as a cheetah. And then it suddenly strikes me— a wonderful, warm smell. They're baking bread! And all I want to do is taste it, with melting butter and some crumbly Cheddar cheese.

Adjectives
Help create a more detailed picture.

Adverbs
Bring how something is being done to life.

Onomatopoeia
Helps the reader hear what is happening.

Similes
Comparing two things helps engage the reader.

Senses
Using your senses can help draw the reader in.

Alliteration
Helps set the pace of a piece of writing.

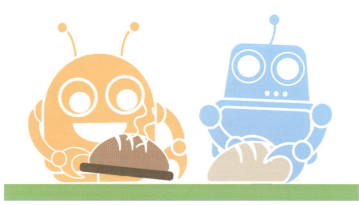

> **TRY IT OUT**
>
> Write your own descriptive piece. Try to describe the flavor of your favorite food or drink. Or explain what it feels like at the movie theater when the lights first go down.

Descriptions in stories and poems

Effective descriptions need to suit both the audience and the purpose that the piece is written for. Here, the character of Magwitch is first introduced to the reader—the writer's choice of words is vital to build tension and create a clear picture of the man.

A fearful man, all in coarse grey, with a great **iron** on his leg. A man **with no hat, and with broken shoes, and with an old rag tied round his head.** A man who had been **soaked** in water, and **smothered** in mud, and **lamed** by stones, and **cut** by flints, and **stung** by nettles, and **torn** by briars; who **limped**, and **shivered**, and **glared**, and **growled**.

Great Expectations by Charles Dickens, 1861

This word provides a clue he's an escaped convict.

The precise description paints a clear picture of the man's simple clothing.

Powerful verbs (see page 119) build an image of a man who has been through a tough ordeal.

Dynamic (or action) verbs create a vivid picture of the man.

Descriptions in nonfiction

Most types of text include descriptive writing. A good description can make writing more persuasive or help you understand something in more detail. It can therefore be invaluable for creating a setting or for sales materials such as a vacation brochure.

Stay at beach villages and swim in the sea all year round. There are trees on the cliffs.

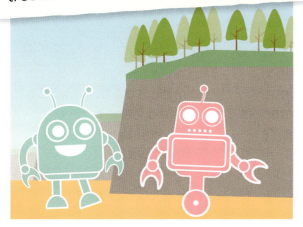

Stay at gleaming white fishing villages nestled close to picturesque beaches, where you can swim in the warm sea all year round. Fragrant pines top the nearby cliffs.

Planning a story

A story can be about anything, and your ideas can come from anywhere. But that freedom also needs structure—and that's where planning comes in.

Planning is important. But remember, it's okay to change your plans!

Where to begin

Sometimes the idea for a story arrives in your imagination fully formed, but most often you need to start by making a plan. It's a little bit like planning a journey using a map—it will give you a better idea which way the story is heading. Some writers don't plan much; others plan a lot.

SEE ALSO
Genres	**126**
Learning from other writers	**240**
Choosing a narrator	**274**

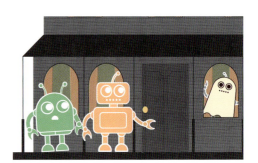

Genre
Think about what type of story you want to write—what genre will it be? It could be an exciting adventure, a heartfelt romance, a magical fantasy, or a spooky ghost story.

Setting
Where will your story be set? Try to build up a picture in your mind. Think of a variety of settings where the characters might play out the events in your story.

Character
Think about who the spotlight will fall on in your story. How old are they? What are they like? Do they have a friend or an enemy? Then start to think about other characters you could include.

Finding inspiration

Writers find inspiration everywhere. Try to keep a notebook handy to jot down ideas—you might just get a spark of inspiration. If there is no magic spark, start with a single letter. Turn it into a word. Keep going … then turn it into a sentence. You're writing!

Changing your mind

Things don't always go to plan. In writing, this can be a good thing. You might change your mind about parts of your story as you go. If things aren't working, you're allowed to make changes to your plan. It's all part of making your story the best it can be.

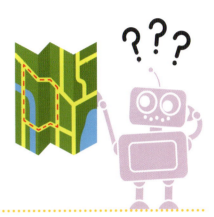

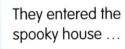

Narration
Who will be the storyteller? It could be the main character or another character in the story who is watching events unfold from the sidelines. Perhaps you'll choose a third-person narrator.

Plot
Now think about what your story will be about and what will happen. You might have an idea for an opening scene. How can you develop it? Will you put your main character in danger?

Beginning and ending
Finally, figure out the best place to begin and end your story. You don't always have to tell the whole story from start to finish—you might want to end on a cliffhanger.

Plot and structure

Reading a story is like going on a journey. When you write a story, you use plot, structure and dramatic tension to build suspense and carry the reader with you.

Story maps are also known as story mountains.

Using a story map

The storyline, or plot line, is the way a novel, play or film develops. We usually mark five or six key plot points from start to end. We can show the main character's journey with a "story map" like the one shown below. The action rises to a peak, or "climax", and then the tension decreases until the drama is resolved at the end.

You can use these plot points to help you plan and write your own story.

> **SEE ALSO**
> Introducing plot   140
> The three-act structure 142
> Planning a story   264

Beginning
The setting and the main character are established.

Dev is at home, watching a storm light up the empty castle on the hill.

Initial incident
A life-changing incident: adventures will begin.

A man Dev knows from the village knocks on his door and asks for help.

Early conflict
Tensions rise as the main character struggles.

He wants Dev to help him recover a stolen key. Dev has doubts, but agrees.

Act 1

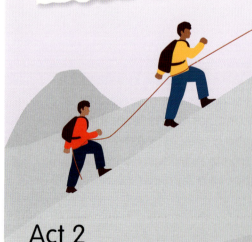

Act 2

How to structure your story

Plot points, such as the "initial incident", can help give structure to your story. This will also help divide up your story into three main parts, or acts. You can then divide the acts into scenes, and drive your plot's action on with sequence words like "soon", "suddenly" or "one day".

Acts and plot points
Having structured a story, using three acts and key plot points, writers have to work hard to keep the reader interested. You can do this by building tension in the story.

Scenes
Each act (beginning, middle and end) will have several scenes. Think about how a film works with different settings: put your main character into each setting.

What happens if you get stuck?
First, don't worry! Every writer gets stuck for a bit. Take a break. Then think: what does your main character want? And then start writing again!

Late conflict
The stakes get higher as the action increases.

Dev and his friend must climb peaks and outwit enemies to reach their goal.

Climax
Problems reach a peak in a dramatic final conflict.

They defeat the baddie to find the key. Dev discovers it is for the castle.

Resolution
All is resolved or explained as the story ends.

Dev's friend is the true owner of the castle. He gives Dev a medal for his bravery.

Act 3

Starting and ending a story

You only get one chance to make a first impression, so create a strong opening to your story. Convincing endings are equally important.

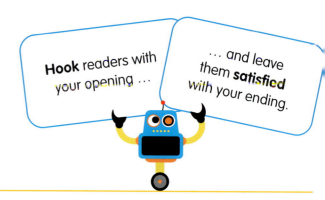

How to start

Begin your story with a bang! Make your readers curious about your story from the start so they will want to read on. Introduce the setting and the main character early. That way, readers will know where they are and who to root for.

> **SEE ALSO**
> Introducing plot — 140
> Organizing ideas — 244
> Plot and structure — 266
> Choosing a narrator — 274

Some openings have already been used a lot. Try to make your opening original.

TRY IT OUT

Look carefully at the beginnings and endings of your favorite books. Which ones really appeal to you? Why? Try using those techniques in your own writing.

How to end

The ending of your story should be satisfying and convincing to the reader. It needs to make sense and be believable within the world of the story. The conclusion usually ties up loose ends, but occasionally a writer leaves some plot points open-ended for readers to interpret in their own way.

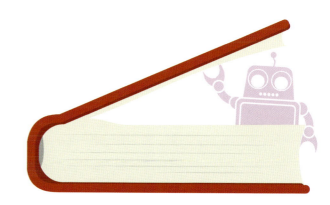

WRITING • STARTING AND ENDING A STORY 269

Interesting openings

Look at the openings of *Wonder* and *Pinocchio*. There's no showing off or fancy vocabulary, but the simple words draw the reader into the story.

I know I'm not an ordinary ten-year-old kid.

Wonder by R. J. Palacio, 2012

In the very first line of *Wonder*, we find out that the narrator is not ordinary. Why? What makes him extraordinary? The reader must keep reading to find out about this remarkable character and his story.

In the opening lines of *Pinocchio*, the narrator intrigues the reader by using the familiar words "once upon a time" but making it clear that the story will be very different from what the reader is expecting.

Centuries ago, there lived …
"A king!" my little readers will say immediately. No, children, you are mistaken. Once upon a time, there was a piece of wood.

The Adventures of Pinocchio by Carlo Collodi, 1883

Excellent endings

Books like *Wonder* and *Pinocchio* have lasting appeal. Their endings are satisfying and their stories stay with readers long after they've finished the books.

She bent down and whispered in my ear. "You really are a wonder, Auggie. You are a wonder."

Wonder by R. J. Palacio, 2012

The uplifting ending of *Wonder* leaves the reader feeling that Auggie, the narrator, has come through some difficulties.

This ending resolves the plot of *Pinocchio* in a way that is satisfying for the characters and the reader. Pinocchio sees what he looked like as a marionette and is glad to have been transformed into a real boy.

After a long, long look, Pinocchio said to himself with great content: "How ridiculous I was as a Marionette! And how happy I am, now that I have become a real boy!"

The Adventures of Pinocchio by Carlo Collodi, 1883

Creating a setting

When you write a story, it has to have a setting—a place, a time, and the conditions where it unfolds. If it's unclear where the action is happening, the reader will be lost.

A **story** can be **set** anywhere, at any time, and in any conditions.

How do you make a setting?

Once you have an idea what your story will be about, follow these four steps to create a memorable setting.

SEE ALSO

Synonyms	118
What is the setting?	130
Why the setting matters	132

1 Use your imagination
Close your eyes and imagine a place—such as a wintry landscape in a bygone era—where your story will unfold.

2 Use the senses
Don't just think about the things you can see. What can you hear, smell, taste, and touch in your setting?

3 Does the story fit the setting?
Make sure the story you plan to write fits in with the setting you've imagined. Do they make sense together?

4 Make notes
Write lots of notes about your setting—whatever comes into your head. Use the best ideas when you start writing.

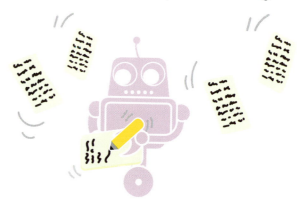

Effective words

When you have a clear idea of your setting, jot down relevant words. If your story takes place in a wintry landscape, for example, choose adjectives and verbs that conjure up cold, harsh conditions.

Writing it down

Use your notes and effective words to write the opening scene of your story. Remember to use the senses to add atmosphere to the setting. Make a rough draft first, change anything you don't think works well, and then write a final version.

> **WORLD OF WORDS**
>
> A particularly memorable setting is the deserted tropical island featured in Robert Louis Stevenson's *Treasure Island*. This tale of pirates and buried treasure is set in the 1700s, with some of the action also taking place in England and on the high seas.

Creating characters

You can create the characters in your stories from a number of sources: yourself, the people you know, people you hear or read about—and your own vivid imagination.

To create a fictional character, ask yourself **questions** about them.

Building up a character

The first thing you may think about when creating a character is what they look like. Or you might start with their personality traits and how these come through in the way the character behaves. You can then fill in more details about them, one by one, until you have a strong, believable character.

SEE ALSO	
Characters	134
Understanding characters	136

1 What do they look like?
Is your character short or tall, and what kind of clothes do they wear? Any little details can stick in a reader's mind.

2 How do they speak?
A character may have a deep voice. They may speak in a slightly strange way, using unusual words or phrases.

3 What do they do?
Does your character go to school? Or, if they're an adult, what job do they do—secret agent or estate agent?

What is a backstory?

You may want to create a backstory for your character—events in their past that happened before the time your story is set. The events may be happy or sad and may explain why a character behaves in a certain way. A character's backstory is often revealed at a key point in a story for dramatic effect. For example, in *Beauty and the Beast*, the reader learns that the Beast used to be a handsome prince before a sorceress transformed him into a hideous beast.

4 What are their likes and dislikes?
Your character may love books or BMX racing. They may hate school or be scared of the dark.

5 Where do they live?
Perhaps your character lives in a beach hut, a caravan, or a huge mansion with a big family and unusual pets.

6 How do they behave?
What's your character like when they're alone? Is it different from how they are when they're in a crowd or at a party?

Choosing a narrator

Before you start writing, you will need to choose a narrator. Imagine how the story of *Little Red Riding Hood* would change if it was narrated by different characters.

Different narrators give different **points of view**.

SEE ALSO
Who's telling the story? 138
Narrative techniques 276

The protagonist

The protagonist narrates in the first person (using "I" and "we") and is the main character. The whole story revolves around them. The protagonist is often trustworthy—and can be easier to relate to because their thoughts and feelings are shared.

Another character

This is another character who narrates in the first person and helps tell the story in which the action revolves around the protagonist. This narrator may be a major character who is also directly involved in the action or a minor character.

Pro
You can immediately connect with the reader.

Con
You can write from only one perspective; your story is limited to what they see (or hear).

Pro
The reader can see the protagonist from a different viewpoint; this may give a more balanced picture.

Con
Another character will not know certain things, such as what your protagonist is feeling or thinking.

See it in *The Last Wild* by Piers Torday.

See it in *The Great Gatsby* by F. Scott Fitzgerald.

WRITING • CHOOSING A NARRATOR

The unreliable narrator

Usually told in the first person but occasionally in the third, an unreliable narrator cannot be trusted. They may be misinformed, biased, troubled, or simply lying. The unreliable narrator misleads the reader by omitting certain vital things about the story and the characters.

 Pro
The unreliable narrator can be an engaging, fun character.

 Con
This narrator may be hard to like and can make the reader feel misled or deceived.

See it in *Liar & Spy* by Rebecca Stead.

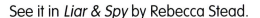

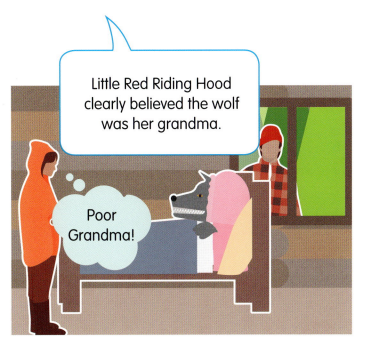

The observer

The observer narrates in the third person, and fairy tales are often told by an omniscient (all-knowing) narrator. The observer witnesses what is happening and sticks to telling the story. They are meant to stay objective without giving their own opinions.

Multiple narrators

Several narrators relate different scenes in a story or different versions of events in the first person. The narration switches between these different characters in order to tell the story from their unique points of view.

 Pro
You can write from a wider perspective.

 Con
The narration is more detached, so it may be more difficult to relate to your characters.

 Pro
You can show a wider view of the world and the relationships between your various characters.

 Con
Your story will become confusing unless you make it clear when you're switching to a different narrator.

See it in *Charlotte's Web* by E. B. White.

See it in *Wonder* by R. J. Palacio.

Narrative techniques

Effective storytelling is all about drawing a reader in and getting them to read on. Writers achieve this by using narrative techniques like dialogue, description, and pacing.

Narrative techniques help a writer tell their story.

Using dialogue

Bring your characters to life with strong dialogue. Give them their own unique voice. A main character's voice can help keep readers hooked.

SEE ALSO	
The effects of language	156
Descriptive writing	262
Plot and structure	266

1 Revealing character
Dialogue should always serve a purpose. The way a character speaks to others shows how they think—and what they are truly like. Tags such as "he sneered" also convey character.

2 Advancing action
Dialogue should never take place in a vacuum. Make it push the plot on, so that what the characters say helps drive the action. Make sure it's lively, too!

> You're tired, too? I'm tired, three!

> That's hilarious! I love jokes!

> We don't have any clues left.

> Let's follow the cat and see where it leads us.

TRY IT OUT

Write a lively, action-packed scene using only description and no dialogue. Now try to write the same scene as dialogue only. Make sure that the words the characters say to each other convey the action to your readers.

Using description

Descriptive writing is a great way to add depth to your story. It can convey atmosphere and feelings and show the reader what the characters are like.

Adjectives can make descriptions clearer or more interesting.

Metaphors can give a more vivid idea of what something is like.

> As Jack Donovan entered the warm, cozy restaurant, the waiter stared at Jack's torn, dripping pants and squelchy shoes with holes in them. With puppy-dog eyes, Jack looked at the waiter, who showed him to a table in the far corner of the room.

Using pacing

Pacing is how slow or fast a scene moves for a reader. It will affect the mood of your story and can create suspense, excitement, and tension.

Use longer sentences for slower pacing or to build up tension or suspense.

Short sentences, which may even be incomplete, help keep the action fresh and fast-paced.

Use **dialogue** to slow pacing and to provide a contrast.

Use **punctuation** to pace the action, convey shock, or create suspense.

> As the sun was setting and my shadow was stretching out in front of me, I looked ahead at the dusty, tree-lined avenue. Something whistled through the air. Right past my ear! "Hey, who's there?" I shouted, my voice cracking.

Managing shifts in time and place

When we write, the action often moves around, shifting from one scene to another. Sometimes it shifts in time, sometimes in place. We need to use the right language for these shifts.

Shift in time

She told him she loved him during the English class *the next day.*

This transitional phrase indicates a change in time.

Shift in place

They boarded a train *to Spain.*

This indicates a change of location.

Planning a poem

Writing a poem is a fantastic way to use your imagination and to express your thoughts and feelings. Writing a good poem usually takes time. Planning is an important part of the process.

Sometimes a poem will just come to you, but usually you'll have to **work at it**!

What is it about?

Poems have a topic or theme, and they often say something personal. Sometimes a great idea will just pop into your head. If you need inspiration, try looking for ideas in the world around you. Choose something that makes you smile, think, cry, gasp, or even laugh out loud.

> **SEE ALSO**
> What is a poem? — 148
> Making sense of poetry — 150
> Figurative language — 158

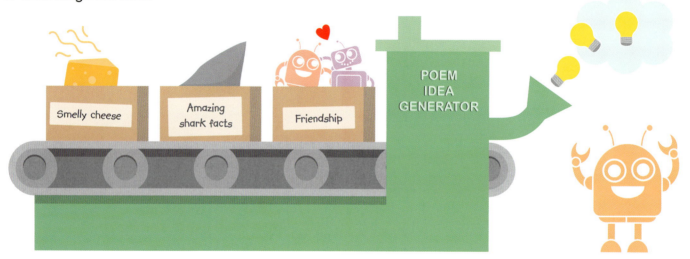

Organizing your ideas

You might find a poem comes spilling out of your pen fully formed straight onto the page. But more often, it's worth taking the time to develop and organize your ideas before you start to write. Thinking time is never wasted.

1 Grab a big sheet of paper. Write your Big Idea at the top. Then scribble down lots of ideas—messy or neat!

2 Think about the language you want to use. Rhyming words? Onomatopoeia? How about metaphors? Add them all to your plan.

What kind of poem will it be?

Poetry can be a lot more flexible than stories. Use your imagination and play with words to present your topic in a new way. It's up to you to choose how!

How long will your poem be?
Will you use rhyme or repetition?
What sort of rhythm will it have?
What kind of figurative language can you use?
Does a specific kind of poem—like a limerick, shape poem, or haiku—suit your theme?

... Why not try a limerick?

There was an Old Man with a beard,
Who said, "It is just as I feared!—
Two Owls and a Hen,
Four Larks and a Wren,
Have all built their nests in my beard."

"There Was an Old Man with a Beard"
by Edward Lear, 1846

Try repeating important words to add more impact.

==Write,== for through your scribbled words come answers yet unspoken,
worlds yet to imagine,
futures yet unknown.
==Write,== for it's through stepping out in bold pursuit of stories
that you come to know your own.
Just ==write.==

"Some Thoughts about Writing" by Helen Dineen, 2021

Varying line lengths makes a poem more interesting to read aloud.

---

3 Now take a pen or a highlighter. Choose which of your notes you want to include in your poem. What's the main idea? What images might support it? Are there particular words or rhymes that you love?

4 Don't expect your poem to be perfect the first time. Poems often change as new thoughts come to you. While you plan or edit, you might even find your first Big Idea changes into something completely different!

5 Don't be afraid to let your poem rest. Sometimes it can help to do something else for a while and come back to it later.

Writing a poem

Writing a poem can feel easy or take serious effort. Thinking about language features you can use can jump-start your creativity and let your poem soar.

A poem **paints a picture** using words and sounds.

Creating strong images and feelings

Poems are all about communication, so you need to help your reader understand what you are thinking or feeling as clearly as possible.

SEE ALSO	
What is a poem?	148
The effects of language	156
Figurative language	158
Planning a poem	278

1 Use words that evoke strong images. A synonym can add interest or spark to your poem.

It was a ~~dangerous climb~~ **death-defying scramble**.

2 Try out unusual comparisons. Can you compare your subject to something fresh and new?

My love is like ~~a red, red rose~~ **bathing in warm sunshine**.

Don't use other people's words—think of your own!

3 Remember you can play with words and even invent your own! There are no rules.

A day! What a day! What a **grin-tastic** day!

Using the right tone

The tone of a poem tells you about the writer's attitude toward their subject. They might feel emotional or be more detached. They might write with humor or seriousness. Think about the tone you want to convey in your poem.

> Twinkle, twinkle, little bat!
> How I wonder what you're at!
> Up above the world you fly,
> Like a tea-tray in the sky.
>
> From *Alice's Adventures in Wonderland* by Lewis Carroll, 1865

The tone of this poem is playful and funny.

Sound it out

Listening to how your poem sounds will help you see how to improve it. Use a range of different effects to bring your poem to life and support your big idea.

> **SPEAK UP**
>
> Tap out the beats of your poem as you read.

1 What's the **rhythm** of your poem? Choose a beat that sets the right pace and tone.

2 Use **onomatopoeia** to help your reader hear what is happening, like sound effects in a film.

3 **Repetition** emphasizes key points or ongoing actions, like the constantly moving ocean.

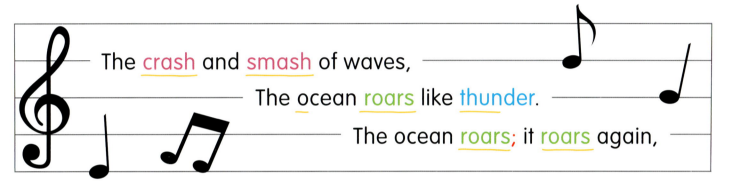

The crash and smash of waves,
The ocean roars like thunder.
The ocean roars; it roars again,

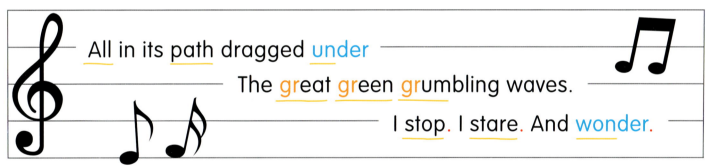

All in its path dragged under
The great green grumbling waves.
I stop. I stare. And wonder.

by Helen Dineen, 2021

4 **Alliteration** helps set the scene. This "gr" sound is harsh, which mimics the sea's cruel nature.

5 Using **rhyme** can make your poem more musical and satisfying to perform.

6 Think about your use of **punctuation**. The semicolon in this poem matches the gap between waves. The periods in the last line ask the reader to pause and think.

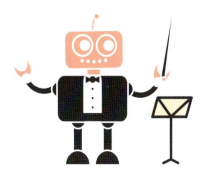

Writing about poetry

Poetry is often open to interpretation, so when you're writing about a poem, it's particularly important to explain your ideas clearly and use evidence from the text to back these ideas up.

When writing about poetry, always explain the **effects** of the poet's choices.

Understanding poetry questions

Questions about poetry often ask you to analyze how a poet has used form, structure, and language for effect. Remember to take time to understand what the question is asking before you answer it.

SEE ALSO
Making sense of poetry — 150
Analyzing poetry — 168
Introduce, cite, explain — 300

1 **Form** is the type of poem. Has the poet written a limerick for comic effect or a sonnet to convey, or put across, feelings of love?

2 **Structure** is the way a poem is organized. Has the poet used short lines to show excitement or used rhyme to highlight certain words?

3 **Language** refers to words and language techniques. Has imagery been used to paint a vivid picture? Or hard sounds to communicate feelings of anger?

How does the form of the poem help convey its meaning?

How has the poet used structure for effect?

How does the poet use language in the poem?

Backing up your ideas

When you write about a poem, focus on any features that contribute to the poem's meaning and their effects on the reader. Using "introduce, cite, explain" (see page 300) will help you back up your ideas.

1 Introduce Start each paragraph by briefly stating your point. It might be that the poet has used metaphors to help the reader relate to the poet's feelings.

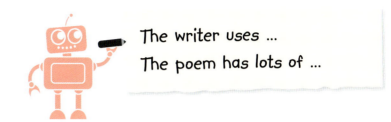

The writer uses …
The poem has lots of …

2 Cite Look for evidence in the poem. Include one or two quotes that demonstrate the point you've made.

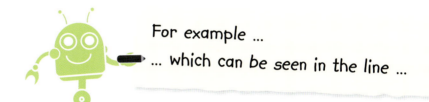

For example …
… which can be seen in the line …

3 Explain Talk about the effect on the reader. How might the poem make them feel? How does this effect help convey the poet's thoughts or add to the poem's meaning?

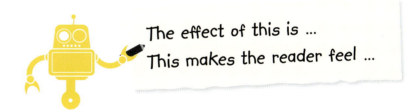

The effect of this is …
This makes the reader feel …

Analysis in action

In his poem "Checking Out Me History," John Agard discusses how, growing up in Guyana, he was taught a lot of British history and very little about his own heritage. Look at the use of metaphor in this line from the poem.

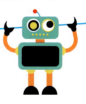

There's no right and wrong **interpretation** of poetry—as long as you can back up your ideas with **evidence** from the poem.

> Bandage up me eye with me own history.

The poet uses a metaphor to compare his own history to a "bandage," which suggests that learning more about his own history would help make him feel better. The metaphor helps the reader understand the poet's feelings.

Writing to inform and explain

When writing informative or explanatory text, rather than telling a story, it's even more important to have a clear overall structure for the whole piece. You should structure each section and paragraph carefully, too.

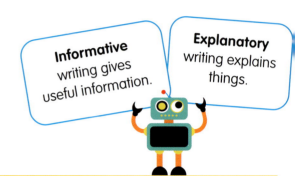

Informative writing gives useful information.

Explanatory writing explains things.

How to structure text

Writing that informs or explains should have three sections: a short introduction, a longer main body text, and a short conclusion.

1 Introduction
Tell the reader what the topic is about and why it's important.

2 Main body text
This section should go through all the points you want to cover in one or more paragraphs.

3 Conclusion
Round off the piece by summarizing the main points or suggesting what might happen next.

How bees make honey

Honey bees make honey to feed on during winter. This food provides energy and plenty of vitamins.

A bee visits a flower and sucks up nectar—which is like sugar water—using its hollow tongue. Inside the bee's stomach, the nectar turns into watery honey. Back at the hive, the bee moves the honey from its stomach to its mouth, then into a honeycomb.

Bees seal the honeycomb with wax to protect it until winter arrives. The honey will keep them alive until spring.

The writer introduces the topic.

WRITING • WRITING TO INFORM AND EXPLAIN

Additional features

Writers use facts and figures to inform readers and evidence from experts to explain. Pictures, diagrams, and charts can be a good way to give information, too. For example, it's easier to show what a pyramid looks like than to describe its shape.

> **WORLD OF WORDS**
>
> An encyclopedia is a book full of informative and explanatory writing on many subjects or on one subject in detail.

The Great Pyramid of Giza

Still standing after 4,500 years

Ancient Egypt is famous for its pyramids—massive tombs for its dead rulers. Built about 2550 BCE, the Great Pyramid of Giza is the largest. Ancient Greek historian Herodotus reported that 100,000 men worked for three months a year for 20 years to build the Great Pyramid. However, modern experts think it was a smaller number. The laborers used stone blocks weighing about 2.8 tons—heavier than an average car today.
The ancient builders did an excellent job: the pyramid is still standing.

Pictures show what the text talks about.

The strapline is a secondary heading.

This is a fact—the date when the pyramid was built.

Evidence from an Ancient Greek historian and modern experts

Writing clear English

You have to write clearly for all your subjects, not just English. If you're writing up a science experiment, for example, you need to explain what you did step by step in a clear and logical order. Tables, charts, and graphs can also help make the results of experiments easy to understand.

SEE ALSO

The stages of writing	234
Coming up with ideas	236
Organizing ideas	244
Transition words	258

How to present information clearly

Always plan your writing so that it will be easy to follow. Write an introduction, then divide the content into sections. Your sections should be in a clear, logical order.

The way you present information on pages is called the **format**.

Formatting text

To make your text easier to read, break it up into sections of just one or a few paragraphs. Give each section a heading so that the reader gets an idea of what the text below it will talk about.

The introduction is clearly visible in a larger font.

Unformatted text can be tricky to read.

What are reptiles?

Reptiles are animals that breathe air and have scales instead of feathers or hair. Most lay eggs. They are cold-blooded – their body temperature varies with the environment. About 6,000 species exist today.
Lizards have four legs and long tails. They are the biggest reptile group and vary in size from tiny geckos to giant Komodo dragons.
Snakes have long, slender bodies and no legs. Some snakes, such as vipers, inject their prey with venom.
Turtles are a group of reptiles that also includes terrapins and tortoises. They have a shell to protect them.

What are reptiles?

Reptiles are animals that breathe air and have scales instead of feathers or hair. Most lay eggs. They are cold-blooded—their body temperature varies with the environment. About 6,000 species exist today.

1 LIZARDS
These reptiles have four legs and long tails. They are the biggest reptile group and vary in size from tiny geckos to giant Komodo dragons.

2 SNAKES
Snakes have long, slender bodies and no legs. Some snakes, such as vipers, inject their prey with venom.

WRITING • HOW TO PRESENT INFORMATION CLEARLY   287

TRY IT OUT

Plan and create your own double-page spread on your favorite kind of animal using the features described on these pages.

Using numbers
Numbering is useful if there's a particular number of items (here, groups of reptiles) or if they need to be read in a certain order.

When formatting, keep in mind that we read across pages from **left to right** and from **top to bottom**.

3 TURTLES
This group also includes terrapins and tortoises. These reptiles have shells to protect them.

4 CROCODILIANS
These large, powerful reptiles include crocodiles and alligators.

Images
You can add images, such as photographs, illustrations, maps, or diagrams, to show information effectively. They break up the text and make your work more appealing.

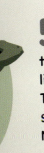

5 TUATARAS
There are only two species of these lizardlike creatures. They live on a few small islands in New Zealand.

Extra information
You can add extra information related to the topic using boxes or charts with facts and figures.

EXTINCT REPTILES
Reptiles have lived on Earth for more than 280 million years. Most early types—including the dinosaurs, which died out about 65 million years ago—are now extinct.

SEE ALSO
What's the writer's purpose?	202
Layout and structure	214
Choosing the form	248

How to write a formal letter

Formal letters are written to ask for help or information or to make a complaint. The better you write, the more likely it is that your letter will be taken seriously.

You can also write a **formal email** asking for help or information or to complain.

Using formal language

Formal letters are written in standard English and should sound polite and businesslike. Use correct words, write in full sentences, and be firm and clear about what you want.

> **SEE ALSO**
> Levels of formality   206
> Identifying your audience
> and purpose   246

1 Avoid slang and informal words
✗ I got the stuff you sent.
✓ I received your letters.

2 Write words in full
✗ can't/won't/I'll/isn't
✓ cannot/will not/I will/is not

3 Use full sentences
✗ Wanna know more? Okay to call me!
✓ Please call me if you have any further questions.

Do not use exclamation marks in formal letters.

4 Be firm but polite
✗ Get this done by Friday so I can take it to the meeting.
✓ Please do this by Friday so I can take it to the meeting.

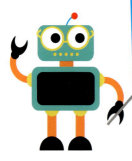

Writing a formal letter

Format your letter correctly, with the address, date, reference, and greetings in the right place. Structure your letter as shown below, using a formal greeting and ending.

Your address in the top-right corner

1234 Main Street
New York, NY 10001

Add the date under the address.

October 10, 2022

The name and address of the person you are writing to

Mr. Robinson
567 Maple Street
Essex, VT 05403

The subject of the letter, or reference number

Environmental poster competition

Dear Mr. Robinson,

If you don't know the name, write "To whom it may concern."

Start by saying why you're writing the letter.

I am writing to inquire about the environmental poster competition that was advertised on your website. I am very interested in designing a poster and would be grateful if you could give me some further information.

Give the details.

Your advertisement states that the competition is open to all children and I would appreciate it if you could confirm the maximum age for entrants. I'll be 16 years old on December 2, so am I eligible to enter?

Say what you would like to know.

Also, on your website, it says that the deadline is on Monday, December 1. Please can you let me know when the winners will be announced?

I look forward to your reply.

Make it clear you want a reply.

Yours sincerely,
Naoko Arai

End with "Yours faithfully" if you started with "To whom it may concern."

> State each point in a separate **paragraph**.

How to write an informal email and letter

A letter to friends or family is more like a face-to-face chat. But it's important to still write clearly so they understand what you're saying.

Writing an informal email

You might write an informal email to a friend or family member to make plans or tell them interesting news. Informal emails still need a beginning, middle, and end.

> **SEE ALSO**
> Letters — 196
> Writing in the right style — 250

Writing **informally** is like **talking** on a screen or page.

Start with an informal greeting.

Use contractions—"we're" rather than "we are."

Finish with an informal sign-off.

You can attach photos.

Write the subject so your reader knows what the email is about.

It's still important to use a line space between paragraphs.

Use informal words or slang—"yummy" rather than "delicious."

Writing an informal letter

Work out the best order for the information, then structure your letter in paragraphs so it is easy to read. Think about the writing style, vary your vocabulary, and use questions to invite your reader to reply, too.

> **TRY IT OUT**
>
> Write a postcard to a friend about an extraordinary animal or place.

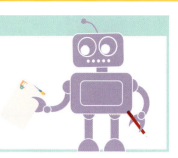

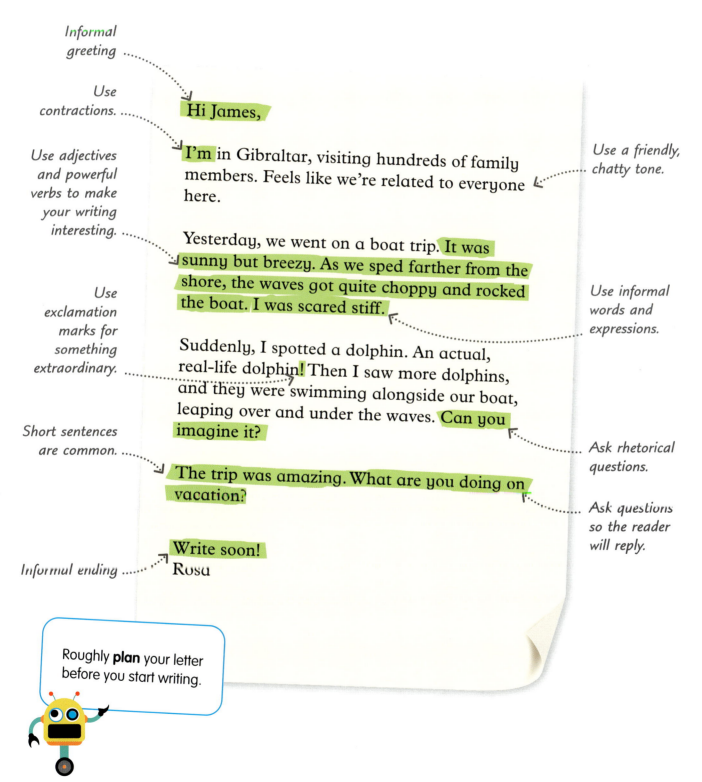

Informal greeting

Use contractions.

Use adjectives and powerful verbs to make your writing interesting.

Use exclamation marks for something extraordinary.

Short sentences are common.

Informal ending

Hi James,

I'm in Gibraltar, visiting hundreds of family members. Feels like we're related to everyone here.

Yesterday, we went on a boat trip. It was sunny but breezy. As we sped farther from the shore, the waves got quite choppy and rocked the boat. I was scared stiff.

Suddenly, I spotted a dolphin. An actual, real-life dolphin! Then I saw more dolphins, and they were swimming alongside our boat, leaping over and under the waves. Can you imagine it?

The trip was amazing. What are you doing on vacation?

Write soon!
Rosa

Use a friendly, chatty tone.

Use informal words and expressions.

Ask rhetorical questions.

Ask questions so the reader will reply.

> Roughly **plan** your letter before you start writing.

Writing persuasively

Persuasive writing is all around you, from political speeches to toy advertisements. Writers use persuasive techniques to convince their audience to agree with their point of view or take action on something.

The art of persuasion

You can use a range of techniques called rhetorical devices to make your writing persuasive. The most important thing is to think about how you can appeal to your audience to encourage them to agree with you.

> **SEE ALSO**
> Using language techniques 260
> Writing to argue 294

Personal pronouns
Use personal pronouns like "you," "your," "we," and "our" to make your reader feel like they are being spoken to directly.

Emotive language
Words that appeal to a reader's feelings are called emotive language. It can make a reader feel guilty, excited, or angry.

Exaggeration
You can make your points sound more important or impressive by using exaggeration. Make sure you don't overdo it, though!

SAVE OUR PLANET!

Our planet is dying
It is vital that we act now to save our planet before there is no planet left to save.

The world is going to end! Earth is over 4 billion years old, but if we don't make changes NOW, it won't survive much longer.

WRITING • WRITING PERSUASIVELY

WORLD OF WORDS

Swedish environmental activist Greta Thunberg made headlines in 2018 thanks to a powerful speech she delivered at the United Nations Climate Change Conference. The speech was packed with persuasive language to encourage world leaders to act more urgently on climate change.

*The key to persuasion is to appeal to your **audience**.*

Rhetorical questions
Sometimes questions don't need an answer. They can be used to stress a point and get the reader to think about what you're saying.

Are you going to help us?

You may feel like a small part of a big world, but if we all make small changes, together these changes will be big!

✓ Educate yourself and others.

✓ Use greener transport, such as a bicycle, to reduce the harmful gases being put into the atmosphere.

✓ Reduce, reuse, recycle! Cut down on waste and avoid buying plastic.

✓ Every day, countless trees in lush, pristine rainforests are torn down for grazing livestock. Eating less meat means less deforestation.

If we act smart, act fast, and act now, we can create a happier planet.

Lists of three
Listing three words together can add impact because it makes your point more memorable.

Imagery
Try to paint a vivid picture in your reader's head using descriptive writing, called imagery.

Repetition
Repeating words and phrases can be very powerful. It adds rhythm and emphasis to convince your readers.

TRY IT OUT
Write a speech for a cause you believe in and perform it to a friend. How many persuasive techniques can you include?

Writing to argue

In writing, remember that an argument is not about picking a fight with someone—it is about persuading your reader. This can be a useful skill when writing an assignment or campaigning for something.

Preparing your argument

When writing to argue, planning and organizing your ideas are essential. A strong argument shows consideration of the other side of the argument (called the counterargument) and uses well-reasoned arguments against it.

> **SEE ALSO**
> Research 238
> Organizing ideas 244
> Answering an essay prompt 298

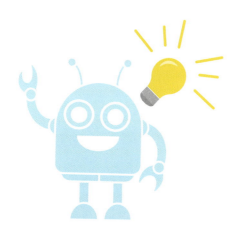

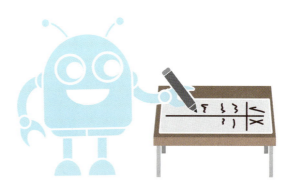

1 Pick your argument
Choose your topic and work out your opinion or stance on the matter. Start to identify what you want your argument to achieve.

2 Identify reasons
Why do you feel that way about the argument? Scribble down a handful of reasons and explain them as best as you can.

3 Gather evidence
Backing up your reasons with evidence will make your argument more convincing. Find evidence for each of your reasons.

Structuring your argument

When you are writing out your argument, keep your audience in mind to make sure your tone and language are suitable. Always include the counterargument in your writing.

> **SPEAK UP**
> Always read your argument out loud to help you check the pace, tone, and balance of the whole piece. Go back and improve any parts that sound awkward.

1 Opening
Start with a clear opening paragraph. Make a statement that outlines your position. Aim for clarity and impact.

2 Building and balancing
Write a paragraph for each reason. Start by making a clear point, then use evidence to expand and argue your point.

3 Closing
The final paragraph should summarize your strongest points. Close with an impactful sentence that sticks in people's minds.

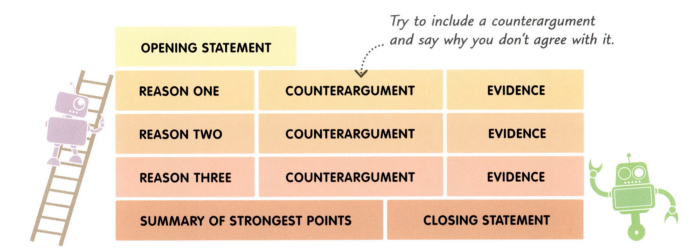

Try to include a counterargument and say why you don't agree with it.

Making an impact

How you deliver your argument is as important as your reasons and evidence.

1 Language
Use persuasive techniques and varied language to create more impact. Avoid too much emotion or exaggeration—just focus on the facts.

2 Pace
Make points clear and brief to keep the interest of your audience. Vary the pace of your sentences.

3 Guiding the audience
Use transition words like "furthermore" and "however" to guide the reader through your points.

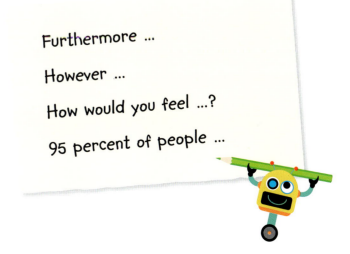

Writing a speech

When you're writing a speech or presentation, think about your audience and the purpose of the talk. It might be to inform, advise, persuade, or entertain.

A **speech** is a formal talk on a topic given to an **audience**.

Planning a speech

Plan your talk carefully, make sure it's the right length, and practice it so you don't need to read from your notes. Make sure you include all the points outlined below.

> **SEE ALSO**
> Reading speeches — 198
> Identifying your audience and purpose — 246

A recent survey showed that just 25 percent of you thought that our school council was effective!

I'm going to outline my three ideas—which may raise a few eyebrows—for how we can help run the school.

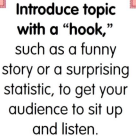

Introduce topic with a "hook," such as a funny story or a surprising statistic, to get your audience to sit up and listen.

Tell your audience what you'll cover in your talk. Keep it simple, such as three ways that the school council could help run the school.

Explain your key idea—for example, because the schools are for children, they should have a significant role in running them.

Convince your audience

Provide evidence so your audience will believe what you say and take it seriously.

1 Evidence Provide facts and figures to back up what you say. For example, the best schools have active school councils.

2 Experts Give quotes from experts, such as professors of education.

3 Stories Tell real stories, such as how a school council raised funds for playground equipment, to show why the issue matters.

Make it lively

You can make your speech more lively and enjoyable with images, sound, or video.

Images Use slides of photographs, drawings, or charts to show what you are talking about.

Sound You could play relevant music or sound effects.

Video Show a short video to introduce the topic or make a point.

And this leads me to the most important point of all—choosing a new principal.

That's a good question—could the pupils run the school themselves? Let me explain my plan …

Go through your points in order. Make sure they flow well from one to another so the audience can follow you easily.

Finish off with a strong conclusion—the message for your listeners. What do you want them to remember from your talk?

Allow time for questions from the audience at the end. Prepare answers for the questions you think people are likely to ask.

Answering an essay prompt

Stuck on a tricky essay prompt? Focus carefully on what is being asked, and you can tackle any writing task.

Keep **referring back** to the essay prompt when you plan your answer.

What are you being asked?

Even a daunting essay prompt can be broken down to make it easier to understand. Take your time to figure out exactly what's being asked of you.

SEE ALSO	
Research	238
Organizing ideas	244
Introduce, cite, explain	300

1 Instruction word
What is the prompt or title asking you to do? Discuss? Compare? Analyze? Check the words in a dictionary to make sure you understand their exact meaning.

2 Subject
What is the subject of the prompt or title? And what particular angle is the prompt asking you to explore?

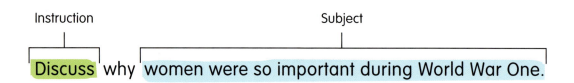

Analyze the role of Siobhan in *The Curious Incident of the Dog in the Night-Time.*

Discuss why women were so important during World War One.

TRY IT OUT

What are the instruction words and subjects of these essay prompts?

Explain how language is used for effect in these two magazine advertisements.

Compare how John Steinbeck presents Curley and Curley's wife in *Of Mice and Men.*

Planning your response

An essay response usually starts with an introduction and ends with a conclusion. But when it comes to planning, decide on the points you want to cover before thinking about your introduction and conclusion.

1 Plan your points and organize them logically. Give a balanced view by considering both sides of the argument.

2 Plan your introduction It should serve as a signpost to your main points, outlining your opinion on the prompt.

3 Plan your conclusion It should summarize your response to the prompt and round off your writing.

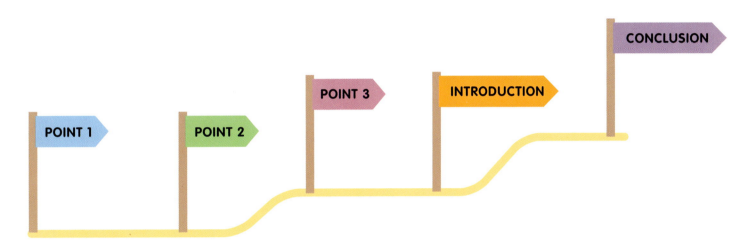

Research and evidence

Carry out research to find evidence, such as quotes or statistics, that support the statements and ideas in your essay response. Providing strong evidence will make your points and reasoning appear much clearer and more convincing to the reader.

Improve your work

Once you have written your essay, read it out loud. This will show you where there are any weaknesses or mistakes in your argument. Cut out any repetition. Does each point flow on to the next? If not, fix them. Edit your work to make your writing as clear and effective as possible.

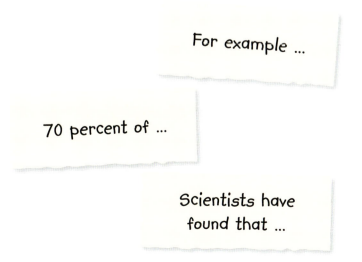

Your argument should convince the reader.

Introduce, cite, explain

When answering an essay prompt, it is important to show that you understand the text. A useful strategy is "introduce, cite, explain," known as ICE.

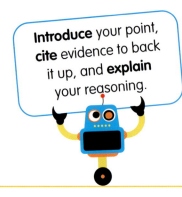

Introduce your point, **cite** evidence to back it up, and **explain** your reasoning.

Using introduce, cite, explain

It is often difficult to know where to start when answering an essay prompt. "Introduce, cite, explain" ensures that you make your point effectively and that it is backed up by the text. Here are the steps to follow for ICE.

SEE ALSO

Proving your point	180
Using evidence from the text	182
Inferring meaning	220
Answering an essay prompt	298

1 Introduce
Introduce your point with a clear, concise statement that sums up your answer to the question.

2 Cite
Provide citation, or evidence, from the text to support your point. Do not use an opinion as evidence.

3 Explain
Explain how the evidence from the text proves the point that you are making.

Types of evidence to cite

Evidence can be explicit or implicit. Each type of evidence requires a different approach to finding it in the text.

Explicit evidence is clearly stated in the text. You can point to the actual words in the text to retrieve this information.

Implicit evidence is found by looking for clues in the text and reading between the lines. A piece of implicit evidence is also called an inference.

Finding implicit evidence is similar to inferring meaning. **See page 220.**

Sentence starters

Once you have read the text and decided on the point that you want to make, you need to put forward your case. Here are some sentence starters to help you. Can you think of other effective sentence starters?

In my opinion …
Arguably …
The writer uses …

An example of this is …
This is demonstrated when …
The evidence for this is …

This shows …
This implies …
This is effective because …

INTRODUCE

CITE

EXPLAIN

Putting ICE into practice

Below you will find an extract from *The Three Musketeers*, plus an essay-style question relating to the main character, d'Artagnan. Read the answer and notice how the ICE method has been used.

Our young men had been waiting about half an hour, amid a crowd of courtiers, when all the doors were thrown open, and His Majesty was announced.

At his announcement, d'Artagnan felt himself tremble to the very marrow of his bones. The coming instant would in all probability decide the rest of his life. His eyes therefore were fixed in a sort of agony upon the door through which the king must enter.

The Three Musketeers
by Alexandre Dumas, 1844

How does d'Artagnan feel when the king's arrival is announced?

In my opinion, d'Artagnan feels frightened by the King's arrival. This is demonstrated when the text states that d'Artagnan "felt himself tremble to the very marrow of his bones." This description conveys his fear and unease.

The introduction is clear and concise.

This is clear evidence from the text in the form of a quotation.

The explanation shows how the evidence supports the point.

302 WRITING • INTRODUCE, CITE, EXPLAIN

›› Analyzing an article

Here is a newspaper article about a camping expedition, plus a question. Note how the "introduce, cite, explain" strategy results in an effective response to the question.

Use **ICE** to answer comprehension questions.

Campers survive

Young campers learned survival skills during an expedition to the Wildwood Forest. The campers erected a tent in the forest as shelter. For dinner, they caught fish in the river and cooked it over a campfire that they made themselves. The campers also practiced their navigation skills while they were hiking through the forest.

"We had fun learning to survive in the wild," said one of the campers. "But I missed my phone."

How successful was the expedition for teaching survival skills?

The answer starts with a clear, concise intro. → The expedition taught valuable survival skills successfully. The evidence for this is the fact that "the campers caught fish" and cooked them "over a campfire that they made themselves." This shows that they learned the survival skills of catching and cooking their food.

Evidence from the text backs up the point.

The explanation shows how the evidence proves the point.

TRY IT OUT

Use the "introduce, cite, explain" method to write about something you have read recently.

WRITING • **INTRODUCE, CITE, EXPLAIN**

Analyzing an informative text

Now use the "introduce, cite, explain" method to analyze this informative website page about playing the violin. Do you think the answer is effective?

> **WORLD OF WORDS**
>
> Citing evidence to explain your point is a valuable skill for speaking, as well as writing. It is used in debates, sales, news reports, and more.

How to play the violin

Hold the violin under your chin. Use the fingers of your left hand to press the strings on the neck of the violin. This produces different pitches when you bow or pluck the strings. To make the strings sound, hold the bow in your right hand and draw it across the strings at right angles. Practice to make beautiful music!

How much coordination is needed to play the violin?

A lot of coordination is needed to play the violin. For instance, the website states that you must place the violin under your chin and use both hands. This shows that coordination is essential, as you are using different parts of your body at the same time.

··· The answer starts with a clear, concise intro.

··· The evidence implies that a lot of coordination is needed to play the violin.

··· The explanation shows how the evidence proves the point.

> Using ICE can help you write about **fiction** and **nonfiction** texts.

Revision, editing, and proofreading

No one writes perfect text the first time. Make time for each of these steps to improve your work: revision, editing, and proofreading.

Revise, edit, and proofread to improve the **quality** and **accuracy** of your writing.

How to improve your writing

Break down the work into stages. First, check what you are saying. Then check how you are saying it. Afterward, check that there are no mistakes.

> **SEE ALSO**
> The stages of writing 234
> Collaboration and synthesis 242

Revision

Check the content: what you are saying

- ✔ Have you written what you intended to write?
- ✔ Does it fit the purpose and audience?
- ✔ Does the writing make sense?
- ✔ Does it flow well?
- ✔ Have you included all the important parts?
- ✔ Are there any parts that you don't need?

Don't worry about spelling, punctuation, or grammar at this stage.

> **TRY IT OUT**
>
> When you revise text, you should make sure it makes sense to someone else. Swap a draft of your writing with a partner. Read each other's work to see if you understand it. If something is not clear, make a note for your partner to check it.

Editing

Check the language: how you have written it

- ✔ Is the style the same all the way through?
- ✔ Check the grammar. For example, make sure that nouns (such as "the bird"/"the birds") agree with verbs (such as "sings"/"sing").
- ✔ Are all of your sentences complete?
- ✔ Are any paragraphs too short or too long?
- ✔ Check the punctuation. Have you used periods, question marks, commas, and capital letters correctly?
- ✔ Check the spelling is all correct.

Proofreading

Tips for the final check

- ✔ Leave your writing for a day before you check it.
- ✔ If you're working on screen, change the text to another font to help you proofread it with fresh eyes.
- ✔ Print it out to read.
- ✔ Ask a friend or family member to read it and mark any mistakes.
- ✔ Check a last time for grammar, punctuation, and spelling.

WORLD OF WORDS

Revision, editing, and proofreading are important for professional writers, too! Most write a first draft, then revise it. An editor suggests ways to improve the text. Finally, a proofreader corrects mistakes.

Glossary

abstract noun A word that refers to a quality rather than a thing or person, e.g. "beauty" or "hope."

academic words and phrases Vocabulary commonly found in written texts but not commonly used in speech, e.g. "justify" or "theory."

active voice When the subject of the sentence does the action of the verb, e.g. "The rat ate the cake." See also passive voice.

adjective A word that describes or modifies a noun or pronoun, e.g. "funny" or "slow."

adverb A word that describes or modifies an adjective, clause, verb, or other adverb, e.g. "gently."

adverb phrase A phrase that, like an adverb, says how, when, where, or why something happened, e.g. "in the park" or "yesterday morning."

affix A morpheme added to the root of a word to modify its meaning or create a new word. See also prefix and suffix.

agreement When the verb form matches the subject, e.g. "He is" = singular subject + singular verb.

alliteration The repetition of the same initial letters or sounds for effect.

allusion A type of figurative language that refers to something familiar, such as a place or person, to make the reader think of that thing.

antagonist A character in a story who is the enemy of, or comes into conflict with, the main character in the story. See also protagonist.

antonym A word with the opposite meaning to another word. For example, "wet" and "dry" are antonyms.

apostrophe The punctuation that shows either belonging (e.g. "John's cat") or the place of missing letters in a contraction (e.g. "I'm happy").

article 1) The words a, an, or the, which show whether something is specific or general. They are types of determiners. 2) A piece of writing that is intended for a wide audience.

audience The people who read, listen to, or watch a performance of a writer's work.

autobiography An account by a writer of their own life story.

auxiliary verb A verb that is used with another verb, e.g. to form tenses. These are be, do, and have and the modal auxiliaries.

backstory Events in a character's past that happened before the time the story is set.

ballad A type of poem, often set to music, that tells a traditional story or legend.

bias A tendency to unfairly favor one thing or person over another.

biography An account by a writer of another person's life story.

blog An online journal that contains the writer's comments and reflections. It is updated regularly.

bound morpheme A part of a word that has to be attached to a root word to have meaning. See also morpheme.

central idea See main idea.

character A person or other being in a story.

claim A statement that is made as part of an argument and that can be supported with evidence.

clause A group of words that contains a subject and a predicate. There are main clauses, subordinate clauses, and relative clauses.

climax The most exciting or dramatic part of a story.

cohesion The way the different parts of a text fit together so that it makes logical sense.

collaboration Working together with others on a shared task.

collective noun A noun that describes a group of things, e.g. "a flock of birds."

colon The punctuation used to introduce an explanation, list, or quotation.

comedy A lighthearted genre with situations and characters designed to make people laugh.

comma The punctuation that separates parts of sentences or items in a list.

command A sentence that tells someone to do something and includes an imperative verb, e.g. "Stop it!"

common noun The name given to objects, places, people, and ideas in general. See also proper noun.

comparison Examining the similarities and differences between two or more things.

compound word A word that contains two or more root words, e.g. "whiteboard" or "supermarket."

conditional tense The verb form used when one event or situation depends on another event or situation happening first, e.g. "If it rains, you'll get wet."

conjunction A word that joins words, phrases, and clauses, e.g. "and," "or," or "because." There are coordinating conjunctions, correlative conjunctions, and subordinating conjunctions.

consonant A letter of the alphabet that is not a vowel.

context The social and cultural situation in which text or speech is made.

contraction A word where letters have been left out to combine or shorten words, e.g. "you'll."

contrast Examining the differences between two or more things.

conventions A series of generally accepted standards for written English.

coordinating conjunction A word that joins two words or clauses of equal importance, e.g. "and" or "but."

correlative conjunction Two conjunctions that work as a pair, e.g. "either" and "or."

couplet Two consecutive lines of poetry, usually rhyming and of similar length.

dash Punctuation used 1) to mark a pause; 2) in pairs to separate extra information from the main text (see parenthetical); or 3) to show spans of time or numbers. A long dash, called the em dash, marks a pause or separates information, and a short dash, called the en dash, shows spans of time or numbers.

determiner A word that comes before a noun and identifies it, e.g. "the" in "the book."

dialect A form of a language that is written and spoken by a particular group or in a particular area.

dialogue Conversation between or among characters in a piece of writing.

direct object The person or thing affected by the action of the verb, e.g. "it" in "I kicked it."

direct speech The words that are actually said to make a statement or question, e.g. "What time is it?"

editing Checking and improving the way in which a text has been written, including its style, grammar, and punctuation.

ellipsis A punctuation mark that tells the reader there are missing words, a pause, or an unfinished sentence.

emotive language Words that are chosen to make the reader or listener feel strongly about something.

GLOSSARY

epic A long poem that tells a story and usually describes a heroic adventure.

etymology The history of a word—the language it comes from and how it has changed.

evidence Facts, data, quotations, or other reliable information that can provide support for a claim or argument made in a text or speech.

exaggeration The suggestion that something is much more or less than it actually is.

exclamation A sentence that expresses strong emotions such as surprise, starts with "what" or "how," and usually ends with an exclamation mark.

expanded noun phrase A noun phrase that gives extra detail about the noun, such as an adjective before it or additional information after it.

explicit evidence Information that is clearly stated in a text. See also implicit evidence.

fact A statement that can be proved.

falling action Events that take place after a story's climax and before its resolution. See also rising action.

farce A highly dramatic subgenre of comedy that uses exaggeration and unlikely situations to entertain the audience.

fiction A piece of writing, such as a story, play, or poem, that is about imaginary events and characters.

figurative language Using words in a different way from their literal meaning to create a strong emotion or impression in the reader or audience. Types of figurative language include metaphor, personification, and simile.

form The overall shape, style, and structure of a piece of writing chosen to suit its purpose and audience.

formal English See Standard English.

free morpheme A word that stands on its own with a single meaning. See also morpheme.

free verse A type of poem with no specific rhythm, line length, or rhyme scheme.

genre A style of writing that is associated with particular characteristics. For example, comedy and romance are genres of writing.

gerund Also called a verbal noun, the -ing form of a verb when it is used as a noun, e.g. "I like dancing."

haiku A short form of poetry that originated in Japan. A haiku is made up of three lines, containing five syllables, seven syllables, and five syllables.

homonym Two different words that sound the same when pronounced and have the same spelling but mean different things.

homophone Two different words that sound the same when pronounced but mean different things.

hyphen The punctuation that is used to join words together to form a single idea (e.g. three-year-old dog) or to clarify meaning (e.g. re-sign as opposed to resign).

idiom An expression, usually spoken, that doesn't mean what it actually says, e.g. The test was a piece of cake. It is a type of metaphor.

imperative The type (mood) of verb used for giving instructions.

implicit evidence Information that is suggested by clues in a text rather than being clearly stated. See also explicit evidence.

implied subject A subject that does not appear in a sentence such as a command but is understood to be "you." For example, the command "Come here!" has the implied subject "you."

indent A space that is left at the start of a line before the start of a new paragraph.

indicative The type (mood) of verb used for stating facts.

indirect object A person or thing that is affected by the action of a verb but is not the direct object, e.g. "my friend" in "I gave my friend a gift."

inference The process of working out meaning in a text, usually not obviously stated by the writer, using information given and reasoning.

infinitive The basic form of the verb, usually following to, e.g. "to swim." Infinitives are verbals, which means they can act as nouns (by being the subject of a sentence), adjectives (by telling us more about a noun), or adverbs (by telling us more about a verb).

interrogative The type (mood) of verb used for asking questions.

intonation The variation of pitch and loudness in a person's voice.

introduce, cite, explain (ICE) A way of showing your how well you understand a text: you make a point about the text, cite evidence from the text to support this point, and explain how the evidence supports your point.

irregular A word that does not follow the usual rules relating to other words like it, e.g. the past simple tense of "make" is "made," not "maked."

language or language features The words chosen and arranged by writers to create certain effects.

layout The way a piece of writing is arranged and presented on a page or a screen.

limerick A funny poem with five lines and a strict rhyme scheme. It usually starts with the words "There was a."

linking verb A verb that provides information about the subject of a sentence by linking it to an adjective or another noun.

main clause A clause that can stand alone as a sentence.

main idea Also known as central idea, the most important idea that runs through a passage or text.

metaphor A type of figurative language that describes one thing as if it is something else, e.g. "The river was a silver thread."

modal auxiliary A verb used in combination with another verb to express degrees of possibility, ability, or necessity, e.g. "will," "can," or "must."

modifier A word or phrase used with another word or phrase to make its meaning more specific, e.g. in "elementary-school teacher," "elementary" specifies the type of school and "elementary-school" specifies the type of teacher.

mood See tone. See also verb mood.

morpheme The smallest individual part of a word that means something, such as a root word. There are free morphemes and bound morphemes.

morphology The study of how words are formed. See also morpheme.

musical A play that contains song and dance to help tell the story.

myth An ancient story that was passed down through many generations and eventually written down.

narrative A spoken or written account of a real or invented sequence of events.

narrative nonfiction A type of nonfiction that uses the structure of a story to tell the reader about real events and people.

narrative poem A poem that tells a story.

narrator The teller of a spoken or written account of something.

near-homophones Words that nearly sound the same but have different meanings and different spellings, e.g. "bowl" and "ball."

noun A word that names a person, place, or thing, e.g. "boy," "city," or "book." There are common nouns and proper nouns.

noun phrase A group of words linked to a noun that, as a unit, acts like a noun in a sentence, e.g. "the house."

object The person or thing that the verb is acting on, e.g. "the ball" in "I kicked the ball."

objective An objective piece of writing is based on facts and is not influenced by personal opinions. See also subjective.

ode A poem that is dedicated to a person, place, or thing that the poet admires. An ode expresses praise, appreciation, or celebration.

omniscient narrator A narrator who knows everything about the people and events they are telling you about, including things the characters themselves don't know.

onomatopoeia A type of figurative language that mimics the sound it describes, e.g. "buzz" or "hiss."

opinion A belief about or judgment on something that may not be based on fact or knowledge.

orthography The rules for writing a language, including capitalization, punctuation, and spelling.

paragraph A group of sentences about the same idea.

paraphrase A description of a written or spoken quotation that uses different words while keeping the original meaning.

parentheses The punctuation most often used to show that words have been added to a direct quotation.

parenthetical A remark or information inserted in the middle of a text that tells more about the topic; usually enclosed by commas, parentheses, or dashes.

parody A subgenre of comedy that makes fun of another work, another author's style, or another genre by imitating it.

participle The form of a verb that ends in "-ing" (present participle) or "-ed" or "-en" (past participle). They can be used with "be" or "have" to form continuous and perfect tenses (e.g. "I am eating" or "I have eaten"). They can also be used as verbals to act like an adjective to describe a noun (e.g. "shining star" or "fallen snow").

parts of speech Also called word classes, the grammatical categories into which words are grouped depending on their use. These are adjective, adverb, conjunction, determiner, interjection, noun, pronoun, preposition, and verb.

passive voice When the action taking place is presented as more important than who or what took the action, e.g. "The cake was eaten." See also active voice.

past continuous See past progressive.

past participle The form of the verb used to make perfect tenses and the passive, e.g. "done," "eaten," or "walked."

past perfect A tense that is formed with "had" and the past participle, e.g. "had walked."

past progressive Also known as past continuous, a tense that is formed with "was" or "were" and the present participle, e.g. "was walking."

personification A type of figurative language that describes nonhuman things with human qualities or characteristics, e.g. "The clouds were weeping."

perspective The point of view expressed by a writer, narrator, speaker, or character.

phoneme The smallest unit of sound in a given language that is heard by native speakers as a distinctive sound, e.g. in "bog" and "dog," "b" and "d" are different phonemes.

phonology The study of sounds in a language.

phrase A group of linked words that does not contain a subject or a verb.

plagiarism Presenting someone else's words or ideas as your own.

plot The storyline of a fictional narrative or play.

plural The form of a word used when there is more than one of something, e.g. "books." See also singular.

possessive Something that shows ownership or belonging. There are possessive determiners (e.g. "my teeth"), possessive pronouns (e.g. "it's mine"), and possessive nouns ("Anton's teeth").

predicate The part of a clause that is not the subject, e.g. "walked to the store" in "She walked to the store."

prefix Letters at the start of a word that change its meaning, e.g. "re-" in "replace." See also suffix.

preposition A short word that links two nouns or pronouns to show a relationship, e.g. "of," "to," or "under."

prepositional phrase A phrase beginning with a preposition and ending with a noun or pronoun (called the object of the preposition), e.g. "in bed" or "under it."

present continuous Also called present progressive, a tense formed with the present of be and the present participle, e.g. "is doing." It expresses an ongoing action in the present.

present participle The form of the verb used to make continuous tenses that ends in "-ing," e.g. "doing" or "writing."

present perfect A tense formed with the present of have and the past participle, e.g. "have done" or "has walked." It expresses an ongoing action that began in the past, or one that happened in the past but has a result in the present.

present progressive See present continuous.

pronoun A word that replaces a noun or noun phrase when the noun has already been mentioned, e.g. "I," "it," or "that."

proofreading Reading a completed text to check it for errors, such as spelling or grammar mistakes.

proper noun A noun that is the name of a specific person, place, or thing such as a day or festival, e.g. "Maria," "France," "Sunday," or "Christmas." See also common noun.

prose Ordinary language used for writing and speaking, usually without rhyme or rhythm (in contrast to poetry).

protagonist A main character in a story or play.

purpose The reason for writing a text, e.g. to argue, to entertain, to inform, or to persuade.

question A sentence that asks something and ends with a question mark.

question tag A very short phrase, such as "isn't it?," that is added to the end of a statement to turn it into a question.

quotation A phrase or short passage written or spoken by one person and repeated word-for-word by someone else.

quotation marks The punctuation used to mark the beginning and end of quotations or direct speech, e.g. "You're late," said Jack.

realism A genre that is based in reality and reflects the real, everyday world. It focuses on familiar situations and everyday experiences.

relative adverb An adverb that introduces a relative clause, e.g. "where," "when," or "why."

relative clause A clause that gives more information about the subject or object of the main clause, often using a relative pronoun, e.g. "The boy who hates spiders."

relative pronoun A pronoun that introduces a relative clause, e.g. "which," "who," or "that."

repetition The use of the same word or phrase more than once, usually for emphasis or effect.

GLOSSARY

resolution The conclusion of a story's plot. Also called the denouement, the resolution is often when any remaining questions in the story are answered.

revision Checking and improving a writer's own work.

rhetorical question A question that is used to make a point or to persuade the reader or audience rather than to obtain an answer.

rhyme The use of two or more words that end with the same or a very similar sound, e.g. "fun" and "sun."

rhyme scheme The pattern of rhymes in a poem. To represent a rhyme scheme, each line of the poem is given a letter; lines that rhyme are given the same letter.

rising action In a plot, the series of events that leads up to the most interesting or exciting point.

root The word or part of it that has meaning to which affixes can be added.

root word A word that can stand alone without having a prefix or suffix added to it.

satire A subgenre of comedy that uses humor to criticize people, ideas, or situations.

script The text of a play.

semicolon Punctuation used to join closely related sentences or to separate items in a list when there are internal commas in the list.

sentence A group of one or more clauses. A sentence may be a statement, a question, a command, or an exclamation.

setting The location and time in which an event or story takes place.

silent letter A letter that can't be heard when we pronounce a word, e.g. the "k" in "knight."

simile A type of figurative language that compares one thing to another using the words like or as, e.g. "as white as snow."

simple past A tense that describes completed actions in the past. Regular verbs take the ending "-ed," e.g. "rested" or "played."

singular The form of word used to refer to only one of something, e.g. "book." See also plural.

sonnet A poem with 14 lines, a regular rhythm, and a rhyme scheme. Sonnets are often about love.

source The text where a quotation or information has come from.

speech A formal talk on a topic.

stage direction An instruction written into the script of a play that gives directions to the actors or information about the scenery, sound effects, or lighting.

Standard English The form of English that is most widely used and understood. It is grammatically correct and can be used in formal and informal situations.

stanza A verse of a poem made up of a certain number of lines that follow a pattern of rhyme and rhythm.

statement A sentence that tells someone something.

story map A visual way of mapping out the beginning, rising action, climax, falling action, and resolution of a story.

structure The way a piece of writing is organized.

style The way a piece of writing is written, depending on its purpose and audience, e.g. formal, informal, personal, or impersonal.

subgenre A genre that is part of a larger genre. For example, satire is a subgenre of comedy.

subheading A heading that is used to break up the text in an article.

subject The person, place, or thing doing or being something in a clause, e.g. "Leila" in "Leila walked to school."

subjective A subjective piece of writing is influenced by the writer's personal opinions. See also objective.

subjunctive A tense used to talk about imaginary things that are unlikely to happen or to express wants or needs in formal or old-fashioned writing.

subordinate clause A clause that needs to be linked to a main clause to make sense, usually introduced by a subordinating conjunction.

subordinating conjunction A conjunction that introduces a subordinate clause, e.g. "because" or "while."

suffix A morpheme attached to the end of a root or root word, e.g. "-less" in "hopeless." It changes the part of speech or tense or makes a plural. See also prefix.

summary A short account showing understanding of the most important points in a text.

syllable Part of a word that sounds like a beat; a syllable can be made up of one or more vowels or at least one vowel and one or more consonants.

synonym A word that has the same or a very similar meaning to another word, e.g. "angry" and "furious" are synonyms.

synthesis Part of the research process in which the writer merges information from different sources into their own work.

tense The form of a verb that shows the time of the action, e.g. past simple or present perfect.

text features The elements of a piece of writing that are not the main text but help the reader's understanding, e.g. headings and illustrations.

theme An idea that runs through a text.

tone (mood) The atmosphere or feeling the writer creates in a text for the reader.

tragedy A genre in which the plot features a lot of suffering and has a sad ending. The main character in a tragedy usually has a fatal flaw.

traits The qualities that make up the personality of a character in a story.

transition words 1) Words or phrases that help link one topic to the next topic, e.g. "furthermore," "meanwhile," or "on the other hand." 2) Words used to show how the different parts of a text fit together, e.g. determiners and pronouns, which can refer back to earlier words.

travel narrative A form of narrative nonfiction that describes a quest to visit a place.

unreliable narrator A narrator who misleads the reader by lying or by omitting vital information about the story and the characters.

unstressed letter A vowel that is pronounced with an unstressed "uh" sound, e.g. "a" in "zebra," "i" in "pencil," and "u" in "circus."

verb A word used to describe an action, state, or event, e.g. "jump," "be," or "happen." Verbs have different tenses.

verb mood The form of verb used to show what job it is doing in a sentence, e.g. imperative, indicative, or interrogative.

verbal A verb that acts as a noun, adjective, or adverb. There are three types: gerunds, participles, and infinitives.

viewpoint The position or perspective from which something is discussed or evaluated. A viewpoint is usually an opinion, but it can be a fact.

vowel The letters "a," "e," "i," "o," "u." The letter "y" can also be used as a vowel. See also consonant.

word family A group of words that has the same root word in common but different prefixes or suffixes. For example, "action," "react," and "activity" share the root word "act."

Further reading

DK English language arts guides

Children's Illustrated Thesaurus

DK Workbooks, Spelling, 2nd Grade

DK Workbooks, Spelling, 3rd Grade

DK Workbooks, Language Arts, 2nd Grade

DK Workbooks, Language Arts, 3rd Grade

English for Everyone: English Grammar Guide

English for Everyone: English Grammar Guide Practice Book

English for Everyone: English Idioms

Help Your Kids With Language Arts, Ages 10–16 (Grades 6–10)

Language Arts Made Easy 10 Minutes a Day Spelling Games, 2nd Grade

Language Arts Made Easy 10 Minutes a Day Spelling, 2nd Grade

Language Arts Made Easy 10 Minutes a Day Spelling, 4th Grade

Language Arts Made Easy 10 Minutes a Day Vocabulary, 2nd Grade

Visual Guide to Grammar and Punctuation

Write Your Own Book

Nonfiction

H. G. Bissinger, *Friday Night Lights: A Town, a Team, and a Dream* (1990)

Georgia Bragg, *How They Choked: The Awful Ends of the Awfully Famous* (2011)

Dieter Braun, *Wild Animals of the North* (2016)

Winifred Conkling, *Radioactive!: How Irène Curie and Lise Meitner Revolutionized Science and Changed the World* (2016)

DK, *Complete Children's Cookbook*

DK, *Cosmic: The Ultimate Pop-Up Guide to Space*

DK, *Eyewitness Titanic*

DK, *DKfindout! Volcano*

DK, *Knowledge Encyclopedia*

DK, *Picturepedia*

Candace Fleming, *Amelia Lost: The Life and Disappearance of Amelia Earhart* (2011)

Benjamin Franklin, *The Autobiography of Benjamin Franklin* (1791)

Russell Freedman, *Lincoln: A Photobiography* (1987)

Henry de B. Gibbins, *An Industrial History of England* (1890)

Ibn Battuta, *The Travels of Ibn Battuta* (1350s, published 2003)

Adam Kay, *Kay's Anatomy* (2021)

Chip Kidd, *Go: A Kidd's Guide to Graphic Design* (2013)

Jack London, *The Road* (1907)

Steve Sheinkin, *Bomb: The Race to Build—and Steal—the World's Most Dangerous Weapon* (2012)

Joshua Slocum, *Sailing Alone Around the World* (1900)

FURTHER READING

If you liked *Speech at the United Nations Climate Action Summit in New York*, try: Greta Thunberg, *No One Is Too Small to Make a Difference* (2019).

Greta Thunberg, *Speech at the United Nations Climate Action Summit in New York* (September 23, 2019)

Sojourner Truth, *Narrative of Sojourner Truth: A Northern Slave* (1850)

Shoshana Weider, *Moon Landings* (2019)

Mary Wollstonecraft, *A Vindication of the Rights of Woman* (1792)

Jacqueline Woodson, *Brown Girl Dreaming* (2014)

Malala Yousafzai, *I Am Malala: The Girl Who Stood Up for Education and was Shot by the Taliban* (2013)

Fiction

Joan Aiken, *A Necklace of Raindrops* (1968)

Louisa May Alcott, *Little Women* (1868)

David Almond, *Skellig* (1998)

Jane Austen, *Pride and Prejudice* (1813)

J. M. Barrie, *Peter Pan* (1911)

L. Frank Baum, *The Wonderful Wizard of Oz* (1900)

Malorie Blackman, *Noughts & Crosses* (2001)

Lewis Carroll, *Alice's Adventures in Wonderland* (1865)

Suzanne Collins, *The Hunger Games* series (2008–2010)

Arthur Conan Doyle, *The Return of Sherlock Holmes* (1905)

Frank Cottrell Boyce, *Framed* (2005)

Roald Dahl, *Matilda* (1988)

Ingri & Edgar Parin d'Aulaire, *D'Aulaires' Book of Greek Myths* (1967)

N. J. Dawood (Translator), *Tales from the Thousand and One Nights* (Arabian Nights) (1973)

Charles Dickens, *A Christmas Carol* (1843)

Charles Dickens, *David Copperfield* (1849)

Charles Dickens, *Great Expectations* (1861)

Charles Dickens, *Oliver Twist* (1838)

Alexandre Dumas, *The Count of Monte Cristo* (1844)

Alexandre Dumas, *The Three Musketeers* (1844)

William Golding, *Lord of the Flies* (1954)

Kenneth Grahame, *The Wind in the Willows* (1908)

E. M. Forster, *A Room With a View* (1908)

Mark Haddon, *The Curious Incident of the Dog in the Night-Time* (2003)

Frances Hodgson Burnett, *The Secret Garden* (1911)

Aldous Huxley, *Brave New World* (1932)

J. K. Jackson, *West African Folktales* (2021)

If you liked *Noughts & Crosses*, try: Malorie Blackman, *Pig Heart Boy* (1997).

FURTHER READING

If you liked the *Harry Potter* books, try: Jessica Townsend, *Nevermoor: The Trials of Morrigan Crow* (2017).

Thomas James, *Aesop's Fables: A New Version, Chiefly from Original Sources* (1848)

Jerome K. Jerome, *Three Men in a Boat* (1889)

Jeff Kinney, *Diary of a Wimpy Kid* series (2007–)

Harper Lee, *To Kill a Mockingbird* (1960)

Michelle Magorian, *Goodnight Mister Tom* (1981)

Logan Marshall, *Favourite Fairy Tales* (1917)

Irfan Master, *A Beautiful Lie* (2011)

L. M. Montgomery, *Anne of Green Gables* (1908)

Michael Morpurgo, *Private Peaceful* (2003)

Beverley Naidoo, *Journey to Jo'burg* (1985)

R. J. Palacio, *Wonder* (2012)

J. K. Rowling, *Harry Potter* series (1997–2007)

Katherine Rundell, *The Explorer* (2017)

Louis Sachar, *Holes* (1998)

Anna Sewell, *Black Beauty* (1877)

Mary Shelley, *Frankenstein* (1818)

Zadie Smith, *White Teeth* (2000)

Lemony Snicket, *A Series of Unfortunate Events* series (1999–2006)

John Steinbeck, *Of Mice and Men* (1937)

Robert Louis Stevenson, *Treasure Island* (1883)

Catherine Storr, *Clever Polly and the Stupid Wolf* (1955)

Robert Swindells, *Stone Cold* (1993)

Mildred D. Taylor, *Roll of Thunder, Hear My Cry* (1976)

J. R. R. Tolkien, *The Hobbit* (1937)

J. R. R. Tolkien, *The Lord of the Rings* (1954–1955)

Piers Torday, *The Last Wild* (2013)

E. B. White, *Charlotte's Web* (1952)

Diana Wynne Jones, *Howl's Moving Castle* (1986)

Gene Luen Yang, *American Born Chinese* (2006)

Poetry

John Agard, "Checking Out Me History" (2003)

Maya Angelou, "Still I Rise" (1978)

Anonymous, "I Eat My Peas with Honey"

Matsuo Bashō, "Bashō's Death Poem" (1694)

Rupert Brooke, "The Soldier" (1915)

Gwendolyn Brooks, "We Real Cool" (1963)

Robert Browning, "The Pied Piper of Hamelin" (1842)

Charles Bukowski, "so you want to be a writer" (1992)

Samuel Taylor Coleridge, "The Rime of the Ancient Mariner" (1798)

Emily Dickinson, "'Hope' Is The Thing with Feathers" (1891)

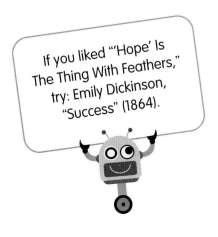

If you liked "'Hope' Is The Thing With Feathers," try: Emily Dickinson, "Success" (1864).

FURTHER READING

> If you liked "From a Railway Carriage", try: Robert Browning, "Porphyria's Lover" (1836).

Carol Ann Duffy, "Text" (2006)

Margarita Engle, "The Surrender Tree" (2010)

Robert Frost, "Fire and Ice" (1920)

Amanda Gorman, "The Hill We Climb" (2021)

Seamus Heaney, "Blackberry-Picking" (1966)

Langston Hughes, "I, Too" (1925)

Philip Larkin, "The Trees" (1974)

Edward Lear, "There Was an Old Man with a Beard" (1846)

Sarojini Naidu, "Street Cries" (1905)

William Shakespeare, "Sonnet 12" (1609)

Lemn Sissay, "Making a Difference" (2018)

Robert Louis Stevenson, "From a Railway Carriage" (1885)

Alfred Lord Tennyson, "The Brook" (1886)

Dylan Thomas, "Do not go gentle into that good night" (1951)

Jacqueline Woodson, "Firefly" (2003)

Benjamin Zephaniah, "Talking Turkeys" (1994)

Drama

Richard Conlon, *Paving Paradise* (2011)

Denise Deegan, *Daisy Pulls It Off* (1985)

Carol Ann Duffy and Tim Supple, *Grimm Tales* (1996)

Gilbert & Sullivan, *The Pirates of Penzance* (1879)

Susan Glaspell, *Trifles* (1916)

Natasha Gordon, *Nine Night* (2018)

David Grant, *Fast* (2011)

Tanika Gupta, *The Empress* (2013)

Lorraine Hansberry, *A Raisin in the Sun* (1959)

Michael Morpurgo, *War Horse* (2007)

J. B. Priestley, *An Inspector Calls* (1945)

Philip Pullman, *Frankenstein* (1990)

Willy Russell, *Blood Brothers* (1985)

Diane Samuels, *Kindertransport* (1995)

William Shakespeare, *Hamlet* (1599–1601)

William Shakespeare, *King Lear* (c. 1605–1606)

William Shakespeare, *Othello* (1604)

William Shakespeare, *Romeo and Juliet* (c. 1595–1596)

William Shakespeare, *The Tempest* (1610)

William Shakespeare, *The Tragedy of Macbeth* (1606)

Sophocles, *Antigone* (c. 441 BCE)

Oscar Wilde, *The Importance of Being Earnest* (1895)

Nicholas Wright (adapted from Philip Pullman), *His Dark Materials* (2005)

Benjamin Zephaniah and Richard Conlon, *Face: The Play* (2008)

> If you liked *The Tragedy of Macbeth*, try: William Shakespeare, *A Midsummer Night's Dream* (1600).

Index

Page numbers in **bold** refer to main entries.

A

a/an 19
ability 57
abstract nouns 12
accents 117
acknowledgments 239
action
   narrative techniques 276
   verbs 26
active sentences **64–65**, 255
actors 125
acts
   plays 125, 141
   three-act structure **142–143**, 267
addition, transition words 258
addresses, letters 196, 197, 289
adjectives **20–21**
   and creating a setting 271
   in descriptions 262, 277
   hyphens 88
   infinitives and participles as 63
   predicate 21
   suffixes 103, 110
   synonyms 118–119
   using more than one **22–23**
adult nonfiction 204, 205
adventure **128**
adverb phrases and clauses **30–31**
adverbs **28–29**
   descriptive writing 262
   infinitives as **63**
   position of 29
   relative 42, **43**
   suffixes 103, 109
advertising 187, 202, 205, 224, 226
   language techniques 211
   online 193
   sales materials **200–201**
advice 187, 188
Aesop's Fables 171, 179, 312
affixes 95, 97
Agard, John 283, 312
Aiken, Joan 311
Alcott, Louisa May 153, 311
alliteration 149, 151, **157**, **159**, 191, 241, 262, 281

allusion **159**
Almond, David 311
alphabet 232
analysis
   dialogue **167**
   poetry **168–169**, 283
   text 180, 182, 302–303
anecdotes 198
Angelou, Maya 312
antagonists **135**
apostrophes
   contractions **76–77**
   possession **74–75**
appearance, characters 136, 137, 272
apps 186
arguments
   structuring 295
   writing to argue **294–295**
articles
   analysis 302
   definite and indefinite 18
   magazine and newspaper **190–191**, 214, 248
atmosphere, building 271
audience **204–205**
   engaging 199, 268
   identifying 204, 224, 226, 227, 232, **246**
   knowledge of topic 246
   language effects on 208–211
   satisfying 268
   and text 205
   writing to argue 295
audiobooks 146
Austen, Jane 167, 311
authorial intent 156
autobiographies 194

B

backstories **273**
balanced arguments 295
balanced viewpoints 212
ballads 148
Barker, G. 183
Barrie, J. M. 311
Bashō, Matsuo 182, 312
Baum, L. Frank 155, 166, 311
behavior, characters 273
biographies 194
Bissinger, H. G. 310
Blackman, Malorie 180, 311

blogs 192
bookstores 123
bound morphemes 97
boxes, text 190, 287
brackets 195
Bragg, Georgina 310
Braun, Dieter 310
brochures 200–201
Brooke, Rupert 312
Brookes, Gwendoline 312
Browning, Robert 133, 312
Bukowski, Charles 312
bullet points 190, 234, 237, 244
bylines 191

C

capital letters 93
   direct speech 73
   proper nouns 13
   sentences 70, 252
captions
   informative texts 189, 218
   newspapers 191, 214
Carroll, Lewis 280, 311
cast lists 145
catchphrases 166
cause and effect
   adverb phrases 31
   adverbs of 28, 29, 43
changes, story-writing 265
chapters 124, 141
characters
   choosing a narrator 274–275
   comparing and contrasting 137, 174, 175, 176, 177
   creating **272–273**
   dialogue **166–167**, **276**
   evolution of 137
   fictional **134–135**
   inferences about **161**, 163
   and main idea 170, 171
   planning a story 264
   plays 145
   style of characterization 241
   understanding **136–137**, 152
charts
   informative/explanatory texts 285, 287
   nonfiction texts 214, 218
   websites 192
children's nonfiction 204, 205
citations 182, 183

clarity
   in information presentation **286–287**
   writing clear English 285
clashing viewpoints 213
clauses **40–41**
   adverb clauses 30
   commas **80**
   conjunctions 46, 47
   multiclause sentences **44–45**
   relative **42–43**
   in sentences 36, 40, 254
climax, plots 143, 267
closing phrases, letters 79
clues
   implicit evidence 181
   inferred meaning 220–221
   in stories 152
Coleridge, Samuel Taylor 312
collaboration 235, **242–243**
collation 235
collective nouns 12
Collins, Suzanne 311
Collodi, Carlo 269
colons **84–85**
columns, newspapers 214
comedy **127**
comma splices 45
commands 39, 60, 61, 70
commas **78–81**
   and clarity of meaning 68
   multiple adjectives 23
   relative clauses 42
comments, online 193
common nouns 13
comparisons
   adjectives 21
   comparing and contrasting fiction **174–177**
   comparing and contrasting nonfiction **224–227**
   unusual 280
compound words 97
Conan Doyle, Arthur 166, 311
conclusions
   arguments 295
   concluding sentences 256
   essay prompts 299
   informative/explanatory texts 284
   transition words 258, 259
   writing 245

conditional tenses **58–59**
conflict, plots 142–143, 266–267
conjunctions **46–49**
  commas before 80
  coordinating 44, **46–47**
  correlative **49**
  joining sentences 252
  semicolons as replacement for 82
  subordinating 41, **47–48**
Conkling, Winifred 310
Conlon, Richard 313
consistency 200, 251
consonant suffixes **108–109**
consonants 104, 106
constructive criticism 243
contents pages 189, 218
context
  comparing nonfiction texts 225
  and meaning of words 154, 155, 216
  and settings 131
contractions
  apostrophes **76–77**
  levels of formality 206, 288, 290
contrasting
  comparing and contrasting fiction **174–177**
  comparing and contrasting nonfiction **224–227**
  transition words 258, 259
conventions, genres 126–129
coordinating conjunctions 44, **46–47**
correlative conjunctions **49**
costumes 147
Cottrell Boyce, Frank 311
counterarguments 294, 295
creative thinking **236**
crime 128
curiosity, creating 268

D

Dahl, Roald 311
dashes 81, 86, **87**
  and hyphens 89
dates, letters 79, 289
d'Aulaire, Ingri and Edgar Parin 311
Dawood, N. J. 311
deck 190
Deegan, Denise 313
definite articles 18
definitions 217
demonstrative pronouns/determiners 19

description
  adjectives **20–23**
  descriptive writing **262–263**
  as narrative technique 276, **277**
  verbs 26
detail, building 254, 262
determiners **18–19**, 24
diagrams 214, 218, 285, 287
dialogue
  exploring **166–167**
  and inference 163
  narrative nonfiction 194
  as narrative technique **276**, 277
  plays 125, 145
  and understanding characters 136
diaries 232
Dickens, Charles 132, 163, 166, 263, 311
Dickinson, Emily 169, 312
dictionaries **93**, 154, 155, **217**
Dineen, Helen 279
direct quotations 183
direct speech
  dialogue **166–167**
  paragraphs 257
  punctuation **72–73**, 80
  rude and polite tones **207**
drafts, first/rough 235, 271, 305
Duffy, Carol Ann 313
Dumas, Alexandre 301, 311
Dunbar-Nelson, Alice Moore 149

E

editing 232, 233, 235, 304, **305**
electronic media 186
ellipses 69, 86, **87**, 253
emails, informal **290**
emotional effect 156
emotional tone 207
emotive language 199, 209, 211, 292
emphasis 146, 147
encyclopedias 222, 238, 285
endings, stories **268–269**
Engle, Margarita 313
entertainment
  language techniques 211
  as writer's purpose 203, 208, 246, 247
epic poems 148
essay prompts **298–303**

etymology 92
events
  ordering 258, 259
  verbs 26
evidence
  arguments 294, 295
  essay prompts 299
  facts and opinions 223
  implicit and explicit 223
  inferences 160–163
  informative texts 285
  introduce, cite, explain **300–303**
  looking for 213, **218–219**, 220
  proving your point **180–181**
  research sources 238–239
  summarizing 229
  using evidence from the text **182–183**
  writing about poetry 283
exaggeration 209, 211, 292
excitement, creating 255
exclamation marks 38, 39, 69, 70, **71**, 73, 252
exclamations 38, 71
exclamatory fragments 38
expanded noun phrases 24, 25
explanation
  colons and 84
  introduce, cite, explain **300–303**
  as writer's purpose 202
  writing about poetry 283
  writing to explain **284–285**
explicit evidence 160, 180, 181, 223, 300
explicit text 220
expressive language 262
extent, adverbs of 28, 29
extra information
  parentheses and dashes to mark 86–87, 89
  commas to mark 81

F

facts and figures
  informative/explanatory texts 285, 287
  speeches 198
facts, vs. opinions 201, **222–223**
fairy tales **127**
FANBOYS 46–47
fantasy **128**
farce 127
feelings, emotions and qualities

abstract nouns 12
characters 136
inferred 221
fiction
  characters **134–137**, **272–273**
  choice of form 248, 249
  comparing and contrasting **174–177**
  features of **124–125**
  further reading **311–312**
  genres **126–129**
  main idea **170–171**
  narrators **138–139**
  plot **140–141**
  reading **120–183**
  research 238–239
  settings **130–133**
  themes **172–173**
  why to read **122–123**
  see also plays; poetry; stories
figurative language 157, **158–159**, 260, 261
  nonfiction texts 209
  poetry 151, 279
  speeches 199
first-person narrators 124, 138, 274, 275
Fitzgerald, F. Scott 274
Fleming, Candace 310
flow, of text 233, 259
flowcharts 234, 237
font, choice of 286
form
  choice of 232, 233, 241, **248–249**
  comparing and contrasting 175
  nonfiction 224, 226, 227
  poetry 149, 282
formal letters 197
formal register/style 206, 208, 210, 250, 251
formality, levels of **206–207**
formatting text **286–287**
forums 193
Franklin, Benjamin 310
free morphemes 97
free verse 148
Freedman, Russell 310
French language 92
friendship 173
Frost, Robert 313
future tense 50, 51

G

genres **126–129**, 241
    comparing and contrasting 175
    stories, poems, and plays 124, 264
gerunds **62**
Gibbins, Henry de B. 310
Gilbert, W. S. 133, 313
Glaspell, Susan 145, 313
glossaries 189, 218
goals 141
Golding, William 173, 311
good vs. evil 173
Gorman, Amanda 169, 313
Grahame, Kenneth 165, 311
grammar **8–65**
    checking 233, 235, 305
    rules **10–11**
    stories, poems, and plays 124–125
Grant, David 313
graphs 218, 285
Greek language 92, 94, 96
greetings
    emails 290
    letters 79, 196, 197, 289, 291
groups of things 12
Gupta, Tanika 313

H

Haddon, Mark 311
haiku 148, 182, 232, 279
handwriting, and punctuation 69
Hansberry, Loraine 313
headings
    informative/explanatory texts 189, 285
    nonfiction texts 214, 215, 218
    sales materials 201
headlines 191, 214, 225
Heaney, Seamus 313
historical fiction 128
history, narrative 195
Hodgson Burnett, Frances 311
homonyms 115
homophones **114–115**
    silent letters in 116
horror 128
Hughes, Langston 313
humor 164
hyperlinks 193
hyphens **88–89**, 93
    and dashes 89
    with prefixes 99

I

Ibn Battuta 195, 310
ICE *see* introductions
ideas
    coming up with **236–237**
    main **170–171**, 178, 278, 279
    organizing 233, 234, **244–245**, 278–279, 294
    in paragraphs 256
    transition words 258, 259
idioms **159**
illustrations *see* pictures
imagery 280, 282, 293
images *see* pictures
imaginary events 59
imagination 122, 232, 248, 264, 270, 272, 279
imaginative effect, of language 156
imperative mood 39, 59, 60, **61**
implicit evidence 160, 181, 223, 300
implicit text 220
incidents, initial 142, 266
indefinite articles 18
indentation, paragraphs 256
indexes 189, 218
indicative mood **60**
inferences **160–161**
    inferring meaning 181, **220–221**
    making **162–163**
infinitives 62, **63**
informal letters 196
informal register/style 206, 211, 250, 251
information
    finding **218–219**
    inferred 160–163, 220
    summarizing **228–229**
informative texts 186–187, **188–189**, 204
    analysis 303
    choice of form 249
    clarity of presentation **286–287**
    different viewpoints 212
    language techniques 210
    writer's purpose 202, 208, 246, 247
    writing **284–285**
    see also nonfiction
-ing endings 55, 62
inspiration, sources of 237, 240, 241, 265
instructions
    essay prompts 298
    imperative mood 60, **61**
    informative texts 186, 188, 210, 219, 249
intellectual effect, of language 156
intensive pronouns 17
intention 57
interactive features 192
interpreting texts 182, 282–283
interrogative mood 60, **61**
introductions
    essay prompts 299
    informative/explanatory texts 189, 284, 286
    introduce, cite, explain (ICE) **300–303**
    nonfiction texts 215
    speech openings 198
    story openings **268–269**
    writing 245
irregular verbs
    present 27
    simple past 53
it/it's 77

J

Jackson, J. K. 312
James, Thomas 312
Jerome, Jerome K. 181, 312

K

Kay, Adam 310
key message, speeches 198
Kidd, Chip 310
Kinney, Jeff 312

L

language
    for different purposes **208–211**
    effect of **156–157**, 208
    facts and opinions 223
    figurative **158–159**
    levels of formality **206–207**, 288, 290, 291
    persuasive writing 292–293
    poetry 149, 151, 168, 169, 282
    speeches 198–199
    and tone 164–165
    writing to argue 295
language techniques **157**, 209, 241, 282
    comparing and contrasting 175, 176, 225, 226, 227
    using **260–261**
Latin language 92, 94, 96
layout **214–215**, 225, 226, 227, 286–287
leaflets 188, 200–201, 249
Lear, Edward 279, 313
legends *see* myths and legends
letters 187, **196–197**, 232, 238
    commas in 79
    writing formal **288–289**
    writing informal 290, **291**
letters (of the alphabet)
    missing 76
    silent and unstressed **116–117**
lexicographers 93
libraries 123
limericks 148, 279, 282
line length, poems 149, 279, 282
linguists 92
linking verbs 27
lists
    bullet point 215, 234, 237, 244
    colons to introduce 85
    commas in **78**
    finding information 219
    organizing ideas 244
    semicolons in 82, **83**
    of three 293
Lloyd Webber, Andrew 144
London, Jack 310
loose ends, tying up 268
lyrical poetry 148

M

magazines 186, **190–191**, 214, 235, 248
Magorian, Michelle 312
main characters *see* protagonists
main clauses 41, 44, 45
main ideas **170–171**, 178, 228, 229
manner
    adverb phrases 31
    adverbs of 28, 29
maps
    informative texts 189, 287
    websites 192
Marshall, Logan 312
Master, Irfan 312
meaning
    commas and **81**
    dictionaries 93
    grammar rules 11
    homophones **114–115**
    how to work out **154–155**
    inferring **220–221**
    of poetry 150, **168–169**
    punctuation and **68**, 78

metaphors **158**, 169, 199, 211, 241, 277, 278
meter 149
mind-maps 234, 237
mistakes, correcting **304–305**
modal auxiliary verbs **56–57**, 58
monsters, overcoming 140
Montgomery, Lucy Maud 177, 312
mood *see* tone
moods (verbs) 59, **60–61**
morals, of stories 170–171
morphemes 92, **97**, 155
morphology 92
Morpurgo, Michael 312, 313
movement
　in performance 147
　prepositions of 34
movies 146
multiple narrators 275
musicals 144
mysteries 128
myths and legends 126, **129**, 171

N

Naidoo, Beverley 312
Naidu, Sarojini 313
names, contractions 77
narrative nonfiction 186–187, **194–195**
narrative perspective 175, 176, 177
narrative poems 148
narrative sequences 244–245
narrative structure 175
narrative techniques **276–277**
narratives 248
narrators 124–125, 138–139
　choice of 241, 265, 274–275
near-homophones 114
negative possibility 56
neutral style 250
newsletters 235, 251
newspapers 186, **190–191**, 214, 227, 248, 302
nonfiction
　audience **204–205**
　choice of form 248, 249
　comparing and contrasting **224–227**
　descriptions in 263
　different viewpoints **212–213**
　facts and opinions **222–223**
　finding information **218–219**
　further reading **310–311**
　inferring meaning **220–221**

informative texts **188–189**
language for different purposes **208–211**
layout and structure **214–215**
letters **196–197**
levels of formality **206–207**
magazines and newspapers **190–191**
narrative **194–195**
online media **192–193**
presenting information clearly **286–287**
reading **184–229**
research 237, **238–239**
sales materials 200–201
specific words and terms 216
speeches **198–199**
summarizing multiple paragraphs **228–229**
types of **186–187**
writer's purpose **202–203**
notes, making 237, 241, 244, 270, 271
noun phrases **24–25**
nouns **12–13**
　of address 39
　adjectives and **20–23**
　gerunds 62
　infinitives 63
　plurals **112–113**
　suffixes 102, 111
novels 124
numbers
　hyphens in 88
　numbering for clarity 215, 287
　ranges of 87

O

object
　nouns 13
　pronouns 15, **17**
　sentences 36, 37
objective adjectives 23
objective summaries **179**, 229
obligation 57
observer, as narrator 275
odes 148
omniscient narrators 139
online media 186, **192–193**, 238, 239
onomatopoeia 157, 260, 261, 262, 278, 281
open-ended stories 143, 268
openings, stories **268–269**
opinions 179, 202, 212, 213
　facts and **222–223**

inferred 221
ordering text
　sequencing points 244–245
　transition words 258, 259
orthography 93
ownership, apostrophes **74–75**

P

pace
　pacing as narrative technique 276, **277**
　varying sentence length 254
　writing to argue 295
Palacio, R. J. 269, 275, 312
panels, text 190, 287
paragraphs
　in arguments 295
　emails and letters 289, 290, 291
　purpose of 257, 286
　structuring 256
　summarizing multiple **228–229**
　transition words 258–259
　writing **256–257**
paraphrasing 178, 239, 243
parentheses 81, **86**
parody 127
participles 62, **63**
parts of speech, suffixes and 102, 103, 110
passive sentences **64–65**, 255
past participles 63, 65
past perfect **54**
past progressive **55**
past subjunctive **59**
past tenses 50, 51, **52–55**
pauses
　dashes and 87
　ellipses and 86, 87
people
　nouns 12, 13
　pronouns 14
performance 144, **146–147**
periods 70, 252
permission 57
personal beliefs 222
personal style 250, 251
personification **158**
perspective, research 238, 239
persuasion
　language techniques 211
　persuasive writing 292
　sales materials 200–201
　as writer's purpose 202, 205, 208
　writing persuasively **292–293**
phonology 93

photographs 238
phrases
　and clauses 40
　conditional 58
　repeated 258
　in sentences 36
pictures
　children's texts 205
　informative/explanatory texts 189, 285, 287
　magazines and newspapers 190, 191
　nonfiction texts 214, 218, 225
　sales materials 201
　websites 192
Pinter, Harold 144
place
　adverb phrases 31
　adverbs of 28, 29, 43
　managing shifts in 277
　nouns 12, 13
　paragraphs 257
　prepositions of 34
　settings 130–133
　subordinating conjunctions 48
plagiarism 229, 234, **241**
planning
　essay prompts 299
　recording your ideas 237
　a story **264–265**
　writing 234
plays
　features of **125**
　as form 249
　further reading **313**
　performance 144, **147**
　plot 141
　reading **144–145**
　settings 133
　three-act structure 142–143
plot pyramids *see* story maps
plots
　building 141
　classic 140
　dialogue and 166, 167
　main idea **170–171**
　stories **140–141**, 265, **266–267**
　themes **172–173**
　three-act structure **142–143**, 267
　twists and turning points 141
plurals
　apostrophes 75
　irregular 113
　nouns 12, **112–113**
　verbs 51
poetry

analyzing **168–169**
descriptions in 263
features of **125**
as form 249
further reading **312–313**
haikus 232
making sense of **150–151**
performance 146
personal experience/
  interpretation of 150
planning a poem **278–279**
settings 133
what is a poem? **148–149**
writing about **282–283**
writing a poem 232, **280–281**
points
  organizing 244–245, 299
  proving **180–181**
  stating 283
polite tones 207, 288
possessive determiners 19
possessive pronouns 15, **17**, 18, 19
possibility
  adverbs of 28, 29
  modal auxiliary verbs **56–57**
practice, writing 233
predicate 37
predicate adjectives 21
predictions, making 163
prefixes 94, 95, 96, 97, **98–101**
  hyphens with 89, 99
  negative **100–101**
prepositions **34–35**
  position of 35
present participles 63
present perfect **53**
present subjunctive **59**
present tense 27, 50, 51
presentation *see* layout
presentations 187, 243
Priestley, J. B. 313
primary sources 234
printed media 186
printed publications **190–191**
progressive (continuous) tense **51**, 63
pronouns **14–15**
  noun phrases 25
  relative 42, **43**
  transition words 258
  using **16–17**
pronunciation 93
proofreading 233, **235**, 304, **305**
proper nouns 13
props 147
prose 124
protagonists **134**, 274

Pullman, Philip 313
punctuation **66–89**
  apostrophes **74–77**
  checking 233, 305
  colons **84–85**
  commas **78–81**
  creating interest 253, 260, 261
  dialogue 167
  direct speech **72–73**
  hyphens **88–89**
  multiple adjectives 23
  and pacing 277
  parentheses, dashes, and ellipses **86–87**
  and performance 147
  in poems 281
  purpose of **68–69**
  semicolons **82–83**
  starting and ending sentences **70–71**, 252
purpose, writer's **202–203**, 224, 226, 227, 232, 246, **247**

Q

quantifiers 19
quest 140
question marks 39, 69, 70, **71**, 73, 252
question tags 39, 80
questions
  about nonfiction texts **218–219**
  about poetry **168–169**, **282–283**
  about stories **152–153**
  answering essay prompts **298–299**
  interrogative mood 60, **61**
  in letters 291
  pronouns 15
  punctuation 70, 71
  rhetorical 199
  sentences 39
quotation marks **72–73**, 183
quotations
  colons and 85
  as evidence from text 183
  from sources 239, 243
  in speeches 198

R

radio 186
rags to riches 140
reading
  between the lines 144, 160, 181
  fiction **120–183**
  inference **160–163**

nonfiction **184–229**
out loud 124, 125, 146, 249, 255, 261, 281, 299
plays **144–145**
poetry **148–151**
and punctuation 69, 78, 80
silently 124
stories **152–153**
why to read **122–123**
realism 126, **127**
rebirth 140
recording your ideas 237
reference texts 186, 187, 188, 214, 215, 249
references
  letters 289
  sources 239
reflexive pronouns 17
register, formal and informal 206
relative adverbs 42, **43**
relative clauses 15, **42–43**
relative pronouns 42, **43**
reliability
  online media 191, 192–193
  printed media 191
  research sources 239
  sales materials 201
repetition
  for emphasis or effect 157, 165, 251, 260, 261
  in nonfiction texts 209, 211
  persuasive writing 293
  poetry 151, 169, 279, 281
  speeches 199
  transition words 258
reported speech 72
rereading 235, 253
research 234, **238–239**, 243, 299
resolution, plots 143, 267, 269
revision, of writing 232, 233, **304**, 305
rhetorical devices 292
rhetorical questions 199, 211, 291, 293
rhyme 148, 149, 157, 278, 279, 281, 282
rhyme schemes 149, 168, 169
rhyming couplets 149, 151
rhythm 157
  poetry 148, 149, 150, 151, 168, 279, 281
  and sentence length 254
Rice, Tim 144
romance **126**
root words **94–95**, 96, 98
  doubling letters for suffixes 106–107
  prefixes 98–101

suffixes 102–103, 110–111
  vowel suffixes 104–105
  and working out meaning 155, 217
roots **94–95**, 96, 97
Rowling, J. K. 128, 134, 135, 312
rude tones 207
run-on sentences 45
Rundell, Katherine 312
Russell, Willy 313

S

Sachar, Louis 312
sadness 164
sales materials **200–201**
Samuels, Diane 313
satire 127
scanning 219
scenes
  plays 125, 141
  setting the scene 131, 145
  stories 267
schwa 117
science fiction 126, **129**
scripts, understanding 145
search bars 193
search engines 193
second-person narrators 138
secondary characters **134**
secondary sources 234
sections, nonfiction texts 215
self pronouns 17
semicolons **82–83**
senses, using 262, 270, 271
sentence fragments 45, 253
sentences **36–37**
  active and passive **64–65**
  clauses 40–41
  common mistakes 253
  conditional 58
  conjunctions 46–49, 252
  grammar rules 10
  ICE starters 301
  interesting 253
  joining with semicolons 82
  length in nonfiction texts 209, 211
  multiclause **44–45**
  nouns in 13
  in paragraphs 256
  punctuation and capital letters **70–71**
  transition words 258–259
  types of **38–39**
  using effectively **254–255**
  varying length and structure 157, 254, 255, 260, 261, 277
  writing 250, **252–253**

INDEX

sequence words 267
sets, stage 147
settings **130–131**
   choice of 264
   comparing and contrasting 175, 176, 177
   creating 266, **270–271**
   importance of **132–133**
Sewell, Anna 165, 312
Shakespeare, William 126, 133, 147, 170, 180, 240, 313
Sheinkin, Steve 310
short stories 124
sign-offs, letters 196, 197, 289, 291
silence 144, 146
silent letters **116**, 117
similes 151, **158**, 211, 262
simple past tense **52–53**
singulars
   apostrophes 75
   nouns 12, 112
   verbs 51
Sissay, Lemn 313
skimming 219
slang 206, 288
sleep, reading and 123
Slocum, Joshua 310
Smith, Zadie 183, 312
Snicket, Lemony 312
social media 192, 193
sonnets 148, 149, 282
Sophocles 313
sound recordings 238
sources
   research **238–239**
   synthesis 242–243
speech
   characters 272
   difference between writing and 251
   direct and reported 72–73
   giving information/advice 187
   inference in 161
speeches **198–199**, 249, 293, 303
spelling rules
   checking spelling 233, 235, 305
   consonant suffixes 108–109
   doubling letters for suffixes **106–107**
   orthography 93
   plurals 112–113
   silent and unstressed letters 116–117
   vowel suffixes 104–105, 110
square brackets 195
stage directions 133, 144, 145

standfirst 190
stanzas 125, 168, 169
state (verbs) 26
statements 38, 60, 70
Stead, Rebecca 275
Steinbeck, John 312
Stevenson, Robert Louis 150, 151, 271, 312, 313
stories
   asking questions about **152–153**
   characters **134–137**
   choosing a narrator **274–275**
   creating a setting **270–271**
   descriptions in 263
   dialogue **166–167**
   features of **124**
   genres **126–129**
   ideas for **237**
   narrative nonfiction 194–195
   narrators **138–139**
   performance 146
   planning **264–265**
   plot and structure **140–141**, **266–267**
   settings 130–132
   starting and ending 265, **268–269**
   three-act structure **142–143**
   writing 232, **264–277**
Storr, Catherine 312
story maps 142–143, 266–267
straplines 285
stress 107
   in poetry 150, 169
   silent and unstressed letters **116–117**
structure
   choice of 241, 250
   nonfiction texts **214–215**, 225, 226, 227
   plays 124
   poetry 124, 149, 150, 168, 282
   stories 124, **266–267**
style
   choice of 232, 233
   writing in the right **250–251**
subgenres 127
subheadings 214, 215, 218
subject
   essay prompts 298
   stories, poems, and plays 124–125
subject (grammar)
   active and passive sentences 64–65
   clauses 40
   implied 37
   nouns 13

pronouns 15, **16**
sentences 36, 37, 252, 253
verbs 27
subjective adjectives 23
subjunctive tenses **58–59**
subordinate clauses 41, 42, 45, 83, 254
subordinating conjunctions 41, **47–48**
suffixes 94, 95, 96, 97, **102–103**
   consonant **108–109**
   doubling letters for **106–107**
   plurals **112–113**
   power of **110–111**
   vowel **104–105**
Sullivan, Arthur 133, 313
summarizing 153, 170, 171, **178–179**, 232
   multiple paragraphs **228–229**
summing up 258, 259
Supple, Tim 313
supporting sentences 256
suspense
   ellipses and 86, 87, 253
   language and tone 164, 211
   plots 142
Swindells, Robert 312
syllables 93, 106, 107
   stressed and unstressed 169
synonyms **118–119**, 155, 280
synthesis **242–243**

T

tables 218, 285
tabs 193
Taylor, Mildred D. 176, 312
technical language 209, 210
television 186
Tennyson, Alfred Lord 313
tenses 27, **50–51**
   conditional and subjunctive **58–59**
   past 52–55
   progressive (continuous) **51**, 63
tension, building 254, 255
text type *see* genres
themes
   comparing and contrasting 175
   in fiction **170–171**
   identifying **172–173**
   in poetry 278, 279
thesauruses 118
things (nouns) 12
third-person narrators 124, 139, 275
Thomas, Dylan 313
three-act structure **142–143**

thrillers 128
Thunberg, Greta 293, 311
time
   adverb phrases 31
   adverbs of 28, 29, 43
   managing shifts in 277
   paragraphs 257
   prepositions of 34
   settings 130–133
   subordinating conjunctions 48
timetables 219
titles
   and main idea 171
   poems 168
to be 27
   passive sentences 65
   progressive (continuous) tense 51
to have
   present 27
   present perfect 53
Tolkien, J. R. R. 312
tone
   comparing and contrasting 175, 176, 177, 225
   language for different purposes 208, 210–211
   performances 146
   poems 280
   punctuation and **69**
   rude and polite **207**
   sales materials 200
   understanding **164–165**
   writing style 251
   writing to argue 295
topic sentences 256
topics
   paragraphs and change of 257
   of poems 278, 279
Torday, Piers 274, 312
Townsend, Jessica 312
tragedy **126**
traits, character **135**
transition words 48–49, 175, 177, **258–259**, 295
travel narratives 195
true stories 248
truth, facts 222–223
Truth, Sojourner 194, 311
turning points, plot 141
twists, plot 141

U

unreliable narrators 275
unstressed letters 116, **117**
URLs 192, 193

V

verbals **62–63**
verbs **26–27**
  and adverbs 28
  clauses 40
  conditional and subjunctive **58–59**
  creating a setting 271
  gerunds, participles, and infinitives **62–63**
  hyphens in 89
  modal **56–57**
  moods 59, **60–61**
  in sentences 36, 37, 252, 253
  suffixes 102
  synonyms 119
  tenses **50–55**
verses 125
videos 192, 238
viewpoints, different 203, **212–213**
visuals 234
vocabulary
  choice of 253
  synonyms **118–119**
voice
  expression of 165
  reading dialogue 167
  varying 255
vowel suffixes **104–105**
vowels 104, 106
voyage and return 140

W

websites **192–193**, 219
Weider, Shoshana 195, 311
White, E. B. 173, 275, 312
Wilde, Oscar 313
Williams, Tennessee 144
Wollstonecraft, Mary 311
Woodson, Jacqueline 311, 313
word families 95
words **90–119**
  breaking into parts **96–97**
  choosing 232, 253, 260, 261
  compound 97
  homophones **114–115**
  inference and choice of 162
  inventing your own 280
  missing 87
  new words and terms **216–217**
  plurals **112–113**
  prefixes **98–101**
  roots and root words **94–95**
  studying **92–93**
  suffixes **102–111**
  synonyms **118–119**
  to create a setting 271
  and tone 165
  transition 258
  working out meaning of unfamiliar **154–155**
Wright, Nicholas 313
writer's purpose 149, **202–203**
writing **230–305**
  about poetry **282–283**
  answering essay prompts **298–299**
  choosing a narrator **274–275**
  collaboration and synthesis **242–243**
  comparisons of fiction 177
  comparisons of nonfiction 227
  creating characters **272–273**
  creating a setting **270–271**
  descriptive **262–263**
  formal letters **288–289**
  how to write well **232–233**
  identifying your audience and purpose **246–247**
  informal emails and letters **290–291**
  introduce, cite, explain **300–303**
  learning from other writers **240–241**
  narrative techniques **276–277**
  paragraphs **256–257**
  planning a story **264–265**
  plot and structure **266–267**
  poetry **280–281**
  presenting information clearly **286–287**
  research **238–239**
  revising, editing, and proofreading **304–305**
  in the right style **250–251**
  sentences **252–253**
  stages of **234–235**
  starting and ending a story **268–269**
  stories **264–277**
  summaries 229
  to argue **294–295**
  to inform and explain **284–285**
  to persuade **292–293**
  transition words **258–259**
use of synonyms 118, 119
  using language techniques **260–261**
  using sentences effectively **254–255**
writing styles **250–251**
Wynne Jones, Diana 312

Y

Yang, Gene Luen 312
young adult fiction 128
Yousafzai, Malala 123, 311

Z

Zephaniah, Benjamin 313

Acknowledgments

Dorling Kindersley would like to thank Madeleine Barnes, Elise Solberg, and Justine Willis for editorial help; Nicola Erdpresser and Ali Scrivens for design help; Gus Scott for additional illustrations; Harish Aggarwal, Senior DTP Designer; Priyanka Sharma Saddi, Senior Jackets Coordinator; Tommy Callan for technical help; Oliver Drake for proofreading; and Helen Peters for indexing.

Excerpts from WONDER by R. J. Palacio, copyright © 2012 by R. J. Palacio. Used by permission of Alfred A. Knopf, an imprint of Random House Children's Books, a division of Penguin Random House LLC. All rights reserved.

Excerpts from ROLL OF THUNDER, HEAR MY CRY by Mildred D. Taylor, text copyright © 1976 by Mildred D. Taylor. Used by permission of Dial Books for Young Readers, an imprint of Penguin Young Readers Group, a division of Penguin Random House LLC. All rights reserved.